The Michigan Historical Reprint Series

Reprints from the collection of the University of Michigan University Library

This volume is produced from digital images created through the University of Michigan University Library's preservation reformatting program. The Library seeks to preserve the intellectual content of items in a manner that facilitates and promotes a variety of uses. The digital reformatting process results in an electronic version of the text that can both be accessed online and used to create new print copies. This book and thousands of others can be found in the digital collections of the University of Michigan Library. The University Library also understands and values the utility of print, and makes reprints available through its Scholarly Publishing Office.

For access to the University of Michigan Library's digital collections, please see http://www.lib.umich.edu.

The Scholarly Publishing Office seeks to disseminate high-quality, cost-effective scholarly content through both print and electronic publishing. Information about the Scholarly Publishing Office can be found at http://spo.umdl.umich.edu.

The Scholarly Publishing Office
the University of Michigan
University Library

ORIGINS OF CHRISTIANITY.

VOL. II

THE APOSTLES.

THE

APOSTLES.

BY

ERNEST RENAN,

MEMBRE DE L'INSTITUT.

AUTHOR OF "THE LIFE OF JESUS," ETC., ETC.

TRANSLATED FROM THE ORIGINAL FRENCH.

NEW YORK:

Carleton, Publisher, Madison Square.

PARIS: MICHEL LEVY FRERES.

M DCCC LXXV.

JOHN F. TROW & SON, PRINTERS,
205-213 EAST 12TH ST., NEW YORK.

TABLE OF CONTENTS.

THE APOSTLES.

INTRODUCTION

CRITICAL EXAMINATION OF ORIGINAL DOCUMENTS.

THE first book of our *History of the Origins of Christianity* brought us down to the death and burial of Jesus; and we must now resume the subject at the point where we left it—that is to say, on Saturday, the fourth of April, in the year 33. The work will be for some time yet a sort of continuation of the life of Jesus. Next to the glad months, during which the great Founder laid the bases of a new order of things for humanity, these few succeeding years were the most decisive in the history of the world. It is still Jesus, who, by the holy fire kindled in the hearts of a few friends from the spark He himself has placed there, creates institutions of the highest originality, stirs and transforms souls, and impresses on everything His divine seal. It shall be ours to show how, under this influence, always active and victorious over death, the doctrines of faith in the resurrection, in the influence of the Holy Spirit, in the gift of tongues, and in the power of the Church, became firmly established. We shall describe the organization of the Church of Jerusalem, its first trials, and its first triumphs, and the earliest missions to which it gave birth. We shall follow Christianity in its rapid progress through Syria as far as Antioch, where it established a second capital in some respects more important than Jerusalem, and destined, even, to supplant the latter. In this new centre, where converted heathen were in the majority, we shall see Christianity separate itself definitively from Judaism, and receive a name of its own; and we shall note, above all, the birth of the grand idea of distant missions destined to carry the name of Jesus throughout the Gentile world. We shall pause at the solemn moment when Paul, Barnabas, and Mark depart to carry this great design into execution; and then, interrupting for a while our narrative, we shall cast a glance at the world which these brave missionaries sought to convert. We shall endeavor to give an account of the intellectual, political, moral, religious, and social condition of the Roman Empire at about the year 45, the probable date of the departure of St. Paul on his first mission.

Such is the scope of this second book which we have called *The Apostles*, because it is devoted to that period of common action, during which the little family created by Jesus acted in concert and was grouped morally around a single point—Jerusalem. Our next and third book, will lead us out of this company, and will have for almost its only character the man who, more than any other, represents conquering and spreading Christianity—St. Paul. Although from a certain epoch he may be called an apostle, Paul, nevertheless, was not so by the same title as the Twelve;[1] he was, in fact, a laborer of the second hour, and almost an intruder.

Historical documents, as they have reached us, are apt to cause some misapprehension on this point. As we know infinitely more of the affairs of Paul than of those of the Twelve, as we possess his authentic writings and original memoirs relating with minute precision certain epochs of his life, we are apt to award him an importance of the first order, almost superior even to that of Jesus. This is an error. Paul was a very great man, and played a considerable part in the foundation of Christianity; but he should neither be compared to Jesus, nor even to his immediate disciples. Paul never saw Jesus, nor did he ever taste the ambrosia of the Galilean's preaching; and the most mediocre man who had partaken of that heavenly manna, was through that very privilege, superior to him who had, as it were, only an after-taste. Nothing is more false than an opinion which has become fashionable in these days, and which would almost imply that Paul was the true founder of Christianity. Jesus alone is its true founder; and the next places to Him should be reserved for His grand yet obscure companions—for affectionate and faithful friends who believed in Him in the face of death. Paul was to the first century a kind of isolated phenomenon. Instead of an organized school, he left vigorous adversaries, who, after his death, wished to banish him from the Church, to place him on the same footing with Simon the Magician,[2] and would even have denied him the credit of that which we consider his special work—the conversion of the Gentiles.[3] The church of Corinth, which he alone had founded,[4] professed to owe its origin to him and to St. Peter.[5] In the second century Papias and St. Justin do not men tion his name; and it was not till later, when oral tradition was lost and Scripture took its place, that Paul assumed a leading position in Christian theology. Paul, indeed, had a theology. Peter and Mary Magdalene had none. Paul has left elaborate works, and none of the writings of the other apostles can dispute the palm with his in either importance or authenticity.

At the first glance, the documents relating to the period embraced in this volume would seem scanty and quite insufficient. Direct testimony is confined to the earlier chapters of the Acts of the Apostles, the historical value of which is open to grave objections. The light thrown upon this obscure interval by the last chapters of the Gospels, and above all by the Epistles of St. Paul, however, somewhat dissipates the shadows. An ancient writer serves to make us acquainted not only with the exact epoch when he wrote, but with the epoch which preceded it. Every written work suggests, in fact, retrospective inductions upon the state of society whence it proceeded. Though written for the most part between the years 53 and 62, the Epistles of St. Paul are replete with information about the first years of Christianity. While speaking here of great events without precise dates, the essential point is to show the conditions in which they originated; and while on this subject, I should state, once for all, that the running dates given at the head of each page (of the French edition) are only approximative. The chronology of those early years has but very few fixed points. Nevertheless, thanks to the care which the compiler of the Acts has taken not to interrupt the series of facts; thanks to the Epistle to the Galatians, where there are several numerical indications of marked value; and thanks to Josephus, who furnishes us with the dates of events in profane history allied to undoubted facts concerning the apostles—it is possible to arrange a probable chronology where the chances of error are confined within tolerably restricted limits.

I will repeat here at the beginning of this book what I said at the beginning of my Life of Jesus. Hypothesis is indispensable in histories of this character, where only the general effect is certain, and where almost all the details are more or less dubious, in consequence of the legendary nature of the authorities. There is no hypothesis at all to be made in regard to epochs of which we know nothing. To attempt to reproduce a group of antique statuary which has certainly existed, but of which we have not even a fragment, and about which we possess no written information, is a purely arbitrary work; but what can be more legitimate than to try to re-arrange the frieze of the Parthenon from the portions which remain, and with the aid of ancient descriptions of drawings made in the seventeenth century, and all other possible means of information—in a word, to become inspired with the style of these inimitable sculptures, and to endeavor to grasp their soul and spirit? It need not be said after the effort that the work of the ancient sculptor has been reproduced; but that everything possible has been done to approach it. Such a procedure is much more legitimate in history, because the doubtful forms of language permit that which the marble does not. Nothing prevents us from proposing to the reader a choice between different suppositions. The conscience of the writer need not trouble him as long as he presents as certain, that which is certain; as probable, that which is probable; as possible, that which is possible. When history and legend glide together, it is only the general effect which need be followed out. Our third book, for which we shall have documents absolutely historical, and in which it will be our function to depict characters clearly defined, and to relate facts distinctly set forth, will thus present a firmer narrative. It will be seen, however, that the physiognomy of that period is, upon the whole, not known with certainty. Accomplished facts speak louder than biographical details. We know very little about the incomparable artists to whom we are indebted for the masterpieces of Greek art; yet these masterpieces really tell us more of the individuality of their authors, and of the public that appreciated them, than could the most circumstantial narrations or the most authentic text.

The documents to which we must look for information concerning what was done immediately after the death of Jesus, are the last chapters of the Gospels, containing the account of the apparitions of the risen Christ.[6] I do not attend to repeat here my estimate of the value of these documents given in the "Life of Jesus." We have, happily, in this question, features wanting too often in that work: I would refer to a prominent passage in St. Paul (I. Corinthians xv. 5–8), which establishes—first, the reality of the apparitions or appearances of Christ; second, the duration of these apparitions, differing from the accounts in the synoptic Gospels; third, the variety of localities where these apparitions were manifest, contrary to Mark and to Luke.

The study of the fundamental text, in addition to many other reasons, confirms us in the views we have already expressed upon the reciprocal relation of the synoptical Gospels and the fourth Gospel. As regards the resurrection and subsequent appearances of Christ, the fourth Gospel maintains the same superiority which it shows throughout its entire history of Jesus. It is to this Gospel that we must look for a connected and logical narrative, suggestive of that which remains hidden behind it. I would touch upon the most difficult of questions relating to the origins of Christianity, in asking, "What is the historical value of the fourth Gospel?" My views on this point in my "Life of Jesus" have elicited the strongest objections brought against the work by intelligent critics. Almost all the scholars who apply the rational method to the history of theology reject the fourth Gospel as in all respects apocryphal; but though I have reflected much of late on this problem, I cannot modify to any material degree my previous opinion, though, out of respect to the general sentiment on this point, I deem it my duty to set forth in detail the reasons for my persistence; and I will devote to these reasons an Appendix to a revised and corrected edition of the "Life of Jesus" which is shortly to appear.

For the history we are about to dwell upon, the Acts of the Apostles form the most important documentary reference; and an explanation of the character of this work, of its historical value, and of interpretations I put upon it, is here desirable.

There can be no doubt that the Acts of the Apostles were written by the author of the third Gospel, and form a continuation of that work. It is not necessary to stop and prove this proposition, which has never been seriously contested.[7] The preface which is at the beginning of each work, the dedication of both to Theophilus, and the perfect resemblance of style and ideas, are abundant demonstration of the fact.

A second proposition, not as certain, but which may nevertheless be regarded very probable, is that the author of the Acts was a disciple of Paul, who accompanied him in most of his travels. At first glance this proposition appears indubitable. In several places, after the 10th verse of Chapter XVI., the author of the Acts uses in the narrative the pronoun "we," thus indicating that the writer thenceforth formed one of the apostolic band which surrounded Paul. This would seem to demonstrate the matter; and the only issue which appears to lessen the force of the argument is the theory that the passages where the pronoun "we" is found, had been copied by the last compiler of the *Acts* in a previous manuscript, in the original memoirs of a disciple of Paul, and that this compiler or editor had inadvertently forgotten to substitute for "we" the name of the narrator. This explanation is, however, hardly admissible. Such an error might naturally exist in a more careless compilation; but the third Gospel and the Acts form a work well prepared, composed with reflection, and even with art; written by the same hand, and on a connected plan.[8] The two books, taken together, are perfectly the same in style, present the same favorite phrases, and exhibit the same manner of quoting Scripture. So gross a fault in the editing would be inexplicable; and we are forced to the conclusion that the person who wrote the close of the work, wrote the beginning of it, and that the narrator of the whole is the same who used the word "we" in the passages alluded to.

This will appear still more probable on remembering under what circumstances the narrator thus refers to his association with Paul. The use of the word "we" begins when Paul for the first time enters Macedonia (xvi. 10), and closes when he leaves Philippi. It occurs again when Paul, visiting Macedonia for the last time, goes once more to Philippi (xx. 5, 6); and thenceforward to the close, the narrator remains with Paul. On further remarking that the chapters where the narrator accompanies the apostle are particular and precise in their character, there will be little reason to doubt that the former was a Macedonian, or more probably, perhaps, a Philippian,[9] who came to Paul at Troas during the second mission, remained at Philippi after the departure of the apostle, and on his last visit to that city (the third mission) joined him, to leave him no more during his wanderings. Is it probable that a compiler, writing at a distance, would allow himself to be influenced to such a degree by the reminiscences of another? These reminiscences would not harmonize with the general style. The narrator who used the "we" would have his own style and method,[10] and would be more like Paul than the general editor of the work; but the fact is, that the whole work is perfectly homogeneous.

It seems surprising that any one should be found to contradict a proposition apparently so evident. But the critics of the New Testament bring forward plenty of commentaries which are found on examination to be full of uncertainty. As regards style, ideas, and doctrines, the Acts are by no means what one would expect of a disciple of Paul. In no respect do they resemble the Epistles, nor can there be found therein a trace of those bold doctrines which showed the originality of the Apostle to the Gentiles. The temperament of St. Paul is that of a rigid Protestant; the author of the Acts produces the effect of a good and docile Catholic, with a tendency to optimism; calling each priest "a holy priest," each bishop "a great bishop," and ready to adopt every fiction rather than to acknowledge that these holy priests and these great bishops quarrelled, and sometimes most bitterly, among themselves. Though always professing the greatest admiration for Paul, the author of the Acts avoids giving him the title of apostle,[11] and is disposed to award to Peter the credit of the initiative in the conversion of the Gentiles. One would deem him a disciple of Peter rather than of Paul. We shall soon show that in two or three instances his principles of conciliation led him to grave errors in his biography of Paul. He was inexact,[12] and above all, guilty of omissions truly strange in one who was a disciple of that apostle.[13] He does not at all allude to the Epistles; he omits important facts.[14] Even in the portions relating to the period when he was supposed to be a constant companion of Paul's, he is dry, ill-informed, and far from entertaining;[15] and on the whole, the vagueness of certain portions of the narrative would imply that the writer had no direct or even indirect relation with the apostles, but wrote about the year 100 or 120.

Is it necessary to pause here to discuss these objections? I think not; and I persist in believing that the last writer or editor of the Acts is really that disciple of Paul who used the "we" in the concluding chapters. All the discrepancies, however inseparable they may appear, should be at least held in suspense, if not wholly done away with, by the argument resulting from the use of this word "we." It may be added, that in attributing the Acts to a companion of Paul, two peculiarities are explained—the disproportion of the parts of the work, three-fifths of which are devoted to Paul; and the disproportion which may be observed in the biography of Paul, whose first mission is very briefly spoken of, while certain parts of the second and third missions, especially the concluding travels, are related with minute details. A man wholly unfamiliar with the apostolic history would not have practised these inequalities. The general design of the work would have been better conceived. It is this very disproportion that distinguishes history written from documents, from that wholly or in part original. The historian of the closet takes for recital events themselves, but the writer of memoirs avails himself of recollections or personal relations. An ecclesiastical historian, a sort of Eusebius, writing about the year 120, would have left us a book quite differently arranged, after the thirteenth chapter. The eccentric manner in which the *Acts* at that period leave the orbit in which they had until then revolved, cannot, in my opinion, be explained in any other way than by the particular situation of the author, and his relations with Paul. This view will be naturally confirmed if we find among the co-workers known to Paul, the name of the autl or to whom tradition attributes the book of Acts.

And this is really what has taken place. Both manuscript and tradition give for the author of the third Gospel, a certain Lucanus[16] or Lucas. From what has been said, it is evident that if Lucas is really the author of the third Gospel, he is also the author of the Acts. Now, that very name of Lucas we also find mentioned as that of a companion of Paul, in the Epistle to the Colossians, IV. 14; in the Epistle to Philemon, 24; and in the Second Epistle to Timothy, IV. 11. This last Epistle is of more than doubtful authenticity. The Epistles to the Colossians and to Philemon, on the other hand, although very probably authentic, are not the most indubitable of the Epistles of St. Paul; but nevertheless, in any event, they date from the first century, and that is sufficient to positively establish the fact that among the disciples of Paul there existed a Lucas. The fabricator of the Epistles to Timothy is certainly not the same one who fabricated those to the Colossians and Philemon (conceding, contrary to our opinion, that these last are apocryphal). To admit that writers of fiction had attributed to Paul an imaginary companion, would hardly appear probable; but certainly the different false writers would hardly have fallen on the same name for this imaginary personage. Two observations will give a special force to this reasoning. The first is, that the name of Lucas or Lucanus is an unusual one among the early Christians; and the second, that the Lucas of the Epistles is not known elsewhere. The placing of a celebrated name at the head of a work, as was done with the Second

Epistle of Peter, and very probably with the Epistles of Paul to Titus and Timothy, was in no manner repugnant to the custom of the times; but no one would have thought of using in this way a name otherwise unknown. If it were the intention of the writer to invest his book with the authority of Paul, why did he not take the name of Paul himself, or at least the names of Timothy and Titus, well known disciples of the apostle of the Gentiles? Luke had no place either in tradition, legend, or history. The three passages in the Epistles previously alluded to were not enough to give him the reputation of an admitted authority. The Epistles to Timothy were probably written after the Acts; and the mention of Luke in the Epistles to the Colossians and to Philemon are really equal to only one allusion, these two works being by one hand. We believe, then, that the author of the third Gospel was really Luke, the disciple of Paul.

This very name of Luke or Lucanus, and the medical profession practised by the so-called disciple of Paul,[17] fully accord with the indications which the two books furnish in regard to their author. We have already stated that the author of the third Gospel and the Acts was probably from Philippi,[18] a Roman colony, where the Latin tongue was in use.[19] Besides this, the author of the third Gospel and the Acts was but indifferently acquainted with Judaism[20] and the affairs of Palestine.[21] He knew but little of Hebrew;[22] he was familiar with the ideas of the heathen world,[23] and he wrote Greek in a tolerably correct manner. The work was composed far from Judea, for a people unfamiliar with geography, and who had respect[24] neither for a marked Rabbinical science nor for Hebrew names.[25] The dominant idea of the author is, that if the people had been free to follow their inclination, they would have embraced the faith of Jesus, and that the Jewish aristocracy prevented them from so doing.[26] He always imparts to the word Jew a malevolent signification, as if it were synonymous with an enemy of the Christians;[27] and on the other hand he is decidedly favorable towards the heretic Samaritan.[28]

To what epoch can we refer the composition of this important work? Luke appears for the first time in the company of Paul, after the first journey of the apostle to Macedonia, about the year 52. Allowing that he was then twenty-five years old, it would have been nothing more than natural had he lived until the year 100. The narrative of the Acts closes at the year 63,[29] but the compiling of the work was evidently done after that of the third Gospel; and the date of the editing of this third Gospel being evidently referable to the years immediately following the fall of Jerusalem (year 70),[30] it is not possible the book of Acts was written earlier than the year 71 or 72.

If it were quite certain that the Acts were written immediately after the Gospel, we might stop there. But some doubt exists. Several facts lead us to the belief that quite an interval elapsed between the compositions of the two works; and there is, indeed, a singular contradiction between the last chapter of the Gospel and the first chapter of the Acts. In the former, the Ascension seems to be recorded as taking place on the same day as the Resurrection;[31] in the latter,[32] the Ascension only occurred after a lapse of forty days. It is clear that this second version presents us with a more advanced form of the legend, adopted when it was found necessary to make room for the different apparitions of Christ, and to give to the post-resurrection life of Jesus a complete and logical form. It may be presumed, therefore, that this new method of arranging the history only occurred to the author's mind during the interval between the composition of the two works. In any event, it is somewhat remarkable that the author should feel himself obliged, a few lines further on, to develop his narrative by the recital of additional statements. If his first book was yet in his hands, would he have made additions which, viewed separately, are so awkwardly devised? Yet this even is not decisive, and an important circumstance gives occasion for the belief that Luke conceived the plan of both works at the same time. This circumstance is found in the preface to the Gospel, which appears common to the two works.[33] The contradiction to which we have alluded can probably be explained by the little care taken to account for every moment of time. Indeed, all the recitals of the post-resurrection life of Jesus are thoroughly contradictory in regard to the duration of that existence. So little effort was made to be truly historical, that the same narrator did not shrink from proposing successively two irreconcilable systems. The three descriptions of the Conversion of St. Paul in the *Acts*[34] also show little differences, which only prove that the author was not at all anxious about precision in details.

It would appear, then, that we are very near the truth in supposing that the Acts were written about the year

80. The tone of the book accords with the times of the first Flavian emperors. The author seemed to avoid everything that could annoy the Romans. He loves to show how the Roman functionaries were favorable to the new sect; how they even embraced its doctrines;[35] how, at least, they defended its adherents from the Jews, and how equitable and superior to the partisan passions of the local authorities was the imperial justice of Rome.[36] He lays special stress on the advantages inuring to Paul as a Roman citizen.[37] He abruptly cuts short his narrative at the moment when Paul arrives at Rome, probably to be relieved from recording the cruelties practised by Nero towards the Christians.[38] Striking, indeed, is the contrast between this narrative and the Apocalypse, written in the year 68, replete with memories of the infamies of Nero, and breathing throughout a terrible hatred for Rome. In the former case we recognise a quiet, amiable man, living in a time of peaceful calm. From about the year 70 until the close of the first century, the Christians had little to complain of. Members of the Flavian family had adopted Christianity. It is even possible that Luke knew Flavius Clemens, perhaps was one of his household, and may have written the work for this powerful personage. There are several indications which lead us to believe that the work was written in Rome, and it might be said that the author was influenced by the Roman Church, which, from the earliest centuries, possessed the political and hierarchical character that has ever since distinguished it. Luke could well enter into this feeling, for his views upon ecclesiastical authority were far advanced, and even

contained the germ of the Episcopate. He wrote history in the apologetic tone characteristic of the officials of the Court of Rome. He acted as an ultramontane historian of Clement XIV. might have done, praising at the same time the Pope and the Jesuits, and trying to persuade us that both parties in their debate observed the rules of charity. Two hundred years hence it will be maintained that Cardinal Antonelli and M. de Merode loved each other like two brothers. The author of the Acts was the first of these complacent narrators, piously convinced that everything in the Church must happen in a thoroughly evangelical manner. He was, too, the most artless of them all. Too loyal to condemn Paul, too orthodox to place himself outside the pale of prevalent opinion, he passed over real differences of doctrine, aiming to show only the common end which all these great founders were pursuing, though by methods so opposite, and in face of such energetic rivalries.

It will readily be understood that a man who possesses such a disposition is, of all others, the least capable of representing things as they really are. Historic fidelity is to him a matter of indifference; he is only anxious to edify the reader. Luke scarcely concealed this tendency; he writes "that Theophilus should understand the truth of that which the catechists had taught him."[39] He thus had already a settled ecclesiastical system which he taught officially, and the limit of which, as well as that of evangelical history[40] itself, was probably fixed. The dominant characteristics of the Acts, like that of the third Gospel,[41] are a tender piety, a lively sympathy for the Gentiles,[42] a conciliatory spirit, a marked tendency towards the supernatural, a love for the humble and lowly, a large democratic sentiment, or rather a persuasion that the people were naturally Christian, and that the upper class prevented them from following out their good instincts,[43] an exalted idea of the power of the Church and of its leaders, and a remarkable leaning towards social com munism.[44] The methods of composition are the same in the two works; and indeed in regard to the history of the apostles, are about as we would be in relation to evangelical history, if our only idea of the latter were derived from the Gospel according to St. Luke.

The disadvantages of such a situation are apparent. The life of Jesus, told only by the writer of the third Gospel, would be extremely defective and incomplete. We know so, because in this case, comparison is possible. Besides Luke, we possess (without speaking of the fourth Gospel) Matthew and Mark, who, relatively to Luke, are at least partially original. We can place our finger on the places where Luke dislocates or mixes up anecdotes, and can perceive the manner in which he colors facts according to his personal views, and adds pious legends to the most authentic traditions. Could we make a similar comparison as regards the Acts, would we not perceive analogous faults? The earliest chapters of the Acts appear to us even inferior to the third Gospel; for these chapters were probably composed from the fewer and less universally documentary references.

A fundamental distinction is here necessary. In a historic point of view the book of Acts is divided into two parts—one comprising the first twelve chapters, and recounting the principal events in the history of the primitive Church; and the other containing the seven remaining chapters, all devoted to the missions of St. Paul.

This second part, in itself, includes two kinds of narrative: one portion related by the narrator from his ocular testimony, and the other consisting only of what he has heard.

It is clear that even in this last case his authority is very important. The conversation of St. Paul himself is often drawn upon for information. Particularly towards its close, the narrative is characterized by remarkable precision; and the last pages of the Acts form indeed the only completely historical record that we have of the origins of Christianity.

The first chapters, on the contrary, are the most open to attack of all in the New Testament. In regard to these early years, particularly, the author betrays discrepancies still more remarkable than those existing in his Gospel.

His theory of forty days; his account of the Ascension, closing by a sort of final abduction and theatrical solemnity; the fantastic life of Jesus; his manner of describing the descent of the Holy Ghost, and of miraculous preaching; his method of understanding the gift of tongues—all are different from St. Paul:[45] all betray the influence of an epoch relatively inferior, and of a period when legendary lore finds wide credence.

Supernatural effects and startling accessories are characteristic of this author, who we should remember writes half a century after the occurrences he describes; in a country far from the scene of action; upon events which neither he nor his master, Paul, has witnessed; and following traditions partly fabulous, or at least modified by time and repetition. Luke not only belonged to a different generation from the founders of Christianity, but he was also of a different race; he was a Greek, with very little of the Jew in him, and almost a stranger to Jerusalem and to the secrets of Jewish life; he had never mingled with the primitive Christians, and indeed scarcely knew their later representatives. The miracles he relates, give the impression of inventions *à priori* rather than of exaggerated facts; the miracles of Peter and Paul form two series, which respond to each other,[46] and in which the personages have a family resemblance Peter differs in nothing from Paul, nor Paul from Peter.

The words which he puts in the mouth of his heroes, although adapted to varying circumstances, are all in the same style, and characteristic of the author himself rather than those to whom he attributes them. His text even contains impossibilities.[47] The *Acts*, in a word, form a dogmatic history so arranged as to support the orthodox doctrines of the time or inculcate the ideas which most fully accorded with the pious views of the author. Nor could it be otherwise. The origin of each religion was only known through the statements of its adherents. It is only the sceptic who writes history *ad narrandum.*

These are not simply the suspicions and conjectures of a carping and defiant criticism. They are well founded inductions; every time that we have reviewed the *Acts* we have found the book systematically faulty. The control which we can demand of the synoptical texts, we can demand also of St. Paul, and particularly of the Epistle to the Galatians. It is clear, then, where the Acts and the Epistles do not accord, preference should always be given to the latter, which are older, possess absolute authenticity, thorough sincerity, and freedom from legendary corruption. The most important doctrines for history are those which possess in the least degree the historic form. The authority of chronicles must give place to medals, maps, or authentic letters. Viewed in this light, the epistles of undoubted authors and well-authenticated dates form the basis of all the history of Christian origins. Without them, doubts would weaken and destroy all faith even in the life of Jesus. Now, in two very important instances, the Epistles display in broad light the peculiar tendencies of the author of the *Acts*, and his desire to efface every trace of the dissensions which had existed between Paul and the apostles at Jerusalem.[48]

And firstly, the author of the *Acts* makes out that Paul, after the accident at Damascus (x. 19, and following verses; XXII. 17, and following verses), came to Jerusalem at an epoch when his conversion was hardly known; that he had been presented to the apostles; that he had lived with them and the faithful brethren on the most cordial terms; that he had disputed publicly with the Hellenistic Jews, and that a conspiracy on their part and a celestial revelation led to his departure from Jerusalem. Now Paul informs us that the matter was quite different. To prove that he owes to Jesus Himself and not to the Twelve his doctrine and mission, he says (Gal. I. 11, and following verses) that after his conversion he avoided taking counsel with any one,[49] or going to Jerusalem to consult with those who had been apostles before himself; but that of his own accord he went to preach and to carry out his personal mission in Hauran; that three days later, it is true, he journeyed to Jerusalem, but only to make the acquaintance of Cephas; that he remained fifteen days, but saw no other apostle, excepting, perhaps, James, the brother of the Lord; so that, really, his countenance was quite unknown to the churches of Judea. The effort to soften the asperities of the severe apostle and present him as a co-worker of the Twelve, laboring in concert with them at Jerusalem, hence seems without evidence. It has been given to appear that Jerusalem was his capital and point of departure; that his doctrine was so identical with that of the apostles that he was able, to a great degree, to take their place as preachers; that his first apostolate was confined to the synagogues of Damascus; that he had been a disciple and listener, which was not the fact;[50] that the time between his conversion and his first journey to Jerusalem was very short; that his sojourn in that city was quite protracted; that his preaching was received with general satisfaction; that he lived on intimate terms with all the apostles, though he assures us that he had seen but two of them; and that the faithful of Jerusalem took care of him, though Paul declares that they were unknown to him.

The same disposition to prove that Paul was a frequent visitor to Jerusalem, which had induced our author to prolong the apostle's stay in Jerusalem, seems also to have induced him to credit the apostle with one journey too many. He says that Paul came to Jerusalem with Barnabas, bearing the offerings of the faithful after the year 44 (Acts xi. 30; xii. 25). Now, Paul expressly declares that between the journey made three years after his conversion and that made in relation to the subject of circumcision, he did not go to Jerusalem at all (Gal. i. and ii.); in other words, between Acts ix. 26, and xv. 2, Paul makes no mention of any travel. One could wrongly deny the identity of the journey described in the second chapter of Galatians with that mentioned in the fifteenth chapter of Acts, and yet not be subject to contradiction. "Three years after my conversion," says St. Paul, "I went to Jerusalem to make the acquaintance of Cephas, and fourteen years afterwards I went again to Jerusalem." There has been some doubt whether this period of fourteen years dates from the conversion, or from the journey three years subsequent to that event. We will assume the first hypothesis as being most favorable to those who defend the account as given in Acts. There would then, according to St. Paul, have been at least eleven years between his first and second journey to Jerusalem; now surely there are not eleven years between that which is related in Acts ix. 26 and the following verses, and the account which we find in Acts xi. 30, etc. By maintaining it against all show of truth, one would fall into another impossibility. The truth is, that which is related in Acts xi. 30 is contemporaneous with the death of James, the son of Zebedee,[51] which having just preceded the death, in the year 44, of Herod Agrippa I., furnishes us with the only fixed date in the Acts of the Apostles.[52] The second journey took place at least fourteen years after his conversion; and if he had really made that journey in the year 44—the conversion must have occurred in the year 30—a theory which is manifestly absurd. It is then impossible to allow any credence to the statements in Acts XI. 30 and XII. 35.

All of these journeyings to and fro appear to be reported by our author in a very inexact manner; and in comparing Acts XVII. 14–16, and XVIII. 5, with 1 Thessalonians III. 1–2, another discrepancy will be found. As this last, however, has nothing to do with doctrinal matters, we shall not discuss it here.

An important feature of the subject now before us, and one which throws much light on this difficult question of the historical value of the *Acts*, is a comparison of the passages relative to the discussion concerning circumcision in the fifteenth chapter of Acts and the second chapter of the Epistle to the Galatians. According to the *Acts*, certain of the brethren of Judea coming to Antioch and maintaining the necessity of the rite of circumcision for converted heathen, Paul, Barnabas, and several others were appointed as a deputation to go from Antioch to Jerusalem to consult the apostles and elders on this question. They were warmly received by their brethren at the Holy City, and a great convention was held. The sentiments of reciprocal charity which prevailed, and the great satisfaction experienced by these co-religionists at thus meeting again together, dispelled all feeling of dissension. Peter gave utterance to the opinion which had been anticipated from the mouth of Paul, viz. that the converted heathen were not subject to the law of Moses.

James modified this only by a very light restriction.[53] Paul did not speak, and indeed had no reason to do so, because his views were fully expressed by Peter; and the theory of the Judean brethren found no supporters. According to the advice of James, a solemn decree was made and communicated by deputies expressly chosen to the various churches.

Let us now examine the account given by Paul in the Epistle to the Galatians. It was his desire that this journey to Jerusalem should have the effect of a spontaneous movement, or even be deemed the result of a revelation. On his arrival at Jerusalem he communicated his gospel to whom it concerned, and had private interviews with many important personages. No one criticised his actions nor troubled him with communications, but only begged him to remember the poor of Jerusalem. Titus, who accompanied him, consented to be circumcised, but only through the representations of "two false intruding brethren." Paul permitted this incidental concession, but he would not submit to them. As to the more prominent men (and Paul never speaks of them excepting with a shade of bitterness and irony), they learn nothing new from him. He even disputed with Cephas "because he was wrong." At first, indeed, Cephas mingled with every one without distinction. Emissaries arrived from James; and Peter hid himself, avoiding the uncircumcised. Paul publicly apostrophized Cephas, bitterly reproaching him for his conduct, "seeing that he did not keep in the narrow path of gospel truth."

Observe the difference. On the one side holy concord; on the other, extreme susceptibility and half-restrained anger. On one side a harmonious council; and on the other, nothing resembling it. On the one side a formal decree emanating from a recognised authority; on the other, antagonistic opinions reciprocally conceding nothing excepting for form's sake. It is needless to say which version merits our preference. The account given in the Acts is scarcely truthful, because the dispute in which the Council was engaged is not alluded to after the Council was reunited. The two orators here make use of expressions contradictory to what they had elsewhere said. The decree which the Council is reported to have made, is assuredly a fiction. If this decree, emanating from the pen of James, had really been promulgated, why should the good and timid Peter have been afraid of the messengers sent by James? Why should he hide himself? He, as well as the Christians of Antioch, was acting in entire conformity with this decree, the terms of which had been dictated by James himself. The discussion relating to circumcision took place about 51; yet several years after, about the year 56, the quarrel which this decree should have terminated, was more lively than ever. The Church of Galatia was troubled by new emissaries sent by the Jewish party of Jerusalem.[55] Paul answers to this new attack of his enemies by his terrible Epistle. If the decree reported in the fifteenth chapter of the *Acts* had existed, Paul, by referring to it, would have had a much simpler method of bringing the debate to a close. Now, everything that he says, intimates the non-existence of this decree; and in 57, Paul writing to the Corinthians, not only ignores it, but even violates its directions. The decree commands abstinence from flesh offered to idols; but Paul, on the contrary, thinks it no wrong to eat of this flesh as long as no one is scandalized by the act, though he advises abstinence should it give offence to any one.[56] In 58, at last, after the last journey of Paul to Jerusalem, James was more obstinate than ever.[57] One of the characteristic traits of the book of *Acts*, clearly proving that the author is less anxious to present historic truth or even to satisfy logical reasoning than to edify pious readers, is this fact, that the question of the admission of the uncircumcised is always on the point of being resolved without ever attaining that consummation. The baptism of the eunuch of Candia, the baptism of the centurion Cornelius, both miraculously ordered; the foundation of the Church at Antioch (xr. 19; and following verses); the pretended Council at Jerusalem—all leave the question yet in suspense. In truth, it always remained in that state. The two fractions of budding Christianity never came together; and that one which maintained the practices of Judaism proved unfruitful, and soon vanished in obscurity. So far from finding general acceptation, Paul after his death was calumniated. and even anathematized, by no inconsiderable portion of Christianity.[58]

In our third book we shall dwell at length on the subject to which these singular incidents refer. Our object at present is only to give a few examples of the manner in which the author of the *Acts* interprets history, and to show how he reconciles it with his preconceived ideas. Must we therefore agree with certain celebrated critics that the first chapters of the *Acts* are without authenticity, and that his leading characters, such as the eunuch, the centurion Cornelius, and even the deacon Stephen, and the pious Tabitha, are mere creations of fiction? By no means. It is not probable that the author of the *Acts* invented his personages;[59] but he is a skilful lawyer who writes to prove, and who, from facts of which he has heard, tries to deduce arguments in favor of his cherished theories, which are the legitimacy of the calling of the Gentiles and the divine institution of the hierarchy. Though such a document should be used with great care, its entire rejection would show as little critical acumen as its blind acceptation. Several paragraphs even in the first part possess a value universally recognised as representing authentic memoirs quoted from the last compiler. The twelfth chapter, in particular, is without alloy, and seems to emanate from St. Mark.

It would indeed be unsatisfactory if for this history we had as our documents of reference only this legendary book. Happily there are others which, though they relate directly to the period to which our third book will be devoted, yet throw much light upon this epoch. Such are the Epistles of St. Paul; the Epistle to the Galatians, above all, is really a treasure: the basis of all the chronology of that period, the key which unlocks all, the testimony which assures the most sceptical of the reality of things which cannot be doubted. I wish that the serious readers who may feel tempted to regard me as too bold or too credulous, would re-peruse the first two chapters of this singular Epistle; these chapters are certainly the two most important pages in the history of budding Christianity. The Epistles of St. Paul indeed possess in their absolute authenticity an unequalled advantage in this history Not the slightest doubt has been raised by serious criticism against the authenticity of the Epistle to the Galatians, the two Epistles to the Corinthians, or the Epistle to the Romans; while the arguments on which are founded the attacks on the two Epistles to the Thessalonians and that to the Philippians are without value. At the beginning of our third book we shall discuss the more specious though equally indecisive objections which have been raised against the Epistle to the Colossians and the little note to Philemon; the particular problem presented by the Epistle to the Ephesians; and at last the proofs which have led us to reject the two Epistles to Timothy and that to Titus. The Epistles which shall serve our need in the present volume are all of indubitable authority, while the deductions we shall draw from the others are quite independent of the question whether they were or were not dictated by St. Paul. It is not necessary to revert here to the rules of criticism which have been followed in the composition of this work, and which has already been done in the introduction to the Life of Jesus. The twelve first chapters of the *Acts* form a document analogous to the synoptical Gospels and to be treated in the same manner. This species of document, half historical and half legendary, can be accepted neither as legend nor as history; while in detail nearly everything is false, we can nevertheless exhume therefrom precious truths. A pure and literal translation of these narratives, which are often contradicted by better authenticated texts, is not history. Often in cases where we have but one text there is fear that if others existed it would be contradicted. As regards the life of Jesus, the narrative of Luke is always controlled and corrected by the two other synoptical Gospels and by the fourth. Is it not probable, I repeat, that if we had a work bearing the same relation to the *Acts* that the synoptical Gospels do to the fourth Gospel, the book of *Acts* would be defective in many points on which we now receive it as testimony? Entirely different rules will guide us in our third book, where we shall be in the full light of positive history, and shall possess original and sometimes autographical information. When St. Paul himself relates some episode of his life, regarding which his interest demanded no special interpretation, of course we need only insert his identical words in our work, as Tillemont does. But, when we have to do with a narrator identified with a certain system, writing in support of certain ideas, preparing his work in the vague blunt style and with the highly wrought colors peculiar to legendary lore, the duty of the critic is to free himself from the thraldom of the text and to penetrate through it o the truths which it conceals, without, however, being too confident that he has discovered that truth. To debar criticism from similar interpretations would be as unreasonable as to limit the astronomer to the visible state of the heavens. Does not astronomy, on the contrary, involve an allowance for the parallax caused by the position of the observer, and construe from apparent deceptive appearances the real condition of the starry skies?

Why, then, should a literal interpretation of documents containing irreconcilable discrepancies be urged?

The first twelve chapters of the Acts are a tissue of miracles. It is an absolute rule of criticism to deny a place in history to narratives of miraculous circumstances; nor is this owing to a metaphysical system, for it is simply the dictation of observation. Such facts have never been really proved. All the pretended miracles near enough to be examined are referable to illusion or imposture. If a single miracle had ever been proved, we could not reject in a mass all those of ancient history; for, admitting that very many of these last were false, we might still believe that some of them were true. But it is not so. Discussion and examination are fatal to miracles. Are we not then authorized in believing that those miracles which date many centuries back, and regarding which there are no means of forming a contradictory debate, are also without reality? In other words, miracles only exist when people believe in them. The supernatural is but another word for faith. Catholicism, in maintaining that it yet possesses miraculous power, subjects itself to the influence of this law. The miracles of which it boasts never occur where they would be most effective; why should not such a convincing proof be brought more prominently forward? A miracle at Paris, for instance, before experienced savants, would put an end to all doubts! But, alas! such a thing never happens. A miracle never takes place before an incredulous and sceptical public, the most in need of such a convincing proof. Credulity on part of the witness is the essential condition of a miracle. There is not a solitary exception to the rule that miracles are never produced before those who are able or permitted to discuss and criticise them. Cicero, with his usual good sense and penetration, asks: "Since when has this secret force disappeared; has it not been since men have become less credulous?"[60]

"But," it may be urged, "if it is impossible to prove that there ever was any instance of supernatural power, it is equally impossible to prove that there was not. The positive savant who denies the supernatural, argues as gratuitously as the credulous one who admits it!" Not at all. It is the duty of him who affirms a proposition to prove it, while he to whom the affirmation is made has only to listen to the proof and to decide whether it is satisfactory. If any one had asked Buffon to give a place in his *Natural History* to sirens and centaurs, he would have answered: "Show mea specimen of these beings and I will admit them; until then, I do not admit their existence." "But can you prove that they do not exist?" the other may say, and Buffon would reply: "It is your province to prove that they do exist." In science the burden of proof rests on those who advance alleged facts. Why, although innumerable historic writings claim their existence, do people no longer believe in angels and demons? Simply because the existence of an angel or a demon has never yet been proved.

In support of the reality of miraculous agency, appeal is made to phenomena outside of the course of natural laws, such, for instance, as the creation of man. This creation, it has been said, could only have been compassed by the direct intervention of the Divinity, and why was not this intervention manifested at other decisive crises of the development of the universe? I shall not dwell upon the strange philosophy and sordid appreciation of the Divinity manifested in such a system of reasoning. History should have its method, independent of all philosophy. Without at all entering upon the domain of theology, it is easy to show how defective is this argument. It is equivalent to maintaining that everything which does not happen in the ordinary conditions of the world, everything that cannot be explained by the present rules of science, is miraculous. But, according to this, the sun is a miracle, because science has never explained the sun; the conception of mankind is a miracle, because physiology is silent on that point; conscience is a miracle, because it is an absolute mystery; and every animal is a miracle, because the origin of life is a problem of which we know next to nothing. The reply that every life, every soul, is of an order superior to nature, is simply a play upon words. So we understand it, and yet the word miracle remains to be explained. How is that a miracle which happens every day and hour? The miraculous is not simply the inexplicable, it is a formal derogation from recognised laws in the name of a particular desire. What we deny to the miracle is the exceptional state or the results of particular intervention, as in the case of a clockmaker who may have made a clock very handsome to look at, but requiring at intervals the hand of its maker to supply a deficiency in its mechanism. We acknowledge heartily that God may be permanently in everything, particularly in everything that lives; and we only maintain there has never been convincing proof of any particular intervention of supernatural force. We deny the reality of supernatural agency until we are made cognizant of a demonstrated fact of this nature. To search for this demonstration anterior to the creation of man ; to go outside of history for historical miracles, dating back to epochs when all proof is impossible—all this is to seek refuge behind a cloud, to prove one doubtful proposition by another equally obscure, to bring against a recognised law an alleged fact of which we know nothing. If miracles, which only took place so long ago that no witness of them now exists, are invoked, it is simply because none can be cited for which competent witnesses can be claimed.

In far distant epochs, beyond doubt, there occurred phenomena which, on the same scale at least, are not repeated in the world of to-day. But there was at the time they happened a cause for these phenomena. In geological formations may be met a great number of minerals and precious stones which nature seems no longer to produce; and yet most of them have been artificially recomposed by Messieurs Mitscherlich, Ebelman, De Sénarmont, and Daubrée. If life cannot be artificially produced, it is because the reproduction of the conditions in which life commenced (if it ever did commence) will probably be always beyond human grasp. How can the planet that disappeared thousands of years ago be brought back? How form an experience, which has lasted for centuries? The diversity of thousands of ages of slow evolution is what one forgets in denominating as miracles the phenomena which occurred in other times, but which occur no more. Far back in the vast range of heavenly bodies, are now perhaps taking place movements which, nearer us, have ceased since a period infinitely distant. The formation of humanity, if we think of it as a sudden instantaneous thing, is certainly of all things in the world the most shocking and absurd; but it maintains its place in general analogies (without losing its mystery) if it is viewed as the result of a long-continued progress, lasting during incalculable ages. The laws of matured life are not applicable to embryotic life. The embryo develops all its organs one after another. It creates no more, because it is no longer at the creative age; just as language is no longer invented, because there is no more to invent. But why longer follow up adversaries who beg the question? We ask for a proven miracle, and are told that it took place anterior to history. Certainly, if any proof were wanting of the necessity of supernatural beliefs to certain states of the soul, it would be found in the fact that many minds gifted in all other points with due penetration, have reposed their entire faith in an argument as desperate as this.

There are some persons who yield up the idea of physical miracles, but still maintain the existence of a sort of moral miracle, without which, in their opinion, certain great events cannot be explained. Assuredly the formation of Christianity is the grandest fact in the religious history of the world; but for all that, it is by no means a miracle. Buddhism and Babism have counted as many excited and resigned martyrs as even Christianity. The miracles of the founding of Islamism are of an entirely different character, and I confess have very little effect on me. It may, however, be remarked that the Mussulman doctors deduce from the remarkable establishment of their religion, from its marvellously rapid diffusion, from its rapid conquests, and from the force which gives it so absolute a governing power, precisely the same arguments which Christian apologists bring forward in relation to the establishment of Christianity, and which, they claim, show clearly the hand of God. Let us allow that the foundation of Christianity is something utterly peculiar. Another equally peculiar thing, is Hellenism; understanding by that word the ideal of perfection realized by grace in literature, art, and philosophy. Greek art surpasses all other arts, as the Christian religion surpasses all other religions; and the Acropolis at Athens a collection of masterpieces beside which all other attempts are only like gropings in the dark, or, at the best, imitations more or less successful, is perhaps that which, above everything else, defies comparison. Hellenism, in other words, is as much a prodigy of beauty as Christianity is a prodigy of sanctity.

A unique action or development is not necessarily miraculous. God exists in various degrees in all that is beautiful, good, and true; but he is never so exclusively in any one of His manifestations, that the presence of His vitalizing breath in a religious or philosophical movement should be deemed a privilege or an exception.

I am not without hope that the interval of two years and a half that has elapsed since the publication of the Life of Jesus, has led many readers to consider these problems with calmness. Without knowing or wishing it, religious controversy is always a dishonesty. It is not always its province to discuss with independence and to examine with anxiety; but it must defend a determined doctrine, and prove that he who dissents from it is either ignorant or dishonest. Calumnies, misconstructions, falsifications of ideas or words, boasting arguments on points not raised by the opponent, shouts of victory over errors which he has not committed — none of these seem to be considered unworthy weapons by those who believe they are called upon to maintain the interests of an absolute truth. I would be ignorant indeed of history, if I had not known all this. I am indifferent enough, however, not to feel it very deeply; and I have enough respect for the faith, to kindly appreciate whatever was touching or genuine in the sentiments which actuated my antagonists. Often, after observing the artlessness, the pious assurance, the frank anger, so freely expressed by so many good people, I have said as John Huss did at the sight of an old woman perspiring under the weight of a faggot she was feebly dragging to his stake: "*O sancta simplicitas!*" I have only regretted at times the waste of sentiment. According to the beautiful expression of Scripture: "God is not in the fire." If all this annoyance proved instrumental in aiding the cause of truth, there would be something of consolation in it. But it is not always so; Truth is not for the angry and passionate man. She reserves herself for those who, freed from partisan feeling, from persistent affection, and enduring hate, seek her with entire liberty, and with no mental reservation referring to human affairs. These problems form only one of the innumerable questions with which the world is crowded, and which the curious are fond of studying. No one is offended by the announcement of a mere theoretical opinion. Those who would guard their faith as a treasure can defend it very easily by ignoring all works written in an opposing spirit. The timid would do better by dispensing with reading.

There are persons of a very practical turn of mind, who, on hearing of any new scientific work, ask what political party the author aims to please, and who think that every poem should contain a moral lesson. These people think that propagandism is the only object that a writer has in view. The idea of an art or science aspiring only after the true and beautiful, without regard either to policy or politics, is something quite strange to them. Between such persons and ourselves misapprehensions are inevitable. "There are people," said a Greek philosopher, "who take with their left hand what is offered to them with their right." A number of letters, dictated by a really honest sentiment, which have been sent me, may be summed up in the question, "What is the matter with you? What end are you aiming at?" Why, I write for precisely the same reason that all historical writers do. It I could have several lives, I would devote one to writing a life of Alexander, another to a history of Athens, and a third to either a history of the French Revolution or the monkish order of St. Francis. In writing these works I would be actuated by a desire to find the truth, and would endeavor to make the mighty events of the past known with the greatest possible exactness, and related in a manner worthy of them. Far from me be the thought of shocking the religious faith of any person! Such works should be prepared with as much supreme indifference as if they were written in another planet. Every concession to the scruples of an inferior order, is a derogation from the dignity and culture of art and truth. It can at once be seen that the absence of proselytism is the leading feature of works composed in such a spirit.

The first principle of the critical school is the allowance in matters of faith of all that is needed, and the adaptation of beliefs to individual wants. Why should we be foolish enough to concern ourselves about things over which no one has any control? If any person adopts our principles it is because he has the mental tendency and the education adapted to them; and all our efforts will not be able to impart this tendency and this education to those who do not naturally possess them. Philosophy differs from faith in this, that faith is believed to operate by itself independently of the intelligence acquired from dogmas. We, on the contrary, hold that truth only possesses value when it comes of itself, and when the order of its ideas is comprehended. We do not consider ourselves obliged to maintain silence in regard to those opinions which may not be in accord with the belief of some of our fellow-creatures; we will make no sacrifice to the exigencies of differing orthodoxies, but neither have we any idea of attacking them; we shall only act as if they did not exist. For myself, it would be really painful to me for any one to convict me of an effort to attract to my side of thinking a solitary adherent who would not come voluntarily. I would conclude that my mind was perturbed in its serene liberty, or that something weighed heavily upon it, if Iwere no longer able to content myself with the simple and joyous contemplation of the universe.

It will readily be supposed that if my object was to make war upon established religions, I should adopt different tactics, and should confine myself to exposing the impossibilities and the contradictions in texts and dogmas that are viewed as sacred. This work has been often and ably done. In 1865[61] I wrote as follows: "I protest once for all against the false interpretation which has been given to my writings, in accepting as polemical works the various essays and religious and historical matters which I have published, or may hereafter publish. Viewed as polemical works, these essays, I am well aware, are very unskilful. Polemics demand a strategy to which I am a stranger; it requires the writer to choose the weak point of his adversaries, to hold on to it, to avoid uncertain questions, to beware of all concession, and practically renounce even the essence of scientific spirit. Such is not my method. Revelation and the supernatural—those fundamental questions around which must revolve all religious discussion—I do not touch upon; not because I may not answer these questions with thorough certainty, but because such a discussion is not scientific, or, rather, because independent science presupposes that such questions are already answered. For me to pursue any polemical or proselyting end, would be to bring forward among the most difficult and delicate problems, a question which can be more satisfactorily treated in the more practical phraseology in which controversialists and apologists usually discuss it. Far from regretting the advantages which I thus deprive myself of, I would be well pleased thereat, if I could thus convince theologians that my writings are of a different order to theirs, that they are only intended as scholarly researches, open to attack as such, when they sometimes attempt to apply to the Christian and Jewish religions the same principles of criticism which are adopted towards other branches of history and philology. Questions of a purely theological nature I am no more called upon to discuss, than are Burnouf, Creuzer, Guizniaut, and other critical historians of ancient religions, to defend the creeds which they have made their study. The history of humanity seems to me to be a vast grouping where everything, though unequal and diverse, is of the same general order, arises from the same causes, and is subject to the same laws. These laws I seek without any other intention than to understand them exactly as they are. Nothing will ever induce me to leave a sphere, humble it may be, but valuable to science, for the paths of the controversialist, who is always certain of the countenance of those interested in opposing war to war.

For the polemic system, the necessity of which I do not deny, though it is neither adapted to my tastes nor to my capabilities, Voltaire was enough. One cannot be, at the same time, a good controversialist and a good historian. Voltaire, so weak in mere erudition; Voltaire who, to us initiated into a better method, seems so poorly to comprehend the spirit of antiquity, is twenty times victorious over adversaries yet more destitute of true criticism than himself. A new edition of the works of this great man would furnish a reply that is now much needed to the usurpations of theology—a reply poor in itself, but well suited to that which it would combat; a weak, old-fashioned reply to a weak, old-fashioned science. Let us, who possess a love of the true and an inquiring spirit, do better. Let us leave these discussions to those who care for them; let us work for the limited class who follow the true path of the human mind. Popularity, I know, is more easily gained by those writers who, instead of pursuing the most elevated form of truth, devote their energies to combating the opinions of their age; yet by a just compensation, they are of no value after the theories they combat are abandoned. Those who, in the sixteenth and seventeenth centuries, refuted magic and astrology, rendered an immense service to right and truth; and yet their writings are to-day unknown, and their very victory has consigned them to oblivion.

I shall always hold to this rule of conduct as the only one suitable to the dignity of the *savant*. I know that researches into religious history always bring one face to face with vital questions which seem to demand a solution. Persons unfamiliar with free speculation do not at all comprehend the calm deliberation of thought; practical minds grow impatient of a science which does not respond to their desires. Let us guard against this vain ardor; let us remain in our respective Churches, profiting by their secular teachings and their traditions of virtue, participating in their charitable works, and enjoying the poetry of their past. Let us only reject their intolerance. Let us even pardon this intolerance, for like egotism it is one of the necessities of human nature. The formation of new religious families or beliefs, or any important change in the proportions of those existing to-day, is contrary to present indications. Catholicism will soon be scarred and seamed by great schisms; the days of Avignon, of the anti-popes, of the Clementists and the Urbanists, are about to return. The Catholic Church will see another sixteenth century; and yet, notwithstanding its divisions, it will remain the Catholic Church. It is not probable that for a hundred years to come the relative proportions of Protestants, Catholics, and Jews, will be materially varied. But a great change will be accomplished, or, at least, people will become sensible of it. Every one of these religious families will have two classes of adherents; the one believing simply and absolutely after the manner of the middle ages, the other sacrificing the letter of the law and maintaining its spirit. In every communion this latter great class will increase; and as the spirit draws together quite as much as the letter separates, the spiritually-minded of each faith will be brought nearer. Fanaticism will be lost in a general tolerance. The theory of the dogma will become merely a mysterious vault which no one will ever care to open; and if the vault be empty, of what importance is it? Only one religion—Islamism alone, I fear—will resist this mollifying process. Among certain Mahommedans of the old school, several eminent men in Constantinople, and above all among the Persians, there are the germs of a tolerant and conciliatory spirit. If these germs of good be crushed by the fanaticism of the Ulemas, Islamism will perish; for two things are evident—that modern civilization does not wish to see the old religions entirely die out; and that, on the other hand, it will not be impeded in its work by senile religious institutions; these latter must either bend or break.

And why should pure religion, which cannot be

deemed the exclusive attribute of any one sect or church, encumber itself with the inconveniences of a position the advantages of which are denied it? Why should it array standard against standard, all the time knowing that safety and peace are in the reach of all, according to the merits of each. Protestantism, which proceeded from a very absolute faith, led in the sixteenth century to an open rupture. So far from showing any reduction of dogmatism, the reform was marked by a revival of the most rigid Christian spirit. The movement of the nineteenth century, on the other hand, arises from a sentiment which is the inverse proposition of dogmatism. It will not do away with any sect or church, but will lead to a general concentration of all the churches. Divisions and schisms increase the fanaticism and provoke reaction. The Luthers and Calvins made the Caraffas, the Ghislieri, Loyolas, and Philip II. If our church repels us, do not let us recriminate; let us the better appreciate the mildness of modern manners which has made this hatred impotent; let us console ourselves by reflecting on that invisible church which includes excommunicated saints, and the noblest souls of every age. The banished of the church are always its best blood; they are in advance of their times; the heresy of the present is the orthodoxy of the future. And what, after all, is the excommunication of men? The heavenly Father only excommuicates the narrow-minded and selfish. If the priest refuses to admit us to the cemetery, let us prohibit our families from beseeching him to alter his decision. God is the Judge; and the Earth is a kind and impartial mother. The body of the good man, placed in ground not consecrated, carries there a consecration with it.

There are, without doubt, positions when the application of these principles is difficult. The spirit of liberty, like the wind, bloweth wherever it listeth. There are often people like clergymen, riveted, as it were, to an absolute faith; but even among them, a noble mind rises to the full extent of the issue. A worthy country priest, through his solitary studies and the simple purity of his life, comes to a knowledge of the impossibilities of literal dogmatism; and must he therefore sadden those whom he formerly consoled, and explain to the simple folk those mental processes which they cannot comprehend? Heaven forbid! There are no two men in the world whose paths of duty are exactly alike. The excellent Bishop Colenso showed an honesty which the Church since her origin has not seen surpassed, in writing out his doubts as they occurred to him. But the humble Catholic priest, surrounded by timid and narrow-minded souls, must be quiet. Oh! how many close-mouthed tombs about our village churches, hide similar poetic reticence and angelic silence! Do those who speak when duty dictates, equal, after all, in merit, those who in secret cherish and restrain the doubts known only to God?

Theory is not practice. The ideal should remain the ideal, for it may become soiled and contaminated by contact with reality. Sentiments appropriate enough to those who are preserved by their innate nobleness from all moral danger, are not as suitable to those who are of a lower grade. It is only from ideas strictly limited that great actions are evolved; and this is because human capacity is limited. A man wholly without prejudice would be powerless and uninfluential. Let us enjoy the liberty of the sons of God; but let us also beware that we are not accomplices in diminishing the sum-total of virtue in the world—a result which would necessarily arise, were Christianity to be weakened. What, indeed, would we be without it? What would replace the noble institutions to which it gave birth, such as the association of the Sisters of Charity? How cold-hearted, mean, and petty mankind would become! Our disagreement with those who believe in positive religions, is, after all, purely scientific; we are with them at heart; and we combat but one enemy, which is theirs as well as ours—and this enemy is vulgar materialism.

Peace, then, in the name of God! Let the different orders of men live side by side, and pass their days, not in doing injustice to their own proper spirit by making concessions which would only deteriorate them, but in mutually supporting each other. Nothing here below should rule to the exclusion of its opposite; no one force should have the power to suppress other forces. The true harmony of humanity results from the free use of discordant notes. We know too well what follows when orthodoxy succeeds in overpowering science. The Mussulman element in Spain was extirpated because it clung too fondly to its orthodox views. The experience of the French Revolution shows us what we may expect when Rationalism attempts to govern people without reference to their religious needs. The instinct of art, carried to a high pitch of refinement, but without honesty, made of Italy a den of thieves and cut-throats. Stupidity and mediocrity are the bane of certain Protestant countries, where, under the pretext of common sense and Christian spirit, art and science are both absolutely degraded. Lucretia of Rome and Saint Theresa, Aristophanes and Socrates, Voltaire and Francis of Assisi, Raphael and St. Vincent de Paul, all enjoyed, to an equal degree, the right of existence, and humanity would have been lesened, had a single one of these individual elements been wanting.

CHAPTER I.

FORMATION OF BELIEFS RELATIVE TO THE RESURRECTION OF JESUS.—THE APPARITIONS AT JERUSALEM.

JESUS, although constantly speaking of resurrection and of a new life, had not declared very plainly that he should rise again in the flesh.[1]

The disciples, during the first hours which elapsed after his death, had, in this respect, no fixed hope. The sentiments which they so artlessly confide to us show that they believed all to be over. They bewail and bury their friend, if not as one of the common herd who had died, at least as a person whose loss was irreparable ;[2] they were sorrowful and cast down ; the expectation which they had indulged of seeing him realize the salvation of Israel, is proved to have been vanity ; we should speak of them as of men who have lost a grand and beloved illusion.

But enthusiasm and love do not recognise situations unfruitful of results. They amuse themselves with what is impossible, and, rather than renounce all hope, they do violence to every reality. Many words of their Master which they remembered—those, above all, in which he had predicted his future advent—might be interpreted to mean that he would rise from the tomb.[3] Such a belief was, otherwise, so natural, that the faith of the disciples would have been sufficient to have invented it in all its parts. The great prophets Enoch and Elijah had not tasted death. They began to imagine that the patriarchs and the chief fathers of the old law were not really dead, and that their bodies were sepulchred at Hebron, alive and animated. To Jesus had happened the same fortune which is the lot of all men who have riveted the attention of their fellow-men. The world, accustomed to attribute to them superhuman virtues, could not admit that they had submitted to the unjust, revolting, iniquitous law of the death common to all. At the moment at which Mahomet expired, Omar rushed from the tent, sword in hand, and declared that he would hew down the head of any one who should dare to say that the prophet was no more.[5]

Death is so absurd a thing when it smites the man of genius or the man of large heart, that people will not believe in the possibility of such an error on the part of nature. Heroes do not die. What is true existence but the recollection of us which survives in the hearts of those who love us? For some years this adored Master had filled the little world by which He was surrounded with joy and hope; could they consent to allow Him to the decay of the tomb? No; He had too entirely lived in those who surrounded Him, that they could but affirm that after His death He would live for ever.[6]

The day which followed the burial of Jesus (Saturday, the 15th of the month Nisan), was occupied with such thoughts as these. All manual labor was forbidden on account of the Sabbath. But never was repose more fruitful. The Christian conscience had, on that day, only one object; the Master laid low in the tomb. The women, especially, overwhelmed him in spirit with the most tender caresses. Their thoughts leave not for an instant this sweet friend, lying in His myrrh, whom the wicked had slain! Ah! doubtless, the angels are surrounding Him, and veiling their faces with His shroud. Well did He say that He should die, that His death would be the salvation of the sinner, and that He should live again in the kingdom of His father. Yes! He shall live again; God will not leave His Son a prey to hell; He will not suffer His elect to see corruption.[7] What is this tombstone which weighs upon Him? He will raise it up; He will reascend to the right hand of His Father, whence He descended. And we shall see Him again; we shall hear His charming voice; we shall enjoy afresh His conversations, and they will have slain Him in vain.

The belief in the immortality of the soul, which through the influence of the Grecian philosophy has become a dogma of Christianity, is easily permitted to take the part of death; because the dissolution of the body, by this hypothesis, is nothing else than a deliverance of the soul, hereafter freed from the troublesome bonds without which it is able to exist. But this theory of man, considered as a being composed of two substances, was by no means clear to the Jews. The reign of God and the reign of the spirit consisted, in their ideas, in a complete transformation of the world and in the annihilation of death.[8] To acknowledge that death could have the victory over Jesus, over him who came to abolish the power of death, this was the height of absurdity. The very idea that he could suffer had previously been revolting to his disciples.[9] They had no choice, then, between despair or heroic affirmation. A man of penetration might have announced during the Saturday that Jesus would arise. The little Christian society, on that day, worked the veritable miracle; they resuscitated Jesus in their hearts by the intense love which they bore towards him. They decided that Jesus had not died. The love of these passionately fond souls was, truly, stronger than death;[10] and as the characteristic of a passionate love is to be communicated, to light up like a torch a sentiment which resembles it and is straightway indefinitely propagated; so Jesus, in one sense, at the time of which we are speaking, is already resuscitated. Only let a material fact, insignificant of itself, allow the persuasion that his body is no longer here below, and the dogma of the resurrection will be established for ever.

This was exactly what happened in the circumstances which, being partly obscure on account of the incoherence of their traditions, and above all on account of the contradictions which they present, have nevertheless been seized upon with a sufficient degree of probability.[11]

On the Sunday morning, at a very early hour, the women of Galilee who on Friday evening had hastily embalmed the body, repaired to the cave where they had provisionally deposited it. These were, Mary of Magdala, Mary Cleophas, Salome, Joanna, wife of Khouza, and others.[12] They came, probably, each from her own abode; for if it is difficult to call in question the tradition of the three synoptical Gospels, according to which many women came to the tomb,[13] it is certain, on the other hand, that in the two most authentic accounts[14] which we possess of the resurrection, Mary of Magdala plays her part alone. In any case, she had at this solemn moment a part to play altogether out of the common order of events. It is her that we must follow step by step; for she bore on that day during one hour all the burden of the Christian conscience; her witness decided the faith of the future. We must remember that the cave, wherein the body of Jesus was inclosed, had been recently hewn out of the rock, and that it was situated in a garden hard by the place of execution.[15] For this latter reason only had it been selected, seeing that it was late in the day, and that they were unwilling to violate the Sabbath.[16] The first Gospel alone adds one circumstance, viz. that the cave was the property of Joseph of Arimathea. But, in general, the anecdotical circumstances added by the first Gospel to the common fund of tradition are without value, above all when it treats of the last days of the life of Jesus.[17] The same Gospel mentions another detail which, considering the silence of the others, is destitute of probability; viz. the fact of the seals and of a guard detailed to the tomb.[18] We must also recollect that the mortuary vaults were low chambers hewn in the side of a sloping rock, on which was contrived a vertical cutting. The door, usually downwards, was closed by a very heavy stone, which fitted into a rabbet.[19] These chambers had no locks secured with keys; the weight of the stone was the sole safeguard they possessed against robbers and profaners of tombs; thus were they arranged in such a manner that either mechanical power or the united effort of several persons was necessary to remove the stone. All the traditions are agreed on this point, that the stone had been placed at the orifice of the vault on the Friday evening.

But when Mary Magdala arrived on the Sunday morning, the stone was not in its place. The vault was open. The body was no longer there. The idea of the resurrection was with her, as yet, but little developed. That which occupied her soul was a tender regret, and the desire to pay funeral honors to the corpse of her divine friend. Her first feelings then were those of surprise and grief. The disappearance of this cherished corpse had taken away from her the last joy on which she had depended. She could never touch him again with her hands. And what was he become? . . . The idea of a profanation presented itself to her, and she revolted at it. Perhaps, at the same time, a ray of hope beamed across her mind. Without losing a moment, she runs to the house where Peter and John were reunited.[20]

"They have taken away the body of our Master," she said, "and we know not where they have laid him." The two disciples arise hastily and run with all their might. John, the younger, arrives first. He stoops down to look into the interior. Mary was right. The tomb was empty. The linen cloths which had served as his shroud were lying apart in the vault. In his turn Peter arrives. The two enter, examine the linen cloths, no doubt spotted with blood, and remark, in particular, the napkin which had enveloped his head rolled by itself in one corner of the cave.[21] Peter and John returned to their homes overwhelmed with grief. If they did not then pronounce the decisive words, "He is risen!" we may affirm that such a consequence was their irrevocable conclusion, and that the creative dogma of Christianity was already propounded.

Peter and John having departed from the garden, Mary remained alone at the edge of the cave. She wept copiously; one sole thought preoccupied her mind: Where had they put the body?

Her woman's heart went no further from her desire to clasp again in her arms the beloved corpse. Suddenly she hears a light rustling behind her. There is a man standing. At first she believes it to be the gardener. "Oh!" she says, "if thou hast borne him hence, tell me where thou hast laid him, that I may take him away." For the only answer, she thinks that she hears herself called by her name, "Mary!" It was the voice that had so often thrilled her before. It was the accent of Jesus. "Oh, my master!" she cries. She is about to touch him. A sort of instinctive movement throws her at his feet to kiss them.[22]

The light vision gives way and says to her, "Touch me not." Little by little the shadow disappears.[23]

But the miracle of love is accomplished. That which Cephas could not do, Mary has done; she has been able to draw life, sweet and penetrating words from the empty tomb. There is now no more talk of inferences to be deduced, or of conjectures to be framed. Mary has seen and heard. The resurrection has its first direct witness.

Frantic with love, intoxicated with joy, Mary returned to the city; and to the first disciples whom she met, she says, "I have seen Him, He has spoken to me."[24] Her greatly agitated mind, her broken and disconnected accents of speech, caused her to be taken by some persons for one demented.[26] Peter and John, in their turn, relate what they had seen; other disciples go to the tomb and see likewise.[27] The fixed conviction of all this first party was that Jesus had risen again. Many doubts still existed; but the assurance of Mary, of Peter, and of John, imposed upon the others. At a later date, this was called "the vision of Peter."[28]

Paul, in particular, does not speak of the vision of Mary, and attributes all the honor of the first apparition to Peter. But this expression is very indefinite. Peter only saw the empty cave, and the linen cloth and the napkin. Only Mary loved enough to pass the bounds of nature and revive the shade of the perfect master. In these kinds of marvellous crises, to see after the others is nothing; all the merit is in seeing for the first time, for the others afterwards model their visions on the received type. It is the peculiarity of fine organizations to conceive the image promptly, justly, and with a sort of intimate sense of the end. The glory of the resurrection belongs, then, to Mary of Magdala. After Jesus, it is Mary who has done most for the foundation of Christianity. The shadow created by the delicate sensibility of Magdalene wanders still on the earth. Queen and patroness of idealists, Magdalene knew better than any one how to assert her dream, and impose on every one the vision of her passionate soul. Her great womanly affirmation: "He has risen," has been the basis of the faith of humanity. Away, impotent reason! Apply no cold analysis to this *chef-d'œuvre* of idealism and of love. If wisdom refuses to console this poor human race, betrayed by fate, let folly attempt the enterprise. Where is the sage who has given to the world as much joy as the possessed Mary of Magdala?

The other women, meanwhile, who had been to the tomb, spread abroad different reports.[29] They had not seen Jesus;[30] but they told of a man clothed in white, whom they had seen in the cave, and who had said to them: "He is no longer here, return into Galilee: He will go before you, there shall ye see Him." [36]

Perhaps it was the white linen clothes which had given rise to this hallucination. Perhaps, again, they saw nothing at all, and only began to speak of their vision when Mary of Magdala had related hers. According to one of the most authentic texts,[32] indeed, they maintained silence for some time, and their silence was subsequently attributed to terror. However that may be, these stories continued hourly to increase, as well as to undergo strange transformations. The man in white became an angel of God; it was told how that his clothing was glistening like the snow, and his figure like lightning. Others spoke of two angels, of whom one appeared at the head and the other at the foot of the tomb.[33] In the evening, it is possible that many persons believed already that the women had seen the angel descend from heaven, take away the stone, and Jesus then shoot forth with a crash.[34] They themselves, no doubt, varied in their narratives;[35] suffering from the effect of the imagination of others, as always happens to people of the lower orders, they scrupled not to introduce all sorts of embellishments, and were thus participators in the creation of the legend which took its rise amongst them and concerning them.

The day was stormy and decisive. The little company was sadly dispersed. Some of them had already departed for Galilee, others hid themselves from fear.[36] The deplorable scene of the Friday, the heart-rending spectacle which they had before their eyes when they saw Him of whom they had hoped such great things expire upon the gibbet, without His Father having come to deliver him, had, moreover, shocked the faith of many. The news spread by the women and by Peter had been received by many of them with scarce dissembled incredulity.[37] The different stories contradicted one another; the women went hither and thither with strange and conflicting stories, each surpassing the other. The most opposite ideas were propounded. Some of them still deplored the sad event of the previous evening; others were already rejoicing: all were disposed to collect the most extraordinary tales. Meanwhile the mistrust which the excitement of Mary of Magdala caused,[38] the want of authority on the part of the women, together with the incoherence of their several stories, produced great doubts. They were on the watch for new visions, which could not fail to appear. The state of the sect was entirely favorable to the propagation of strange rumors. If the entire little Church had been assembled, the legendary creation would have been impossible; those who knew the secret of the disappearance of the body would probably have protested against the error. But in the confusion which prevailed amongst them, an opportunity was afforded for the most fruitful misunderstandings.

It is the characteristic of those states of mind in which ecstasy and apparitions are commonly generated, to be contagious.[39] The history of all the great religious crises proves that these kinds of visions are catching; in an assembly of persons entertaining the same beliefs, it is enough for one member of the society to affirm that he sees or hears something supernatural, and the others will also see and hear it. Amongst the persecuted Protestants, a report was spread that angels had been heard chanting psalms in the ruins of a recently destroyed temple; the whole company went to the place and heard the same psalm. In cases of this kind, the most excited are those who make the law and who regulate the common atmospheric heat. The exaltation of individuals is transmitted to all the members; no one will be behind or confess that he is less favored than the others. Those who see nothing are carried away by excitement, and come to imagine either that they are not so clear sighted as others, or that they do not give a just account of their feelings; in every case they are careful not to avow their distrust: they would be disturbers of the common joy, they would be causing sadness to the others, and would be themselves acting a disagreeable part. When, then, an apparition is brought forward in such meetings as these, the usual result is, that all either see it or accept it. We must remember, moreover, what degree of intellectual culture was possessed by the disciples of Jesus. What we ca l a weak head is well accompanied by perfect goodness of heart. The disciples believed in phantoms;[41] they imagined that they were surrounded by miracles; they took no part whatever in the positive science of the time. This science flourished amongst a few hundreds of men who were only to be found in the countries to which the civilization of the Greeks had penetrated. But the common people, in all countries, knew very little about it. In this respect Palestine was one of the most backward countries; the Galileans were the most ignorant of the inhabitants of Palestine, and the disciples of Jesus might be counted amongst the number of the most simple people of Galilee. It was to this very simplicity that they owed their heavenly election. Among such a people, belief in the marvellous discovered the most extraordinary channels of propagation. The idea of the resurrection of Jesus being once circulated, numerous visions would be the result. And so, indeed, it came to pass.

Even during the course of that very Sunday, at an advanced period of the forenoon, when the stories of the woman had already been freely circulated, two disciples, one of whom was called Cleopatras or Cleopas, set out on a short journey to a village called Emmaus,[42] situated a short distance from Jerusalem.[43] They were conversing together respecting the recent events, and were full of sadness. On the road an unknown companion joined them and inquired the cause of their deep grief: "Art thou, then, the only stranger at Jerusalem," they said to him, "that thou knowest not what things are come to pass there? Hast thou not heard of Jesus of Nazareth, which was a prophet mighty in deed and word before God and all the people? Knowest thou not how that the chief priests and rulers have condemned him to death and crucified him? We trusted that it had been he which should have redeemed Israel; and besides all this, to-day is the third day since these things were done—yea, and certain women, also, of our company made us astonished who were early at the sepulchre; and when they found not his body, they came, saying that they had also seen a vision of angels who said that he was alive. And certain of them who were with us went to the sepulchre, and found it even so as the women had said; but him they saw not." The stranger was a pious man, well versed in the Scriptures, quoting Moses and the prophets. These three good people became fast friends. As they came near to Emmaus, the stranger proposing to continue his journey through the village, the disciples entreated him to tarry with them and partake of their evening meal. The day was fast drawing to a close; the memories of the two disciples become more vivid. This hour of the evening meal was that which they remembered with the greatest pleasure and regret. How often had they, at this very hour, seen their beloved Master forget the weighty duties of the day in the *abandon* of pleasant conversation, and, cheered by the repast, speak to them of the fruit of the vine which He should drink anew with them in the kingdom of His Father. The gesture which He made while breaking the bread and offering it to them, according to the custom of the head of the house among the Jews, was deeply engraven on their memory. Giving way to a sort of pleasurable sadness, they forget the stranger; it is Jesus whom they see holding the bread, and then breaking it and offering it to them. These remembrances took such a hold on them, that they scarcely perceived that their companion, anxious to continue his journey, had left them. And when they had recovered from their reverie: "Did we not perceive," they said, "something strange? Do you not remember how our heart burned within us, while he talked with us by the way?" "And the prophecies which he cited proved clearly that Messiah must suffer before entering into his glory. Did you not recognise him at the breaking of the bread?" "Yes! up to that time our eyes were closed; they were opened when he vanished." The conviction of the two disciples was that they had seen Jesus. They returned with all haste to Jerusalem. The principal group of the disciples were exactly at that time assembled around Peter.[44]

Night had completely set in. Each one communicated his impressions and the news which he had heard. The general belief already willed that Jesus had arisen. On the entrance of the two disciples, they were immediately informed of what they called "the vision of Peter."[45] They, on their side, related what had happened to them on the road to Emmaus, and how they had recognised him by the breaking of bread. The imagination of all became vividly excited. The doors were closed, for they were afraid of the Jews. Oriental towns are hushed after sunset. The silence accordingly within the house was frequently profound; all the little noises which were accidentally made were interpreted in the sense of the universal expectation. Ordinarily, expectation is the father of its object.[46] During a moment of silence, some slight breath passed over the face of the assembly. At these decisive periods of time, a current of air, a creaking window, or a chance murmur, are sufficient to fix the belief of peoples for ages. At the same time that the breath was perceived they fancied that they heard sounds. Some of them said that they had discerned the word *scha-*

lom, "happiness" or "peace." This was the ordinary salutation of Jesus and the word by which He signified His presence. No possibility of doubt; Jesus is present; He is in the assembly. That is His cherished voice; each one recognises it.[47] This idea was all the more easily entertained because Jesus had said that whenever they were assembled in His name, He would be in the midst of them. It was, then, an acknowledged fact that Jesus had appeared before His assembled disciples, on the night of Sunday. Some pretended to have observed on His hands and His feet the mark of the nails, and on His side the mark of the spear which pierced Him. According to a widely spread tradition, it was the same night as that on which He breathed upon His disciples the Holy Spirit.[48] John xx. 22–23, who is echoed by Luke xxiv. 49. The idea, at least, that His breath had passed over them on their reassembling was generally admitted. Such were the incidents of the day which has decided the lot of the human race. The opinion that Jesus had arisen was thus irrevocably propounded. The sect which was thought to have been extinguished by the death of the Master, was, from henceforth, assured of a wondrous future. And yet some doubts were still existing.[49] The apostle Thomas, who was not present at the meeting of Sunday evening, confessed that he envied those who had seen the mark of the spear and of the nails. We read that, eight days afterwards, he was satisfied.[50] But a little stain, and as it were a mild reproach, have always rested upon him in consequence. By an instinctive view of unerring accuracy, man understands that the ideal is not to be touched with hands, and that there is no occasion for its submission to the control of experience. *Noli me tangere* is the motto of all grand affection. The sense of touch leaves no room for faith; the eye, a purer and more noble organ than the hand—even the eye which nothing soils, and by which nothing is soiled, became very soon a superfluous witness. A singular sensation began to appear; all hesitation was construed into a want of loyalty and love; each was ashamed to be behindhand; the desire to behold was interdicted. The dictum, "Blessed are they who have not seen and yet have believed,"[51] became the word of salutation. It was thought to be more generous to believe without proof. The true-hearted friends would rather not have had the vision.[52] Just as, in later times, St. Louis refused to be a witness to an eucharistic miracle that he might not detract from the merit of faith. Henceforth this credulity became a terrible emulation, and, as it were, a sort of out-bidding one another. The reward consisting in believing without having seen, faith at any price, gratuitous faith—faith approaching to madness—was exalted as if it were the chief gift of the soul. The *credo quia absurdum* is established; the law of Christian dogmas will be an unwonted progression which no impossibility shall be able to arrest. The most cherished dogmas as regards piety, those to which it will attach itself with the most resolute frenzy, will be the most repugnant to reason, in consequence of that touching idea that the moral worth of faith increases in proportion to the difficulty of believing, and because men are not called on to prove any love when they admit one which is evident.

These first davs were like a period of intense fever,

when the faithful, mutually inebriated, and imposing upon each other by their mutual conceits, passed their days in constant excitement, and were lifted up with the most exalted notions. The visions multiplied without ceasing. Their evening assemblies were the usual periods for their production.[53] When the doors were closed and all were possessed with their besetting idea, the first who fancied that he heard the sweet word *schalom*, "salutation," or "peace," gave the signal. All then listened, and very soon heard the same thing. Then it was that there was great joy among these simple souls when they knew that the Master was in the midst of them. Each one tasted of the sweetness of this thought, and believed himself to be favored with some inward colloquy. Other visions were noised abroad of a different description, and recalled that of the travellers of Emmaus. At meal-time they saw Jesus appear, take the bread, bless it and break it, and offer it to the one whom He honored with a vision of Himself.[54] In a few days a complete cycle of stories, widely differing in their details, but inspired by the same spirit of love and absolute faith, was formed and disseminated. It is the greatest of errors to suppose that legendary lore requires much time to mature; sometimes a legend is the product of a single day. The Sunday evening [16 of Nisan, 5 April] had not passed before the legend of Jesus was held as a reality. Eight days afterwards, the character of the resuscitated life which had been conceived for him, was stayed in its progress, at least as regards its essential characteristics.

CHAPTER II.

DEPARTURE OF THE DISCIPLES FROM JERUSALEM.—SECOND GALILEAN LIFE OF JESUS.

The most earnest desire of those who have lost a dear friend is to revisit the places where they have lived with him. It was no doubt this feeling which, some days after the events of Easter, induced the disciples to return to Galilee. From the moment of the arrest of Jesus, and immediately after His death, it is probable that many of His disciples had already taken their departure for the northern provinces. At the period of the resurrection, a report was spread that it was in Galilee that they would see him again. Some of the women who had been at the sepulchre returned with the statement that the angel had told them that Jesus had already preceded them into Galilee.[1] Others said that it was Jesus himself who had told them to meet him there.[2] Sometimes they even fancied that they remembered how that He had told them so in his life-time.[3] It is, however, certain, that at the end of some days, perhaps after they had completed the solemnities of the Paschal feast, the disciples believed that they had received a commandment to return to their own country, and they returned accordingly.[4] Perhaps the visions began to diminish in frequency at Jerusalem. A sort of homesickness possessed them. The short apparitions of Jesus were not sufficient to compensate for the enormous void left to them by His absence. They fancied that they were actuated by a melancholy affection for the lake and the beautiful mountains where they had tasted of the kingdom of God.[5] The women, especially, desired at all hazards to return to the country where they had enjoyed so much happiness. It must be observed that the order for leaving Jerusalem came especially from them.[6] This odious city weighed down their spirits ; they longed to revisit the country where they had possessed Him whom they so well loved, assured aforehand in their own minds that they would need him there. The greater part of the disciples then departed full of joy and hope, perhaps in company with the caravan which was conducting homewards the pilgrims who had attended the Paschal feast. That which they hoped to find in Galilee was not only fleeting visions, but Jesus Himself to continue with them as He had done previous to His death. An intense expectation filled their minds. Was He about to restore the kingdom of Israel, to found in definite form the kingdom of God, and, as it has been said, "reveal His justice?"[7] All this is possible. Already did they recall to their minds the smiling landscapes where they had been happy with Him. Many thought that He had told them that He would meet them on a mountain,[8] probably that one to which so many sweet remembrances of Him were attached. Never certainly was any more cheerful journey undertaken. They were on the eve of realizing all their dreams of happiness. They were going to see Him again.

And indeed they did see him. Hardly restored to their peaceable fantasies, they believed themselves to be placed in the midst of the Gospel dispensation. It was about the end of the month of April. The ground was covered with red anemones, which are probably the "flowers of the field," from which Jesus loved to draw his similes. At every step they recollected His words, attached, as it were, to the thousand events of the way. See this tree, this flower, this seed, from which he took up his parable! here is the little hill on which he delivered his most touching discourses; here is the little ship in which he taught. It was all like a beautiful dream commenced anew, like an illusion which had vanished, and then reappeared. The enchantment seemed to spring up again. The sweet "kingdom of God" to be established in Galilee, took possession of their hearts. This pellucid air, those mornings spent on the bank of the lake or on the mountain, those nights passed on the lake while guarding their nets,—all these returned to their minds in distinct visions. They saw him in every place in which they had lived with him. Doubtless it was not always the joy of possession. Sometimes the lake appeared to them to be very solitary. But a great love is contented with small matters. If all of us, while we are alive, could stealthily once a year calculate on a moment long enough to behold those loved ones whom we have lost, and to exchange but two words with them, death would be no more death.

Such was the state of mind of this faithful company in this short period when Christianity seemed to return for a moment to its cradle to bid Him an eternal adieu. The principal disciples, Peter, Thomas, Nathanael, the sons of Zebedee, returned to the shore of the lake. and henceforth took up their abode together;[9] they had taken up their former trade of fishers at Bethsaida, or at Capernaum. The women of Galilee were, doubtless, with them. More than the others, they had urged the return to Galilee; for with them it was a matter of heartfelt love. This was their last act in the foundation of Christianity. From this moment we see no more of them. Faithful to their affection, they would not quit the country where they had tasted of so great enjoyment.[10] Soon they were forgotten, and as Galilean Christianity had scarcely any posterity, the remembrance of them was completely lost in certain ramifications of the tradition. These touching demoniacs, these converted sinners, these real founders of Christianity, Mary of Magdala, Mary Cleophas, Joanna, Susanna, all passed into the condition of forsaken saints. St. Paul knows nothing about them.[11] The faith which they had created almost threw them into oblivion. We must come down to the middle ages before justice is rendered to them; and when one of them, Mary Magdalene, again assumes her lofty position in the Christian heaven.

The visions on the lake shore appear to have been frequent enough. On these very waters where they had touched God, how was it that the disciples had not again beheld their Divine friend? The most simple circumstances restored Him to them. On one occasion they had toiled all the night without having taken a single fish; all on a sudden the nets are filled: this was a miracle. It seemed to them that some one had told them from the shore, "Cast your nets to the right." Peter and John looked at each other: "It is the Lord," said John. Peter, who was naked, hastily covered himself with his tunic and jumped into the sea, that he might go and rejoin the invisible counsellor.[12] At other times, Jesus came to share their simple repasts. One day, when they had done fishing, they were surprised to find the coals lighted, with a fish upon the fire, and some bread beside it. A lively recollection of their feasts in times past took possession of their minds, for the bread and the fish had always been essential characteristics of them. Jesus was in the habit of offering portions to them. They were persuaded after their meal that Jesus was seated at their side, and had presented them with these victuals, which had become already, in their view, eucharistic and holy.[13]

It was John and Peter, more than all the others, who had been favored with these intimate conversations with the well-beloved phantom. One day Peter, dreaming perhaps (But why do I say this? Was not their life on these shores a perpetual dream?), thought that he heard Jesus ask him, "Lovest thou me?" The question was thrice repeated. Peter, altogether under the influence of tender and sad feelings, imagined that he replied, "Oh! yea, Lord! Thou knowest that I love thee;" and on each occasion the apparition said, "Feed my sheep."[14] On another occasion Peter confided to John a wondrous dream. He had dreamt that he was walking with the Master. John was coming up a few steps behind. Jesus spoke to him in very obscure language, which appeared to tell him of a prison or a violent death, and repeated to him at different times, "Follow me." Then Peter, pointing to John, who was following, with his finger, asked, "Lord, and this man?" Jesus said, "If I wish that this man remain until I come, what is that to thee?

Follow thou me." After the martyrdom of Peter, John recollected this dream, and saw in it a prediction of the kind of death by which his friend suffered. He told it to his disciples; and they on their part fancied that they had discovered an assurance that their master would not die before the final advent of Jesus.[15] These grand and melancholy dreams, these unceasing conversations interrupted and again commenced with the beloved departed One, occupied the days and the months. The sympathy of Galilee in behalf of the prophet whom the Jerusalemites had put to death, was renewed. More than five hundred persons were already devoted to the memory of Jesus.[16] In the absence of the lost Master, they obeyed the chief of the disciples, and above all, Peter. One day, when following their spiritual chiefs, the Galileans had climbed up one of the mountains to which Jesus had often led them, and they fancied that they saw him again. The air on these mountain-tops is full of strange mirages. The same illusion which had previously taken place in behalf of the more intimate of the disciples, was produced again.[17] The whole assembly imagined that they saw the Divine spectre displayed in the clouds; they all fell on their faces and worshipped.[18] The feeling which the clear horizon of these mountains inspires is the idea of the immensity of the world and the desire of conquering it. On one of these neighboring points, Satan, pointing out with his hand to Jesus the kingdoms of the earth, and all the glory of them, it is said proposed to give them to him if he would fall down and worship him. On this occasion, it was Jesus who, from the top of these sacred summits, pointed out to his disciples the whole world, and assured them of the future. They came down from the mountain persuaded that the Son of God had commanded them to convert the whole human race, and had promised to be with them even to the end of the world. A strange ardor, a divine fire, took possession of them when they returned from these conversations. They looked upon themselves as the missionaries of the world, capable of effecting prodigious deeds. St. Paul saw many of those who were present at this extraordinary scene. At the expiration of twenty-five years, the impression on their minds was still as strong and as vivid as it was on the first day.[19]

Nearly a year passed over during which they lived this charmed life, suspended, as it were, between heaven and earth.[20] The charm, far from diminishing, increased. It is the peculiarity of grand and holy enterprises, that they always become grander and more pure of themselves. The feeling towards a beloved one whom we have lost is always more intense than on the day following his death. The more distant it is, the more i tense does this feeling become. The sorrow whi h at first was part of it, and in a certain sense diminished it, is changed into a serene piety. The image of the departed one is transfigured, idealized, and becomes the soul of life, the principle of every action, the source of every joy, the oracle which we consult, the consolation which we seek in times of despondency. Death is a necessary condition of every apotheosis. Jesus, so beloved during His life, was even more so after His last breath; or rather His last breath became the commencement of His actual life in the bosom of His Church. He became the intimate friend, the confidant, the travelling companion, the one who, at the corner of the road, joins you and follows you, sits down to table with you, and reveals Himself as He vanishes out of your sight.[21] The absolute want of scientific exactitude in the minds of these new believers, was the reason why no question was ever propounded as to the nature of His existence. They represented Him as impassible, endowed with a subtle body, passing through open windows, sometimes visible, sometimes invisible, but always alive. Sometimes they thought that His body was not a material body; that it was a pure shadow or apparition.[22] At other times they accorded to Him a material body with flesh and bones; with an unaffected minuteness, and as if the hallucination had wished to be on its guard against itself, they represented Him as drinking and eating; nay even as feeling.[23] Their ideas on this point were as vague and uncertain as the waves of the sea.

With difficulty have we thus far dreamed, in order to propose a trifling question, but one which admits not of easy solution. Whilst Jesus rose again in this real manner, that is to say in the hearts of those who loved Him; while the immovable conviction of the apostles was being formed and the faith of the world being prepared—in what place did the worms consume the lifeless corpse which, on the Saturday evening, had been deposited in the sepulchre? This detail will be always steadily ignored; for, naturally, the Christian traditions can give us no information on the subject. It is the spirit which quickeneth; the flesh is nothing.[24] The resurrection was the triumph of the idea concerning its reality. The idea once entered upon its immortality, what need of discussion about the body?

About the year 80 or 85, when the actual text of the first Gospel received its last additions, the Jews had already formed a fixed opinion in regard to it.[25] According to them, the disciples came by night and stole away the body. The consciences of the Christians were alarmed at this report, and, in order to put an end to such an objection at once, they invented the circumstances of the guard of soldiers and the seal affixed to the sepulchre.[26] This circumstance, related only in the first Gospel, and mixed up with legends of very doubtful authority,[27] is in no respect admissible.[28] But the explanation of the Jews, although unanswerable, is far from altogether satisfactory. We can scarcely admit that those who so bravely believed that Jesus had risen again, were the very ones who had carried off the body. However slight the accuracy with which these men reflected, we can hardly imagine so strange an illusion. It must be remembered that the little Church was at this moment completely dispersed. There was no organization, no centralization, and no open regularity of proceeding. The contradictory stories which have reached us respecting the incidents of the Sunday morning, prove that the reports were spread through different channels, and that there was no particular care on their part to harmonize them. It is possible that the body was taken away by some of the disciples, and by them carried into Galilee. The others, remaining at Jerusalem, would not have been cognizant of the fact. On the other hand, the disciples who carried the body into Galilee,[29] could not have, as yet, become acquainted with the stories which were invented at Jerusalem, so that the belief in the resurrection would have been propounded in their absence, and would have surprised them accordingly. They could not have protested; and had they done so, nothing would have been disarranged. When a question of miracles is concerned, a tardy correction is not the way to a denial.[30] Never did a material difficulty prevent the sentimental development and creation of the desired fictions.[31] In the history of the recent miracle of Salette, the imposture has been clearly demonstrated;[32] this does not damage the prosperity of the temple, nor the increase of belief in it. It is also permissible to suppose that the disappearance of the body was the work of the Jews. Perhaps they thought that in this way they would prevent the scenes of tumult which might be enacted over the corpse of a man so popular as Jesus. Perhaps they wished to prevent any noisy funeral ceremonies, or the erection of a monument to this just man. Lastly, who knows that the disappearance of the body was not effected by the proprietor of the garden or by the gardener?[33] This proprietor, as it would seem from such evidence as we possess,[34] was a stranger to the sect. They chose his cave because it was the nearest to Golgotha, and because they were pressed for time.[35] Perhaps he was dissatisfied with this mode of taking possession of his property, and caused the corpse to be removed. Of a truth, the details related by the fourth Gospel of the linen cloths left in the tomb, and of the napkin folded away carefully by itself in a corner,[36] scarcely agree with such a hypothesis as this. This last circumstance would lead to the conclusion that a female hand had slipped in there.[37]

The five stories of the visit of the women to the tomb are so confused and so embarrassed, that we may well be permitted to suppose that they conceal some misconception. The female conscience, when under the influence of passionate love, is capable of the most extravagant illusions. Often is it the abettor of its own dreams.[8] To introduce these kinds of incidents regarded as miraculous, deliberately deceives no one ; but all the world, without thinking of it, is induced to connive at them. Mary of Magdala had been, according to the parlance of the age, "possessed with seven devils."[39] In all this we must consider the want of precision of eastern women, from their absolute defect of education and the particularly slight knowledge of their sincerity. The conviction of being exalted, renders any return to oneself impossible. When one sees the heaven everywhere, one is induced at times to put oneself in the place of heaven.

Let us draw a veil over these mysteries. In the circumstances of a religious crisis, everything being considered as divine, the very grandest effects can be produced from the very meanest causes. If we were witnesses of the strange facts which lie at the bottom of all works of faith, we should see therein circumstances which seem to us quite out of proportion to the importance of the results, and others at which we could but smile. Our old cathedrals are counted amongst the most beautiful things of the world ; one can scarcely enter them without being in some sort inebriated with the infinite. But these splendid marvels are almost always the blossoming of some little deceit. And what does it matter definitively ? The result alone counts in such a matter. Faith purifies all. The material incident which has produced the belief in the resurrection was not the veritable cause of the resurrection. It was love that made Jesus rise again; and this love was so powerful that a little risk was sufficient to build up the universal faith. If Jesus had been less loved, if the belief of the resurrection had had less reason for its establishment, these sorts of risks would have been incurred in vain; nothing would have come of it. A grain of sand causes the fall of a mountain, when the moment for the fall of the mountain has arrived. The grandest results are produced altogether from causes very grand and very insignificant. The grand results alone are real; the little ones only serve to hasten the production of an effect which has been a long time in a state of preparation.

CHAPTER III.

RETURN OF THE APOSTLES TO JERUSALEM.—END OF THE PERIOD OF APPARITIONS.

The apparitions, in the meanwhile, as is usually the case in all movements of too credulous enthusiasm, began to diminish. Popular chimeras are nearly allied to contagious diseases; quickly do they become stale and change their shape. The activity of these ardent souls was already turned in another direction. That which they believed they had heard from the lips of their beloved and resuscitated friend, was the command to go before him to preach and to convert the world. But where should they commence? Naturally at Jerusalem.[1] The return to Jerusalem was accordingly resolved upon by those who at this time directed the movements of the sect. As these journeys were ordinarily made in caravanseries at the periods of the feasts, we may suppose, with sufficient probability, that the return of which we are treating, took place at the feast of Tabernacles at the end of the year thirty-three or at the Paschal feast of the year thirty-four. Galilee was, accordingly, abandoned by Christianity, and abandoned for all time. The little church which remained there, doubtless, still existed; but we intend to speak no more of it. It was probably crushed, like all the rest, by the frightful catastrophe which overwhelmed the country during the war of

Vespasian; the residue of the dispersed society took refuge, from that time, in Jerusalem. After the war, it was not Christianity which was replanted in Galilee; it was Judaism. In the second, third, and fourth centuries, Galilee was altogether a Jewish country, the centre of Judaism, the country of the Talmud.[2] Thus Galilee was considered as of no account whatsoever in the history of Christianity; but this was the sacred time of the church, *par excellence;* it conferred on the new religion its enduring qualities, its poetry, its penetrating charms. "*The Gospel,*" according to the theory of the synoptics, was a Galilean work. But we shall endeavor to show, further on, that "*The Gospel,*" thus understood, has been the principal cause of the success of Christianity, and continues to be the surest guarantee of its future history.

It is probable that a portion of the little school which surrounded Jesus during his last days had remained at Jerusalem at the time of their separation. The belief in the resurrection was already established. This belief became accordingly developed from two points of view, each having a perceptibly different aspect, and such, doubtless, is the reason for the completely different variations which are so remarkable in the stories of the apparitions. Two traditions—one Galilean, the other Jerusalemitish—were intended; according to the former, all the apparitions (except those of the earliest period) had occurred in Galilee; according to the latter, they had all taken place at Jerusalem.[3] The agreement of the two portions of the little church respecting the fundamental dogma, only served, as was natural, to confirm the common belief. They were united by the bonds of the same faith; again and again they said, "He is risen!" Perhaps the joy and enthusiasm which were the consequence of this harmony produced for them certain other visions. It is at about this period that we can place the "vision of James" mentioned by St. Paul.[4] James was the brother, or at least the kinsman, of Jesus. It is not clear that he accompanied Jesus during his last sojourn at Jerusalem, but he came there, probably, with the apostles, when they departed from Galilee. All the chief apostles had had their vision; it was hard that this "brother of the Lord" should not also have had his. It would appear that this vision was eucharistic—that is to say, one in which Jesus appeared taking and breaking the bread.[5] Later, those members of the Christian family who attached themselves to James, and who are called the Hebrews, referred that vision to the very day of the resurrection, and pretended that it had been the first of all.[6]

It is, indeed, very remarkable that the family of Jesus, certain members of which during his life had been unbelieving and opposed to his mission,[7] should now have become members of the Church and hold a position of eminence in it. We are compelled to suppose that the reconciliation took place during the sojourn of the apostles in Galilee. The renown with which the name of their kinsman had suddenly become invested—these five hundred persons who believed in him and were assured that they had seen him resuscitated—might have made an impression on their minds.[8] Since the definitive establishment of the apostles at Jerusalem, we see with them Mary, the mother of Jesus, and the brethren of Jesus.[9] As far as Mary is concerned, it appears that John, in the belief that he was thus obeying a recommendation of his Master, had adopted her and taken her into his own house.[10] He perhaps took her to Jerusalem. This woman, whose history and personal characteristics had been veiled in profound obscurity, became henceforth of great importance. The saying which the Evangelist puts into the mouth of some unknown woman: "Blessed is the womb that bare thee, and the paps which thou hast sucked!" began to be verified. It is probable that Mary did not survive her son many years.[11]

In respect to the brothers of Jesus, the question is more obscure. Jesus had brothers and sisters.[12] It seems probable, nevertheless, that in the class of persons who were termed "brothers of the Lord," were comprehended kinsmen of the second degree. It is only in connexion with James that the inquiry possesses any consequence. Was this James the Just, or "brother of the Lord," whom we are about to regard as playing a grand part during the first thirty years of Christianity—was he James the son of Alphæus, who appears to have been a cousin-german of Jesus, or was he a real brother of Jesus? The data, in this respect, are altogether uncertain and contradictory. What we know of this James gives us an idea of a character so far removed from that of Jesus that one can hardly believe that two men so different could be born of the same mother. If Jesus is the true founder of Christianity, James was its most dangerous enemy; he almost ruined it through his narrow mind. Later, it was certainly believed that James the Just was a real brother of Jesus.[13] But perhaps some confusion has always surrounded this subject. However that may be, henceforth the apostles only separated to undertake temporary journeys. Jerusalem became their centre,[14] they seem to be afraid to disperse, and certain traits appear to manifest amongst them a determination to prevent a return into Galilee, which would have dissolved their little society. They expected an express order from Jesus, forbidding them to quit Jerusalem, at least until the grand manifestation which awaited them.[15] The apparitions became more and more infrequent. They spoke of them far less often, and they began to think that they should no more see the Master until his solemn return in the clouds. Their imaginations were forcibly impressed by a promise which they supposed that Jesus had made. During His lifetime, they said Jesus had frequently spoken of the Holy Spirit, conceived as a personification of divine wisdom.[16] He had promised His disciples that this Spirit should be their strength in the battles which they would have to fight, their inspiration in difficulties, their advocate if they were called upon to speak in public. When these visions became rare, they relied on this Spirit, viewed as a Comforter, as another self whom Jesus would doubtless send to his friends. Sometimes they fancied that Jesus, displaying himself suddenly in the midst of his assembled disciples, had breathed upon them from His own mouth a current of vivifying air.[17] On other occasions, the disappearance of Jesus was regarded as the condition of the coming of the Spirit.[18] They thought that in these apparitions he had promised the descent of this Spirit.[19] Many set up an intimate connexion between this descent and the restoration of the kingdom of Israel.[20] All the activity of imagination which the sect had displayed in the creation of the legend of Jesus resuscitated, it now began to apply to the creation of a similar pious belief respecting the descent of the Spirit and His marvellous gifts.

It seems, meanwhile, that a grand apparition of Jesus had again taken place at Bethany, or on the Mount of Olives.[21] Certain traditions referred to that vision the final recommendations, the reiterated promise of the sending of the Holy Spirit, and the act by which He invested His disciples with power to remit sins.[22] The characteristic features of these apparitions became more and more vague; one was confounded with another, and the result was, that they ceased to think much about them.[23] It was a received fact that Jesus was alive, that he had manifested himself by a number of apparitions sufficient to prove His existence, and that he would continue still to manifest Himself in partial visions, until the grand final revelation when everything would be consumed.[24] Thus St. Paul represents the vision which he saw on the route from Damascus as being of the same order as those which have been related.[25] At any rate, it was admitted that in an ideal sense the Master was with his disciples and would be with them even to the end.[26] In the early days, the apparitions were very frequent; Jesus was imagined as dwelling upon the earth constantly, and more or less fulfilling the functions of an earthly life. When the visions became rare, they inclined to another conception, representing Jesus as having entered into His glory and seated at the right hand of His Father.

"He is ascended into heaven," they said.

This saying, though depending for the most part upon

the state of vague idea in which they indulged, or on a process of induction,[27] was by many converted into a material scene. It was desirable that at the close of the last vision which was common to all the apostles, and when he delivered to them His last commands, Jesus should be taken up into heaven.[28] Afterwards, the scene was developed, and became a complete legend. They related that men of heavenly appearance, surrounded by the most appalling brilliancy,[29] appeared at the moment when a cloud surrounded Him, and consoled His disciples by the assurance of His return in the clouds precisely similar to the scene which they had just witnessed. The death of Moses had been invested by the popular ideas with circumstances of the same sort.[30] Perhaps also they bethought them of the ascension of Elijah.[31] A tradition[32] placed the locality of this scene near Bethany, on the summit of the Mount of Olives, a neighborhood always very dear to the disciples, doubtless because Jesus had dwelt there.

The legend relates that the disciples, after this marvellous scene, returned to Jerusalem "with joy."[33] For our own part, it is with sorrow that we say a last farewell to Jesus. To find Him again still living his shadowy life, has been to us a great consolation. This second life of Jesus, a pale image of the first, is yet full of charms for us. Now all trace of Him is lost. Exalted on His cloud at the right hand of His Father, He leaves us with men; and, heavens! how great is the fall! The reign of poetry is past; Mary of Magdala retired to her hamlet-home, has there buried her recollections of him. In consequence of this never-ending injustice which permits man to appropriate to himself alone the work in which woman has taken an equal share, Cephas eclipses her and sends her to oblivion. No more sermons on the Mount; no more of the possessed ones cured; no more courtezans convinced of sin; no more of those wonderful fellow-laborers in the work of Redemption, whom Jesus had not repulsed. God truly has disappeared. The history of the Church will henceforth be oftener the history of treacheries than subservient to the idea of Jesus. But, such as it is, this history is still a hymn to his glory. The words and the image of the illustrious Nazarene will stand out in the midst of infinite miseries, as a sublime ideal—we shall the better understand how grand He was, when we shall see how paltry were His disciples.

CHAPTER IV.

DESCENT OF THE HOLY SPIRIT ; ECSTATICAL AND PROPHETICAL PHENOMENA.

MEAN, narrow, ignorant, inexperienced they were, as much as was possible for them to be. Their simplicity of mind was extreme; their credulity had no bounds. But they had one quality; they loved their Master to madness. The remembrance of Jesus, the only moving power of their life, had possessed them constantly and entirely; and it was clear that they existed only on account of Him who, during two or three years, had so completely attached and seduced them to Himself. The safety of minds of a secondary class, who are unable to love God directly—that is, to discover the truth, create the beautiful, and do what is right of themselves—is the loving of some one in whom there shines forth a reflection of the true, the beautiful, and the good. The majority of mankind require a graduated worship. The multitude of worshippers pant for a mediator between themselves and God.

When an individual has succeeded in gathering around his person, by a highly elevated moral tie, a number of other individuals, and then dies, it invariably happens that the survivors, who were perhaps up to that time often divided amongst themselves by rivalries and differences of opinion, become bound together by a mutual and fast friendship. A thousand cherished images of the past, which they regret, form a common treasure to them. One way of loving a dead person is to love those with whom we have known him to associate. We court their society that we may recall to our minds the times which are no more. A profound saying of Jesus[1] is then discovered to be true to the letter: "The dead one is present in the midst of those who are united again by his memory."

The affection which the disciples entertained for each other during the lifetime of Jesus, was thus increased tenfold after his death. They formed a little society, very retired, and they lived exclusively within themselves. The number of them at Jerusalem was one hundred and twenty.[2] Their piety was active, and as yet, completely restrained by the forms of Jewish religionism. The temple was their chief place of worship.[3] No doubt, they labored for their living; but manual labor occupied but a small place in the Jewish economy. Every Jew had a trade, and this trade implied no lack of learning or of gentle breeding. With us in our day, our material needs are so difficult to satisfy, that a man who lives by manual labor is obliged to work twelve or fifteen hours a day; the man of leisure alone can apply himself to intellectual pursuits; the acquisition of learning is a rare and expensvie matter. But in these old societies, of which the East of our own day furnishes some idea; in those climates where nature is so lavish for man's wants, and exacts so little in return—the life of a laborer left plenty of leisure. A sort of method of common instruction rendered every man well up in the prevailing ideas. Food and raiment sufficed;[4] a few hours of moderate labor were enough to provide them. The remaining portion of the time was devoted to day-dreaming and to the indulgence of passionate love. The latter had, in the minds of these people, attained to a degree altogether inconceivable by us. The Jews of that period[5] appear to us as if possessed, each one obeying like a blind machine the idea which had taken possession of him.

The prevailing idea in the Christian community at the time of which we are treating, and when the apparitions had ceased, was the coming of the Holy Spirit. They expected to receive Him under the form of a mysterious breath, which passed over the assembly. Many pretended that this was the breath of Jesus Himself. Every inward consolation, every courageous movement, every outburst of enthusiasm, every feeling of lively and pleasant gaiety, which they experienced without knowing its origin, was the work of the Spirit. These worthy consciences referred, as ever, to an outward cause the exquisite feelings which were springing up in them. It was especially in their assemblies that these varied phenomena of illumination were produced. When they were all assembled together and were awaiting in silence the heavenly inspiration, whatever murmur or noise arose was thought to be the coming of the Spirit. In the early times, it was the apparitions of Jesus which were thus produced. Now, there was a change in the course of their ideas. It was the Divine breath which was breathed over the little church and filled it with heavenly emanations. These beliefs were strengthened by notions drawn from the Old Testament. The Spirit of prophecy is represented in the Hebrew books as a breathing which penetrates and lifts up the subject of it. In the beautiful vision of Elijah,[7] God passes by under the form of a light wind, which produces a gentle rustling sound. This ancient imagery had handed down to later epochs systems of belief very similar to those of the spiritualists of our own time. In the Ascension of Isaiah[8] the coming of the Spirit is accomplished by a certain crashing at the doors[9] Later on, they always regarded this coming in the light of another baptism—that is to say, the "baptism of the Spirit," far superior to that of John.[10] The hallucinations of bodily touch being very frequent amongst persons so nervous and so excited as they were, the least current of air, accompanied by a shuddering in the midst of the silence, was considered as the passage of the Spirit. One thought that he felt it; very soon all perceived it;[11] and the enthusiasm was communicated from neighbor to neighbor. The correspondence of these phenomena with those which are found to exist amongst the visionaries of every age is easily demonstrated. They are produced daily, partly under the influence of the reading the book of the Acts of the Apostles, in the English and American sects of Quakers, Jumpers, Shakers, Irvingites;[12] amongst the Mormons,[13] and in the camp meetings and revivals of America;[14] we have seen them reproduced amongst ourselves in the sect called the Spiritualists. But an immense difference should be observed between aberrations, without capacity or future results, and the illusions which have accompanied the establishment of a new code of religion for the human race.

Amongst all these "descents of the Spirit," which appear to have been by no means infrequent, there was one which left a deep impression on the nascent Church.[15] One day when they were assembled together a thunder-storm arose. A violent wind burst the windows open—the sky seemed on fire. Thunderstorms in those countries are accompanied by wonderful illuminations; the atmosphere is furrowed, as it were, on every side with garbes of flame. Whether the electric fluid had penetrated into the very chamber itself, or whether a dazzling flash of lightning had suddenly illuminated all their faces, they were convinced that the Spirit had entered, and that he was poured out upon the head of each one of them under the form of tongues of fire.[16] It was a prevalent opinion in the theurgic schools of Syria that the communication of the Spirit was produced by a divine fire, and under the form of a mysterious glimmering.[17] It was believed to have been present at the display of all the wonders of Mount Sinai,[18] at a manifestation analogous to those of former times. The baptism of the Spirit hence became also a baptism of fire. The baptism of the Spirit and of fire was opposed to and greatly preferred to that of water, the only form with which John had been acquainted.[19] The baptism of fire was only produced on rare occasions; only the apostles and the disciples of the first guest-chamber were supposed to have received it. But the idea that the Spirit was poured forth upon them under the form of strokes of flame resembling burning tongues originated a series of singular ideas, which took firm hold of the imaginations of the period.

The tongue of an inspired man was supposed to have received a sort of sacrament. It was pretended that many prophets before their mission had been stammerers;[20] that the angel of God had passed a coal over their lips, which purified them and conferred on them the gift of eloquence.[21] In his prophetic utterances the man was supposed not to speak at all about himself.[22] His tongue was looked upon merely as the organ of the Divinity who inspired it. These tongues of fire appeared a very striking symbol. The disciples were convinced that God desired to make it known that on the apostles also he had conferred his most precious gifts of eloquence and inspiration. But they did not stop there; Jerusalem was, like most of the great cities of the East, a city where many languages were spoken. The diversity of tongues was one of the difficulties which they there discovered in the way of the propagation of a universal form of faith. Besides, one of the things which most alarmed the apostles at their very entry on a ministry destined to embrace the world, was the number of languages which were spoken in it; they were constantly inquiring how they could learn so many dialects. "The gift of tongues" became thenceforth a marvellous privilege. They believed that the preaching of the gospel would relieve them from the obstacle which the difference of idioms had raised. They pretended that, under certain solemn circumstances, those present had heard, each in his own language, the gospel preached by the apostles; in other words, that the apostolic promise was delivered to each one of the hearers. At other times, this conception was entertained in a somewhat different shape. They ascribed to the apostles the gift of acquiring, by divine illumination, every language spoken, and of speaking those languages at will.

There was in this a liberal conception; they wished it should have no language peculiar to itself, that it should be capable of translation into every language, and that the translation should be of the same standard value as the original. Such was not the opinion of orthodox Judaism. The Hebrew was "the holy language" to the Jew of Jerusalem, and no version could be compared to it. Translations of the Bible were in little esteem; so long as the Hebrew text was scrupulously guarded in the translations, changes and modifications of expression were tolerated. The Jews of Egypt and Hellenists of Palestine, indeed, practised a more tolerant system, and habitually perused the Greek translations of the Bible. But the first plan of the Christians was even broader; according to their idea, the word of God has no language peculiar to it; it is free, unfettered by any idiomatic peculiarity; it is delivered to all spontaneously and without interpretation. The facility with which Christianity became detached from the Semitic dialect which Jesus had spoken, the liberty which it at first accorded to every nation of forming its own liturgy, and its own versions of the Bible in the vernacular, favored this sort of emancipation of languages. It was generally admitted that the Messiah would gather into one, all languages as well as all peoples.[26] Common usage and the promiscuousness of the languages was the first grand step towards this grand era of universal pacification.

Moreover, the gift of languages very soon underwent a considerable variation, and resulted in very extraordinary effects. Ecstasy and prophecy were the fruits of mental excitement. At these moments of ecstasy, the faithful, possessed by the Spirit, uttered inarticulate and incoherent sounds, which were mistaken for the words of a foreign language, and which they innocently attempted to interpret.[27] At other times they supposed that the ecstatically possessed was giving utterance to new and hitherto unknown languages,[28] which were not even the languages of the angels.[29]

These extravagant scenes, which were the fruitful cause of abuse, only became habitual at a later period;[30] but it is probable that they were produced from the earliest years of Christianity. The visions of the ancient prophets had often been accompanied by phenomena of nervous excitement.[31] The dithyrambic state amongst the Greeks abounded in occurrences of the same kind; the Pythia seemed to give a preference to the use of foreign or obsolete words, which were called, as also in the apostolic phenomena, glosses.[32] Many of the pass-words of primitive Christianity, which are precisely bi-linguistic, or formed by anagrams, such as *Abba, Father*, and *Anathema Maranatha*,[33] took their origin perhaps from these fantastic paroxysms, intermingled with sighs[34] from stifled gradus, from ejaculations, prayers, and sudden transports which were interpreted as prophecies. It was like some vague harmony of the soul, thrilling in indistinct sounds, and which the hearers of it desired to transform into determined shapes and words,[35] or rather like spiritual prayers addressed to God in a language understood by God alone, and which God knows how to interpret.[36] The individual in a state of ecstasy understood, in fact, nothing of what he uttered, and had no cognizance of it whatever.[37] His eager listeners ascribed to his incoherent syllables the thoughts which occurred to them at the time. Each one referred to his own dialect, and artlessly strove to explain the unintelligible sounds by what little knowledge of languages he possessed. They were always more or less successful, because the auditor interpolated within these broken accents the thoughts of his own breast. The history of fanatical sects is rich in facts of this description. The preachers of Cévennes displayed many instances of "glossology,"[38] but the most remarkable fact is that of the "readers" of Sweden,[39] about the years 1841–1843. Involuntary enunciations, devoid of sense in the minds of those who uttered them, and accompanied by convulsions and fainting-fits, were for a long time daily practised by the members of this little sect. This phenomenon became quite contagious, and a considerable popular movement became blended with it. Amongst the Irvingites, the phenomenon of tongues is produced with features which reproduce, in the most remarkable manner, the most striking of the stories of the "*Acts*" and of St. Paul.[40] Our own age has witnessed fantastic scenes of the same nature, which need not to be recounted here; for it is always unjust to compare the credulity of a grand religious movement with the credulity which is caused only by dulness of intellect.

Now and then these strange phenomena were produced outside. The extatics, at the very moment when under the influence of their extravagant fantasies, had the hardihood to go out and display themselves to the crowd. They were taken for persons who were intoxicated.[41] However sober minded in point of mysticism. Jesus had more than once presented in his own person the ordina ry phenomena of the extatic state.[42] The disciples, during three or four years, were possessed with these ideas. The prophesyings were frequent, and were regarded as a gift analogous to that of tongues.[43] Prayer, mingled with convulsions, with harmonized modulations, with mystic sighs, with lyrical enthusiasm, with songs of thanksgiving,[44] was a daily exercise among them. A rich vein of "canticles," of "Psalms," and of "Hymns," co pied from those of the Old Testament was thus discovered to be open to them.[45] Sometimes the lips and the heart were in mutual accord; sometimes the spirit sang alone, accompanied by grace in the inner man.[46] Any language which did not afford the new sensations which were being produced, they suffered to become an indistinct stammering, at once sublime and puerile; or that which they could denominate "the Christian language" was wafted aloud in an embryo state. Christianity, not finding in the ancient tongues a weapon appropriate to its needs, has destroyed them. But whilst the new religion was forming for itself an idiom of its own, ages of obscure efforts, and so to speak, of squalling, intervened. What is the characteristic of the style of St. Paul and, in general, that of the writers of the New Testament, but the stifled, panting, misshapen improvisation of the "Glossology?" Language failed them. Like the prophets, they began with the *a*, *a*, *a* of the infant.[47] They knew not how to speak. The Greek and the Semitic tongues equally betrayed them. Thus arose that frightful violence which the new Christianity inflicted upon language. They would call it a stammering of the mouth, by which the sounds are stifled and confused, and wind up with a pantomime confused indeed, but nevertheless wonderfully expressive.

All this was very far from the intention of Jesus; but to those whose minds were imbued with a belief in the supernatural, these phenomena were of the utmost importance. The gift of tongues, in particular, was considered as an essential sign of the new religion, and, as it were, a proof of its verity.[48] In every case it resulted in great fruits of edification. Many pagans were in this manner converted.[49]

Up to the third century, the "Glossology" manifested itself in a manner analogous to that which St. Paul describes, and was considered in the light of a permanent miracle.[50] Some of the sublimest words of Christianity have originated in these incoherent sighings. The general effect was touching and penetrating. This fashion of joining together their inspirations and delivering them over to the community for interpretation was enough to establish amongst the faithful a profound bond of confraternity. Like all mystics, the new sectaries led lives of fasting and austerity.[51] Like the majority of Orientals, they ate little, which fact contributed to maintain their excited state. The sobriety of the Syrian, caused by physical weakness, kept him in a constant state of fever and nervous susceptibility. Such great and protracted intellectual efforts as ours are impossible under such a regimen; but this cerebral and muscular debility is productive, without apparent cause, of lively alternations of sadness and joy, which bring the soul into continual communion with God. Thus that which they called "godly sorrow"[52] passed for a heavenly gift. All the teachings of the Fathers respecting the spiritual life, such as John Chinaticus, as Basil, as Nilus, as Arsenius—all the secrets of the grand art of the inward life, one of the most glorious creations of Christianity—were germinating in that strange state of mind which possessed, in their months of extatic watchfulness, those illustrious ancestors of all "the men of longings." Their moral state was strange; they lived in the supernatural. They acted only on the authority of visions; dreams and the most insignificant circumstances appeared to them to be admonitions from Heaven.[53] Under the name of gifts of the Holy Spirit were concealed also the rarest and most exquisite emanations of the soul—love, piety, respectful fear, objectless sighings, sudden languor, and spontaneous tenderness. All the good that is engendered in man, without man having any part in it, was attributed to a breathing from on high. Tears were often taken for a celestial favor. This charming gift, the privilege only of very good and pure souls, was repeated with an infinity of sweetness. We know what influence delicate natures—above all, women—exercise in the ability to shed copious tears. It is their style of praying, and assuredly it is the most holy of prayers. We must come down quite to the Middle Ages, to that piety watered with tears of St. Bruno, St. Bernard, and St. Francis of Assisi, in order to discover again the chaste melancholy of those early days, when they verily sowed in tears that they might reap with joy. To weep became an act of piety; those who could not preach, who were ignorant of languages, and unable to work miracles, wept. Praying, preaching, admonishing they wept;[54] it was the advent of the kingdom of tears. One might have said that their souls were dissolved, and that they desired, in the absence of a language which could interpret their sentiments, to display themselves to the world by a lively and brief expression of their entire inner being.

CHAPTER V.

FIRST CHURCH OF JERUSALEM; ITS CHARACTER CENOBITICAL.

The custom of living in a community professing one identical faith, and indulging in one and the same expectation, necessarily produced many habits common to all the society. Very soon rules were enacted, and established a certain analogy between this primitive church and the cenobitical establishments with which Christianity became acquainted at a later period. Many of the precepts of Jesus conduced to this; the true ideal of the gospel life is a monastery—not a monastery closed in with iron gratings, a prison of the type of the Middle Ages, with the separation of the two sexes, but an asylum in the midst of the world, a place set apart for the spiritual life, a free association or little confraternity, tracing around it a rampart which may serve to dispel cares that are hurtful to the kingdom of God. All, then, lived in common, having only one heart and one mind.[1] No one possessed aught which individually belonged to him. On becoming disciples of Jesus, they sold their goods and presented to the society the price of them. The chiefs of the society then distributed the common possessions according to the needs of each member. They dwelt in one neighborhood only.[2] They took their meals together, and continued to attach to them the mystic sense which Jesus had ordered.[3] Many hours of the day they spent in prayer. These prayers were sometimes improvised in a loud voice; oftener they were silent meditations. Their states of ecstasy were frequent, and each one believed himself to be incessantly favored with the Divine inspiration. Their harmony was perfect; no quarrelling about dogmas, no dispute respecting precedence. The tender recollection of Jesus prevented all dissensions. A lively and deeply rooted joy pervaded their hearts.[4] Their morals were austere, but marked by a sweet and tender sympathy. They assembled in houses to pray and abandon themselves to ecstatic exercises.[5] The remembrance of those two or three years rested upon them like that of a terrestrial paradise, which Christianity would henceforth pursue in all its dreams, and to which it would endeavor to return in vain. Who, indeed, does not see that such an organization could only be applicable to a very little church? But, later on, the monastic life will resume on its own account this primitive ideal, which the church universal will hardly dream of realizing.

That the author of the "*Acts*," to whom we owe the picture of this first Christianity at Jerusalem, has somewhat overcolored it, and in particular has exaggerated the community of goods which prevailed there, is quite possible. The author of the "*Acts*" is the same as the author of the third Gospel, who, in his life of Jesus, is accustomed to shape his facts according to his own theories,[6] and with whom a tendency to the doctrine of "*ebionism*"[7]—that is to say, of absolute poverty—is very perceptible. Nevertheless, the story of the "*Acts*" cannot be entirely without foundation. Although even Jesus would not have given utterance to any of those communistic axioms which we read of in the third Gospel, certain it is that a renunciation of the goods of this world and a giving of alms, carried so far as even the despoiling of self, was entirely conformable to the spirit of his preaching. The belief that the world is coming to an end has always been conducive to a cenobitical life and to a distaste for the things of this world.[8] The story of the "*Acts*" is, in other respects, perfectly conformable to what we know of the origin of other ascetic religions—of Buddhism, for example. These sorts of religion invariably commence with the cenobitical life. Their first adepts are a species of mendicant monks. The laity are only introduced into them at a more advanced period, and when these religions have conquered entire societies, or the monastic life could only exist under exceptional circumstances.[9] We admit, then, in the Church of Jerusalem a period of cenobitical life. Two centuries later, Christianity produced still on the pagans the effect of a communistic sect.[10] We must remember that the Essenians or Thereapeutians had already produced the model of this description of life, which sprang very legitimately from Mosaism. The Mosaic code being essentially moral, and not political, naturally produced a social Utopia; church, synagogue, and convent—not a civil régime, nation, or city. Egypt had had, for many centuries, recluses both male and female supported by the State, probably in fulfilment of charitable bequests, near the Serapeum of Memphis.[11] Above all, it must be remembered that such a life in the East is by no means such as it has been in our West. In the East, one can abundantly enjoy nature and life without possessing anything. Man, in those countries, is always free because he has few cares;

the slavery of labor is there unknown. We willingly suppose that the communism of the primitive Church was neither so rigorous nor so universal as the author of the "*Acts*" would lead us to believe. What is certain about it is, that it had a large community of poor people at Jerusalem, governed by the apostles, and to whom donations from all the places where Christianity existed were sent.[12] This community was, doubtless, compelled to establish rules of a sufficiently rigorous nature, and some years later it became necessary to keep it in due order, even to employ terror. Frightful legends were circulated, according to which, the simple fact of having retained anything besides that which had been presented to the community, was treated as a capital crime and punished with death.[13]

The porticos of the temple, especially Solomon's porch, which commanded the valley of Cedron, was the place where the disciples usually assembled in the daytime.[14] There they recalled the remembrance of those hours which Jesus had passed in the same spot. In the midst of the immense activity which existed all about the temple, they would be little remarked. The galleries which formed part of this building were the seat of numerous schools and sects, and the arena of many a dispute. The faithful of Jesus would no doubt be taken for devotees of great precision of manner; for they scrupulously observed all the Jewish customs, praying at the appointed hours,[15] and observing all the precepts of the law. They were Jews, only differing from the others in their belief that the Messiah had already come. People who were not well versed in their concerns (and these were the immense majority), looked upon them as a sect of Hasidim, or pious people. By being affiliated with them, they became neither schismatics nor heretics,[16] any more than a man ceases to be a Protestant on becoming a disciple of Spener, or a Catholic because he is a member of the order of St. Francis or St. Bruno. They were beloved by the people on account of their piety, their simplicity, and sweetness of temper.[17] The aristocrats of the temple, no doubt, regarded them with disfavor. But the sect made little noise; it was quiet and tranquil, thanks to its obscurity. At eventide, the brethren returned to their quarters and partook of the meal, divided into groups[18] as a mark of brotherhood and in remembrance of Jesus, whom they always saw present in the midst of them. The head of the table brake the bread, blessed the cup,[19] and handed them round as a symbol of union in Jesus. The commonest act of life thus became the most holy and reverential one. These family repasts, always favorites with the Jews,[20] were accompanied by prayers and pious ejaculations, and abounded in a pleasant sort of joyfulness. They thought again of the time when Jesus cheered them by His presence; they fancied that they saw Him; and soon it was bruited abroad that Jesus had said: "As often as ye break the bread, do it in remembrance of me."[21]

The bread itself became, in a certain manner, Jesus; regarded as the only source of strength for those who had loved him, and who still lived by him. These repasts, which were always the principal symbol of Christianity and the very life of its mysteries,[22] were at first served every night;[23] but soon custom restricted them to Sunday evenings[24] only; and later, the mystic repast was transferred to the morning.[25] It is probable that at the period of the history which we are now treating, the holiday of each week was still, with the Christians even, the Saturday.[26] The apostles chosen by Jesus, and who were supposed to have received from Him a special command to announce to the world the kingdom of God, had, in the little community, an undoubted superiority. One of their first cares, as soon as they saw the sect quietly settled at Jerusalem, was to fill up the void which Judas of Kerioth had left in its ranks.[27] The opinion that this Judas had betrayed his Master and became the cause of his death, became more generally received. The legend was mixed up with him, and daily they learned some new circumstance which increased the blackness of his deed. He had bought for himself a field near the old necropolis of Hakeldama, to the south of Jerusalem, and there he lived a retired life.[28] Such was the artless excitement which pervaded the whole of the little church, that in order to replace him they had recourse to the plan of casting lots. In general, in times of great religious excitement, this method of deciding is preferred, for it is admitted on principle that nothing is fortuitous, that the matter in hand is the principal object of the Divine attention, and that the part which God takes in any matter is greater in proportion to the weakness of man. The only condition was, that the candidates should be selected from the number of the older disciples, who had been witnesses of the entire series of events since the baptism by John. This considerably reduced the number of those who were eligible. Only two were found in the ranks, Joseph Bar-Saba, who bore the name of Justus,[29] and Matthias. The lot fell upon Matthias, who from that time was counted in the number of the Twelve. But this was the only example of such a r placing. The apostles were considered hitherto as having been named by Jesus once for all, and as not proposing to have any successors. The idea of a permanent college, preserving in itself all the life and strength of association, was judiciously rejected for a time. The concentration of the Church into an oligarchy did not occur until much later.

We must guard, moreover, against the misunderstandings which this appellation of "apostle" may induce, and which it has not failed to occasion. From a very remote period the idea was formed, by some passages of the Gospels, and above all by the analogy of the life of St. Paul, that the apostles were essentially travelling missionaries, distributing amongst themselves in a certain way the world in advance, and traversing as conquerors all the kingdoms of the earth.[30] A cycle of legends was invented in respect to this gift, and imposed upon ecclesiastical history.[31] Nothing is more opposed to the truth.[32] The twelve disciples were permanently settled at Jerusalem; up to the year 60, or thereabouts, they did not leave the holy city, except on temporary missions. And in this way is explained the obscurity in which the greater part of the central council remained; very few of them had any particular duty to perform. They formed a sort of a sacred college or a senate,[33] unequivocally destined to represent tradition and a conservative spirit. In the end they were discharged from all active duty, because they had only to preach and to pray;[34] as yet the brilliant feats of preaching had not fallen to their lot. Scarcely were their names known out of Jerusalem; and about the year 70 or 80 the catalogues which were published of these twelve primary elect ones only agreed in the principal names.[35]

The "brothers of the Lord" appear to have been often with the "apostles," although they were distinguished from them.[36] Their authority was at least equal to that of the apostles. These two groups constituted, in the nascent Church, a sort of aristocracy, based entirely upon the greater or less intimacy which they had had with the Master. It was these men whom St. Paul called "pillars" of the Church of Jerusalem.[37] We see, moreover, that no distinctions of ecclesiastical hierarchy were yet in existence. The title was nothing; the personal authority was everything. The principle of ecclesiastical celibacy was already well established;[38] but it required time to conduct all these germs to their full development. Peter and Philip were married, and were the fathers of sons and daughters.[39]

The term by which the assembly of the faithful was distinguished, was the Hebrew word *Kahal*, which was rendered by the essentially democratic word ἐκκλησία, *Ecclesia*, which means the convocation of the people in the ancient Grecian cities, the summons to assemble at the Pnyx or the *Agora*. Commencing about the second or third century before Jesus Christ, Athenian democracy became a sort of common law wherever the Hellenic language was spoken; many of these terms,[40] on account of their being used in the Greek confraternities, were introduced into the language of Christianity. It was in reality the popular life, for centuries kept under restraint, which reasserted its power under entirely different forms. The primitive Church is, in its own way, a little democracy. The election by ballot, however—that mode so cherished by the ancient republics—is only rarely reproduced.[41] Far less harsh and suspicious than the ancient cities, the church readily delegated its authority; like every theocratic society, it had a tendency to abdicate its functions into the hands of the clergy, and it was easy to foresee that one or two centuries would scarcely elapse before all this democracy would resolve into an oligarchy.

The powers which they ascribed to an assembled Church and to its chiefs was enormous. All mission was conferred by the Church, which was entirely guided in its choice by signs given by the spirit.[42] Its authority extended as far as the death penalty. They related how, at the voice of Peter, guilty persons fell backwards and expired immediately.[43] St. Paul, at a later period, was not afraid, when excommunicating an incestuous person, "to deliver him to Satan for the destruction of the flesh, that the spirit may be saved in the day of the Lord Jesus." Excommunication was considered equivalent to a sentence of death. They doubted not that an individual whom the apostles or chiefs of the Church had cut off from the body of the saints and delivered over to the power of the Evil One, was lost.[45] Satan was considered to be the author of the diseases; to deliver to him the infected member was to hand him over to the natural executioner. A premature death was ordinarily considered as the result of one of those secret judgments, which, according to the expressive Hebrew term, "cut off a soul from Israel."[46] The apostles believed themselves to be invested with supernatural powers; while pronouncing such condemnations, they believed that their anathemas could not fail to be effectual.

The terrible impression which these excommunications made, and the hatred of all the brethren towards the members thus cut off, were powerful enough in fact to produce death in many cases, or at least to compel the guilty person to expatriate himself. The same frightful ambiguity was found in the old law. "Extirpation" implied, at once decease, expulsion from the community, exile, and a solitary and mysterious death.[47] To kill the apostate, or blasphemer, to beat his body in order to save his soul, would seem quite lawful. It must be remembered that we are treating of the times of zealots, who considered it a virtuous act to assassinate any one who failed in obedience to the law;[48] nor must we forget that some of the Christians were, or had been, zealots.[49] Stories like that of the death of Ananias and Sapphira[50] raised no scruples. The idea of the civil power was so strange to all this world situated outside of the Roman law, they were so persuaded that the Church was a complete society sufficient for all its own needs, that nobody regarded the death or mutilation of an individual as an outrage punishable by the civil law. Enthusiasm and burning faith covered all, yea, excused all. But the frightful danger which these theocratic maxims entailed on the future was easily perceived. The Church is armed with a sword; excommunication will be a sentence of death. There is henceforth in the world a power above that of the State which disposes of the lives of citizens.

Assuredly if the Roman power had limited itself to the repression among the Jews and the Christians of such abominable principles, it would have been a thousand times in the right. Only in its brutality it confounded the most legitimate of liberties, that of worshipping according to one's own conviction, with abuses which no society has ever been able to endure with impunity

Peter had a certain primacy amongst the apostles the result of his daring zeal and activity.[51] In these early times he is scarcely ever separated from John, the son of Zebedee. They went together almost always,[52] and their perfect concord was doubtless the corner-stone of the new faith. James, brother of the Lord, was nearly their equal in authority, at least in one section of the Church. In respect to certain intimate friends of Jesus, like the women of Galilee and the family of Bethany, we have already observed that we have no more to do with them. Less anxious to organize and found a society, the faithful companions of Jesus were satisfied to love in death Him whom they had loved when alive. Totally occupied with their waiting, these noble women, who have established the faith of the world, were almost unknown to the important men of Jerusalem. When they died, the most important traits in the history of nascent Christianity were buried in the tomb with them. The active characters alone became renowned; those who are content to love secretly remain in obscurity, but assuredly they have the better part.

It is superfluous to remark that this little group had no speculative theology. Jesus kept himself far removed from everything metaphysical. He had only one dogma, His own divine Sonship and the divine authority of His mission. Every symbol of the primitive Church might be contained in one line: "Jesus is the Messiah, the Son of God." This belief rested upon a peremptory argument, the fact of the resurrection, of which the disciples claimed to be witnesses. In reality, no one (not even the Galilean women) declared that they had seen the resurrection.[53] But the absence of the body and the apparitions which had followed appeared to be equivalent to the fact itself. To attest the resurrection of Jesus was the task which all considered as being specially imposed upon them.[54] They quickly entertained the idea that the Master had predicted this event. They recollected different sayings of His, which they fancied that they had never thoroughly understood, and in which they saw too late an announcement of the resurrection.[55] Belief in the next glorious manifestation of Jesus was universal.[56] The secret word which the associated brethren used among themselves for purposes of mutual recognition and confirmation was *Maranatha*, "The Lord will come."[57] They fancied that they remembered a declaration of Jesus, according to which their preaching would not have time to reach to all the towns of Israel before the Son of Man appeared in His majesty.[58] In the meanwhile, Jesus risen is seated at the right hand of His Father. There He remains until the solemn day on which He shall come, seated on the clouds, to judge the quick and the dead.[59]

The idea which they had of Jesus was the very same which Jesus had given them of Himself. Jesus had been a mighty prophet in word and in deed,[60] a man elect of God, having received a special mission in behalf of mankind,[61] a mission the truth of which he had proved by His miracles, and, above all, by His resurrection. God anointed Him with the Holy Spirit and endued Him with power; He went about doing good and healing those who were under the power of the devil;[62] for God was with Him[63] He is the Son of God, that is, a man entirely sent of God, a representative of God on earth; He is the Messiah, the Saviour of Israel announced by the prophets.[64] The perusal of the books of the Old Testament, above all of the Psalms and the prophets, was a constant habit of the sect. In these readings one fixed idea ever accompanied them, and that was to discover, above all other considerations, the type of Jesus. They were persuaded that the ancient Hebrew books were full of Him, and, from the very first, He was moulded into a collection of texts drawn from the prophets and the Psalms and certain of the apocryphal books, wherein they were convinced that the life of Jesus was foretold and described in advance.[65] This arbitrary mode of interpretation was, at that time, that of all the Jewish schools. The Messianic allusions were a description of witty trifling, analogous to the use which the ancient preachers made of passages of the Bible, diverted from their natural meaning, and received as simple ornaments of sacred rhetoric. Jesus, with His exquisite tact in religious matters, had instituted no new ritual movement. The new sect had not, as yet, any special ceremonies.[65] Habits of piety were Jewish habits. The assemblies had nothing precisely liturgic about them; they were the sessions of confraternities, in which they devoted themselves to prayer, to glossological or prophetic[66] exercises, and to the reading of correspondence. There was nothing yet of sacerdotalism. There was no priest (cohen, or ἱερεύς); the *presbyter* is the "elder" of the community, nothing more. The only priest is Jesus;[67] in another sense, all the faithful are priests.[68] Fasting was considered a very meritorious usage.[69] Baptism was the sign of entrance into the sect.[70] The rite was the same in form as the baptism of John, but it was administered in the name of Jesus.[71] Baptism was always considered an insufficient initiation into the society. It should be followed by a conferring of the gifts of the Holy Spirit,[72] which was produced by means of a prayer pronounced over the head of the neophyte with the imposition of hands.

This imposition of hands, already so familiar to Jesus,[73] was the crowning sacramental act.[74] It conferred inspiration, inward illumination, the power of working wonders, of prophesying and of speaking languages. This was what they called the baptism of the Spirit. They believed that they recollected a saying of Jesus: "John baptized you with water: but as for you, you shall be baptized with the Spirit."[75] Little by little these ideas became confused, and baptism was conferred "in the name of the Father, and of the Son, and of the Holy Ghost."[76] But it is not probable that this formula, at the early period which we are describing, was as yet employed. The simplicity of this primitive Christian worship is evident. Neither Jesus nor the apostles had invented it. Certain Jewish sects had adopted, before them, grave and solemn ceremonies, which appear to have come partly from Chaldæa, where they are still practised with special liturgies, by the Sabæans and Mendäites.[77] The Persian religion contained, likewise, many rites of the same description.[78] The beliefs in popular medicine, which had accompanied the strength of Jesus, continued to be held by his disciples. The power of healing was one of the marvellous graces conferred by the Spirit.[79] The first Christians, like all the Jews of the age, regarded diseases as the punishment due to a fault,[80] or the work of a malicious demon.[81] The apostles, as well as Jesus, passed for powerful exorcists.[82] They imagined that anointings with oil, administered by them, with imposition of hands and invocation of the name of Jesus, were all-powerful to wash away the sins which were the causes of the disease, and to cure the sick.[83] Oil has always been in the East the chiefest of medicines.[84] Of itself, moreover, the imposition of hands by the apostles was supposed to have the same effect.[85] This imposition was conferred by immediate contact with the person; and it is not impossible that, in certain cases, the warmth of the hands, being sensibly communicated to the head, produced some little relief to the sick man. The sect being young and few in number, the question of the dead was only subsequently brought under their notice. The effect caused by the first deaths which took place in the ranks of the brotherhood was strange.[86] They disquieted themselves about the condition of the departed; they inquired if they would be less favored than those who were reserved to see with their eyes the second advent of the Son of Man. They generally came to the conclusion that the interval between death and the resurrection was a sort of blank in the recollection of the defunct.[87] The idea, expressed in the *Phædon* that the soul exists before and after death; that death is a benefit; that it is even the state above all others favorable to philosophy, because the soul is then altogether free and disengaged—this idea, I say, was in no respect entertained by the first Christians. They appear generally to have believed that man has no existence apart from his body. This persuasion lasted a long time, and only gave way when the doctrine of the immortality of the soul, in the sense of the Greek philosophy, had been received into the Church, and become associated, for good or for evil, with the Christian dogma of the resurrection and universal restoration. At the time of which we speak, a belief in the resurrection prevailed almost alone.[88] The funeral rites were doubtless Jewish. No importance was attached to them; no inscription pointed out the name of the departed. The great resurrection was at hand; the body of the faithful had only to sojourn for a very short time in the rock. They took but little pains to come to an agreement upon the question whether the resurrection would be universal—that is to say, whether it would embrace both good and wicked, or would apply to the elect only.[89]

One of the most remarkable phenomena of the new religion was the reappearance of prophecy. For a long time previous, prophets in Israel were scarcely mentioned. This peculiar kind of inspiration appeared to revive in the little sect. The primitive Church had many prophets and prophetesses,[90] answering to those of the Old Testament. Psalmists reappeared also. The model of the Christian Psalmody is, no doubt, to be found in the Canticles, which Luke loves to scatter about the pages of his Gospel,[91] and which are imitated from the Canticles of the Old Testament. These Psalms and prophecies are, in point of form, destitute of originality; but an admirable spirit of tenderness and piety animates and pervades them. It is like an attenuated echo of the later productions of the sacred lyre of Israel. The book of Psalms was, in some sort, the calyx of the flower from which the Christian bee stole its first juice. The Pentateuch, on the contrary, was, as it appears, but little read and less pondered; allegories were substituted in the form of Jewish *midraschim*, in which all the historical meaning of the books was suppressed.

The chanting with which they accompanied the new hymns[92] was probably that species of groaning without distinct notes, which is still the chant of the Greek Church, of the Maronites, and of the Eastern Christians in general.[93] It is not so much a musical modulation as a manner of forcing the voice, and of emitting through the nose a sort of groaning, in which all the inflexions follow each other with rapidity. They performed this extraordinary melopœia standing, with fixed eye, knit forehead, and contracted eyebrows, using an appearance of effort. The word *amen*, above all, was uttered in a tremulous voice with bodily shaking. This word was of great importance in the liturgy. After the manner of the Jews,[94] the new faithful employed it to mark the assent of the people to the word spoken by the prophet or precentor.[95] They perhaps already attributed to it concealed virtues, and it was only pronounced with a certain emphasis. We know not whether the primitive ecclesiastical chant was accompanied with instruments.[96] As to the inward chant, which the faithful "sang in their hearts,"[97] and which was nothing else than the overflowing of those tender spirits, ardent and dreamy as they were, they performed it no doubt like the slow chants of the Lollards of the Middle Ages, in a sort of whisper.[98] In general, joyousness manifested itself in these hymns. One of the maxims of the sages of the sect was, "If thou art sad, pray; if thou art merry, sing."[99]

Moreover, this first Christian literature, designed as it was entirely for the edification of the assembled brethren, was not committed to writing. It entered into the mind of none to compose books. Jesus had spoken; they remembered his words. Had he not promised that that generation of his hearers should not pass away before he re-appeared among them?[100]

CHAPTER VI.

THE CONVERSION OF THE HELLENISTIC JEWS AND PROSELYTES.

Up to the present time the Church of Jerusalem has practically been only a little Galilean colony. The friends of Jesus in Jerusalem and its vicinity, such as Lazarus, Martha and Mary of Bethany, Joseph of Arimathea and Nicodemus, had disappeared from the scene. Only the Galilean group gathered around the twelve apostles remained, compact and active; and meanwhile these zealous apostles were indefatigable in the work of preaching. Subsequently, after the fall of Jerusalem, and in places distant from Judea, it was reported that the sermons of the apostles had been delivered in public places and before large assemblages.[1] The authorities who had put Jesus to death would not permit the revival of such stories. The proselytism of the faithful was chiefly carried on by means of pointed conversations, during which their hearty earnestness was gradually communicated to others.[2] They preached under the portico of Solomon to audiences limited in number, but on whom they produced a most marked effect; their sermons consisted chiefly in such quotations from the Old Testament as would support their theory that Christ was the Messiah.[3] Their reasoning, though subtle, was weak; but the entire exegesis of the Jews at that time was of the same character, and the deductions drawn from the Bible by the doctors of the Mischna are no more convincing.

Still more feeble was the proof derived from pretended prodigies, which they brought forward in support of their arguments. It is impossible to doubt that the apostles believed that they possessed the power of performing miracles, which were acknowledged as the tokens of every Divine mission.[4] St. Paul, by far the ablest mind of the primitive Christian school, believed in miracles.[5] It was deemed certain that Jesus had performed them, and it was but natural to suppose that the series of Divine manifestations was to continue. Indeed thaumaturgy was a privilege of the apostles until the end of the first century.[6] The miracles of the apostles were of the same nature as those of Jesus; and consisted principally, though not exclusively, in the healing of the sick and the exorcising of demons.[7] It was maintained that even their shadow sufficed to bring about these marvellous cures.[8] These wonders were deemed direct gifts of the Holy Ghost, and held the same rank as the gifts of learning, of preaching, and of prophecy.[9] In the third century the Church believed herself possessed of the same privileges, and claimed as a permanent right the power of healing the sick, of driving out devils, and of predicting the future.[10] The ignorance of the people encouraged these pretensions. Do we not see in our day persons honest enough, but lacking in scientific intelligence, similarly deceived by the chimera of magnetism and other illusions?[11]

It is not by these *naïve* errors, nor by the meagre discourses found in the *Acts*, that we must form our opinion of the means of conversion employed by the founders of Christianity. The private conversations of these good and earnest men, the reflection of the words of Jesus in their discourses, and above all, their piety and gentleness, formed the real power of their preaching. Their communistic life also had its attractions. Their house was like a *hospice*, where all the poor and forsaken found a refuge and an asylum.

Among the first who attached himself to the young society was a Cypriote called Joseph Hallevi, or the Levite, who, like many others, sold his land and laid the money at the feet of the disciples. He was an intelligent and devoted man, and a facile speaker. The apostles soon attached him to their band, and called him *Bar-naba*, which means the "son of prophecy," or "of preaching."[12] He was numbered among the prophets, that is to say, inspired preachers;[13] and later we shall see him playing an important part. After St. Paul, he was the most active missionary of the first century. A certain Mnason was converted about the same time.[14] Cyprus was marked by many Jewish characteristics.[15] Barnabas and Mnason were undoubtedly of the Jewish race;[16] and the intimate and prolonged relations of Barnabas with the Church of Jerusalem give us reason to believe that he was familiar with the Syro-Chaldaic tongue.

A conversion almost equally as important as that of Barnabas, was that of a certain John, who bore the Roman surname of Marcus. He was cousin to Barnabas, and was a circumcised Jew.[17] His mother, Mary, a woman in easy circumstances, was also converted, and her residence was frequently visited by the apostles.[18] These two conversions appear to have been the work of Peter,[19] who was very intimate with both mother and son, and considered himself at home in their house.[20] Admitting the hypothesis that John-Mark was not identical with the true or supposed author of the second Gospel,[21] he yet played a prominent part, accompanying at a later period Paul and Barnabas, and probably Peter himself, on their apostolic journeys.

The fire thus kindled spread rapidly. The most celebrated men of the apostolic age were gained to the cause in two or three years almost simultaneously. It was a second Christian generation, parallel to that which had been formed five or six years previously on the shores of Lake Tiberias. This second generation, not having seen Jesus, could not equal the first in authority, but surpassed it in activity and in the ardor for distant missions. One of the best known of these new adepts was Stephanus or Stephen, who before his conversion was probably only a simple proselyte.[22] He was a man full of fervor and passion, his faith was very strong, and he was believed to be endowed with all the gifts of the Spirit.[23] Philip, who, like Stephen, was a zealous deacon and evangelist, joined the community at about the same time,[24] and was often confounded with the apostle of the same name.[25] Finally, at this epoch, Andronicus and Junia[26] were converted. They were probably husband and wife, who, like Aquila and Priscilla at a later date, were the very model of an apostolic couple, thoroughly devoted to the missionary cause. They were of Israelitish blood, and enjoyed the warm friendship of the apostles.[27]

Although the new converts were all Jews by religion, when touched by grace, they belonged to two very different classes of Jews. Some were "Hebrews," or Jews of Palestine, speaking Hebrew, or rather *Aramaic*, and reading the Bible in the Hebrew text. The others were "Hellenists," or Jews speaking Greek, and reading the Bible in that tongue. These last were further subdivided into two classes—the one being of Jewish blood; the other proselytes, or people of non-Israelitish origin, affiliated in different degrees to Judaism. The Hellenists, who almost all came from Syria, Asia Minor, Egypt, or Cyrene,[29] inhabited a separate quarter of Jerusalem, where they had their distinctive synagogues, thus forming little communities by themselves. There were a large number of these private synagogues[30] in Jerusalem, and in them the word of Jesus found a soil pre pared for its reception.

The primitive nucleus of the Church was exclusively composed of "Hebrews;" and the Aramaic dialect, which was the language of Jesus, was the only one in use: but during the second or third year after the death of Jesus, Greek was introduced into the little community, and soon became the dominant tongue. Through their daily communication with these new brethren, Peter, John, James, Jude, and the Galilean disciples in general, learned Greek very easily, especially as they probably knew something of it beforehand. An incident soon to be mentioned shows that this diversity of language created at first some division in the community, and that the two fractions could not always readily agree.[31] After the ruin of Jerusalem, we shall see the "Hebrews" retire beyond the Jordan, to the heights of Lake Tiberias, and form a separate Church, which had its individual history. But in the meantime it does not appear that the diversity of language seriously affected the Church. The Orientals learn new languages very easily, and in the towns every one speaks two or three dialects. It is probable that the leading Galilean apostles acquired the use of the Greek so far that they used it in preference to the Syro-Chaldaic whenever the majority of their listeners understood it. It was evident that the dialect of Palestine must be abandoned by those who dreamed of a wide-spread propaganda. A provincial *patois* which was written with difficulty[33] and only in use in Syria, was palpably insufficient for such an undertaking. Greek, on the contrary, was almost a necessity to Christianity. It was the universal language of the age, at least around the eastern basin of the Mediterranean; and it was especially the language of the Jews dispersed throughout the Roman empire. Then, as now, the Jews adopted with facility the idioms of the countries they inhabited. They were by no means purists, and this explains why the Greek used by the primitive Christians was so corrupt. Even the best educated Jews pronounced the classic language badly.[34] Their phraseology was always founded on the Syriac. They never freed themselves from the effect of the corrupt dialects, which dated from the Macedonian conquests.[35]

The conversions to Christianity soon became much more numerous among the "Hellenists" than among the "Hebrews." The old Jews of Jerusalem found little attraction in a provincial sect but poorly versed in the only science appreciated by a Pharisee—the science of the law. The relations of the little Church towards Judaism, like Jesus himself, were rather equivocal. But every religious or political party has an innate force which rules it, and, despite of itself, compels it to travel in its orbit. The first Christians, however great their apparent respect for Judaism, were, in reality, only Jews by their birth or by their outward customs. The true spirit of the sect had disappeared. The Talmud germinated in official Judaism, and Christianity had no affinity with the Talmud school. This is why Christianity found special favor among those nominal adherents of Judaism who were the least Jewish. Rigid orthodoxy did not incline towards the Christian sect; and it was the new-comers, people scarcely catechized, who had not been to the great schools, and were ignorant of the holy language, who lent a willing ear to the apostles and their disciples. Viewed rather contemptuously by the aristocracy of Jerusalem, these *parvenus* of Judaism were not without their revenge. Young and newly formed parties always have less respect for tradition than older members of communities, and are more susceptible to the charms of novelty.

These classes, little subjected to the doctors of the law, were also it seems the most credulous. Credulity is not a characteristic of the Talmudic Jew. The credulous Jew, fond of the marvellous, was not the Jew of Jerusalem, but the Hellenist Jew; who was at the same time very religious and very ignorant, and consequently very superstitious. Neither the half incredulous Sadducee, nor the rigorous Pharisee, would be much affected by the theories popular in the apostolic circle. But the Judæus Apella, of whom the epicurean Horace wrote,[37] was ready to give in his adhesion. Social questions, besides, particularly interested those who received no benefit from the opulence enjoyed by Jerusalem as the locality of the temple and other central institutions of the nation; and it was by a recognition of the needs to which in this day modern socialism seeks to respond, that the new sect laid the solid foundation of its mighty future.

CHAPTER VII.

THE CHURCH CONSIDERED AS AN ASSOCIATION OF POOR PEOPLE.—INSTITUTION OF THE DIACONATE.—DEACONESSES AND WIDOWS.

A comparison of the history of religion shows, as a general truth, that all those religions not contemporary with the origin of language itself, owe their establishment to social rather than theological causes. This was assuredly the case with Buddhism, the prodigious success of which may be traced to its social element, rather than to the nihilistic principle on which it was based. It was in proclaiming the abolition of castes, and establishing, in his words, "a law of grace for all," that Sakya-Mouni and his disciples gained the adherence, first of India, and then of the largest portion of Asia.[1] Like Christianity, Buddhism was a movement of the lower classes. Its great attraction was the facility it afforded the poor to elevate themselves by the profession of a religion which improved their condition and offered them inexhaustible assistance and sympathy.

The poor were a numerous class in Judea during the first century. The country was naturally scantily provided with luxuries. In these countries where industry is almost unknown, almost every fortune owes its origin either to richly endowed religious institutions or government patronage. The riches of the temple were for a long time the exclusive appanage of a limited number of nobles. The Asmoneans gathered around their dynasty a circle of rich families; and the Herods considerably increased the welfare and luxury of a certain class of society. But the real theocratic Jew, turning his back upon Roman civilization, only became poorer. He belonged to a class of holy men, fanatically pious, rigidly observant of the law, and miserably and abjectly poor. From this class, the sects of enthusiasts so numerous at this period, received their recruits. The universal dream of these people shadowed forth the triumph of the poor Jew who remained faithful, and the humiliation of the rich, who were considered as renegades and traitors, because of their civilization and different mode of life. Intense indeed was the hatred entertained by these poor fanatics against the splendid edifices which now began to adorn the country, and against the public works of the Romans.[2] Obliged as they were to toil for their daily bread on these structures, which to them seemed monuments of pride and forbidden luxury, they considered themselves the victims of men who were rich, wicked, corrupt, and infidels to the Divine Law.

In such a social state an association for mutual benefit would naturally receive a warm welcome. The little Christian Church appeared to be a paradise. This family of simple and united brethren attracted people from every quarter, who in return for that which they brought secured a settled future, the society of congenial friends, and precious spiritual hopes. The general custom of converts[3] was to convert into specie their property, which usually consisted of little farms but scantily productive. To unmarried people in particular the exchange of their plots of land for shares in a society which would secure them a place in the Heavenly Kingdom, could not be otherwise than advantageous. Several married persons did likewise. Care was taken that the new associates should contribute their entire effects to the common fund without retaining any portion for private use.[4] Indeed, as each one received from the common treasury in proportion to his needs, and not in proportion to his contributions, every reservation of property was a fraud on the community. Such attempts at organization show a surprising resemblance to certain Utopian experiments made recently; but with the important difference that Christian communism rested on a religious basis, which is not the case with modern socialism. It is evident that an association whose dividends were declared not in proportion to the capital subscribed, but in proportion to individual needs, must rest only upon a sentiment of exalted self-abnegation and an ardent faith in a religious ideal

Under such a social constitution, however, and despite of the high degree of fraternity, the administrative difficulties were necessarily numerous. The difference of language between the two factions of the community inevitably led to misapprehensions. The Jews of higher birth could not restrain a feeling of contempt for their more humble brethren in the faith, and soon expressed their dissatisfaction. "The Hellenists," whose numbers daily increased, complained that their widows received less at the distributions than those of the "Hebrews."[6] Until this time the apostles had attended to the financial affairs of the community;

but, feeling now the necessity of delegating to others this part of their authority, they proposed to confide the administrative duties to seven experienced and leading men. The proposition was accepted, and at the election, Stephanus or Stephen, Philip, Prochorus, Nicanor, Timon, Parmenas, and Nicholas, were chosen. This last was a simple proselyte from Antioch, and Stephen, perhaps, was the same.[7] It seems that, in opposition to the course followed in the election of the Apostle Matthew, the choice of the seven administrators was not made from a group of primitive disciples, but from the new converts, and especially from the Hellenists. The names of all of them, indeed, were purely Greek. Stephen was the leading spirit of the seven, who, in accordance with the established rite, were formally presented to the apostles, and confirmed by them in the ceremony of laying on of hands.

The administrators thus designated received the Syriac name of *Schammaschin*, and were also sometimes called "the seven," in the same manner that the apostles were called "the twelve."[8] Such was the origin of the Diaconate, the most ancient of sacred and ecclesiastical orders. In imitation of the church of Jerusalem, all the other churches introduced the Diaconate, and the institution spread with marvellous rapidity. This institution, indeed, elevated the care of the poor to an equality with religious services. It was a proclamation of the truth that social questions should be the first to occupy the attention of man. It was the introduction of political economy into religious affairs. The deacons were the best preachers of Christianity, and we shall soon see how they played their part as evangelists. As organizers, financial directors, and administrators, they had a still more important part. These practical men in perpetual contact with the poor, the rich, and the women, viisted everywhere, observed everything, and by their exhortations were the most efficient agents of conversion.[9] They did much more than the apostles who remained stationary at the central point of authority in Jerusalem; and to them we are indebted for the most prominent and solid features of Christianity.

From a very early period women were admitted to this employment;[10] and, as in these days, they were called "sisters."[11] At first they were widows;[12] but later, virgins were preferred for this office.[13] Admirable tact was shown by the Church in this movement. These good and simple men, with that profound science which comes from the heart, laid the basis of that grand system of charity which is the peculiar merit of Christianity. They had no precedent for such an institution. A vast system of benevolence and of reciprocal aid, to which the two sexes brought their diverse qualities, and lent their united efforts for the relief of human misery, was the holy creation which resulted from the travail of these two or three first years—the most prolific years in the history of Christianity. It is certain that the vital thoughts of Jesus filled the souls of His disciples and directed all their acts. Justice, indeed, demands that to Jesus should be referred the honor of all the great deeds of His apostles. It is probable that during His life He laid the foundations of those establishments which were successfully developed so soon after His death.

Women, naturally, were attracted towards a community where the weak were so cordially protected. Their position in society had previously been humble and precarious; widows, particularly, notwithstanding several protecting laws, were but little respected,[14] and often even abandoned to misery. Many of the doctors were opposed to giving them any religious education.[15] The Talmud placed along with the other pests of mankind, the gossiping and inquisitive widow, who spent her days in chatting with her neighbors, and the maiden who wasted her time in incessant praying.[16] The new religion offered to these poor and neglected souls a sure and honourable asylum.[17] Several women occupied a prominent place in the Church, and their houses served as places of meeting;[18] while those who had no houses were formed into a species of feminine presbyteral body, comprising probably the virgins, who did important duty in charitable works. Those institutions, regarded as the fruit of a later Christianity, such as congregations of women, nuns, and sisters of charity, were really one of its first creations, the beginning of its influence, and the most perfect expression of its spirit. The admirable idea of consecrating by a sort of religious character and subjecting to regular discipline those women who were not in the bonds of marriage, is peculiarly and entirely Christian. The word "widow" became a synonyme for a person devoted to religious works, consecrated to God, and, consequently, a "deaconess."[20] In those countries, where the wife at her twenty-fourth year already began to fade, and where there was no middle state between the child and the old woman, it was practically a new life which was thus opened for that portion of the human race the most capable of devotion.

The times of the Seleucidæ had been a terrible epoch for female depravity. Never before were known so many domestic dramas, and such a series of poisonings and adulteries. The wise men of that day considered woman as a scourge to humanity; as the first cause of baseness and shame; as an evil genius whose only part in life was to impair whatever there was of good in the opposite sex. Christianity changed all this. At that age which, to our view, is yet youth, but at which the existence of the Oriental woman is so gloomy, so fatally prone to evil suggestions, the widow could, by covering her head with a black shawl,[21] become a respectable person worthily employed, and, as a deaconess, the equal of the most esteemed men in the community. The difficult and dubious position of the childless widow, Christianity elevated even to sanctity.[22] The widow became almost the equal of the maiden. She was καλογρια, "beautiful old age,"[23] venerated and useful, and receiving the respect usually awarded to a mother. These women, constantly going to and fro, were the most useful missionaries of the new religion. Protestants are in error in viewing these facts through the light of the system of modern individuality. Socialism and cenobitism are primitive features of Christianity.

The bishop and priest of later days did not yet exist; but that intimate familiarity of souls not bound by ties of blood, known as the pastoral ministry, was already founded. This was always the special gift of Jesus; and, as it were, a heritage from Him. Jesus had often said that He was more than father and mother, and that those who followed Him must forsake those beloved beings. Christianity placed some things above the family. It created a fraternity and spiritual marriages. The ancient system of marriages, which without restriction placed the wife in the power of the husband, was mere slavery. The moral liberty of woman began when the Church gave her in Jesus a friend and a guide, who advised and consoled her, always listened to her grievances, and sometimes advised resistance. Women need a governing power, and are only happy when governed; but it is necessary that they should love the one who wields that power. This is what neither ancient society, Judaism, nor Islamism, were able to do. Woman never had a religious conscience, a moral individuality, or an opinion of her own, previous to Christianity. Thanks to the Bishops and to monastic life, Radegonda found means for escaping from the arms of a barbarous husband. The life of the soul being all that is really of importance, it is just and reasonable that the pastor who would make the divine chords of the heart vibrate, the secret counsellor who holds the key of the conscience, should be more than a father, more than a husband.

In one sense Christianity was a reaction against the too narrow domestic system of the Aramaic race. The old Aramaic societies only admitted married men, and were singularly strict in their views of the marriage relation. All this was something analogous to the English family—a narrow, closed up, contracted circle—an egotism of several, as withering to the soul as the egotism of an individual. Christianity, with its divine idea of the liberty of God, corrected these exaggerations. And first it allotted to every one the duties common to mankind. It saw that the family relation was not of sole importance in life, or at least that the duty of reproducing the human race did not devolve on every one; and that there should be persons freed from these duties, which are undoubtedly sacred, but not intended for every one. The same exceptions made in favor of the *hetairæ* like Aspasia by Greek society, and of the *cortigiana* like Imperia, in recognition of the necessities of polished society, Christianity made for the priest and the deaconess for the public welfare. It admitted different classes in society. There are people who find it more delightful to be loved by a hundred people than by five or six; and for these the family in its ordinary conditions seems insufficient, cold, and wearisome. Why, then, should we extend to all, the exigencies of our dull and mediocre social system? His temporal family is not sufficient for man; he feels the need of brothers and sisters besides those of the flesh.

By its hierarchy of different social functions, the primitive Church seemed to conciliate for the time these opposing exigencies. We shall never understand, never comprehend, how happy these people were under these holy regulations which sustained liberty without restraining it, and permitted at the same time the advantages of communistic and private life. It was far different from the confusion of our artificial societies, in which the sensitive soul so often finds it cruelly isolated. In these little refuges which they call churches, the social atmosphere was sweet and inviting; the member lived there in the same faith and actuated by the same hopes. But it is clear that these conditions could not apply to a very large society. When entire countries became Christianized, the system of the first churches became a Utopian idea only partially realized in monasteries, and the monastic life in this sense was the continuation of the primitive churches.[26] The convent is the necessary consequence of the Christian spirit; there is no perfect Christianity without the convent, because it is only there that the evangelical idea can be realized.

A large share of the credit, certainly, of these great creations should be given to Judaism. Each one of the Jewish communities scattered along the shores of the Mediterranean was already a sort of church, with its charitable treasury. Almsgiving, always recommended by the elders,[27] was a recognised precept; it was practised in the temple and in the synagogues,[28] and it was deemed the first duty of the proselyte.[29] In every age Judaism was noted for its careful attention to the poor, and the fraternal charity which it inspired.

It would be highly unjust to hold up Christianity as a reproach to Judaism, since to the latter primitive Christianity owes almost everything. It is when we look upon the Roman world that we are the most astonished at the miracles of charity performed by the Church. Never did a profane society, recognising only right for its basis, produce such admirable effects. The law of every profane, or, if I may say so, every philosophic system of society, is liberty, sometimes equality, but never fraternity. To charity, viewed as a right, it acknowledges no obligations, it only pays attention to individuals; it finds charity often inconvenient, and neglects it. Every attempt to apply the public funds to the aid of the poor savors of communism. When a man dies of hunger, when entire classes languish in misery, the policy of the profane social system limits itself to acknowledging that the fact is unfortunate. It can easily show that there is no civil order without liberty; now, as a consequence of liberty, he who has nothing, and can get nothing, perishes from hunger. That is indeed logical; but there is no guard against the abuse of logic. The necessities of the most numerous class always result in dispensing with it. Institutions purely political and civil are not enough; social and religious aspirations claim a religious satisfaction. The glory of the Jewish people is, that they boldly proclaimed this principle. The Jewish law is social, and not political; the prophets, the authors of the Apocalypses, were the promoters of social and political revolutions. In the first half of the first century, in the presence of profane civilization, the absorbing idea of the Jews was to repel the benefits of the Roman system, with its philosophy, democracy, and equality, and to proclaim the excellence of their theocratic law. "The law is happiness," was the idea of such Jewish thinkers as Philon and Josephus. The laws of other people were intended to secure justice, and had nothing to do with the goodness and happiness of man; while on the other hand, the Jewish law descended to the details of moral education. Christianity is only the development of this idea. Each church is a monastery where all possess rights over all the others; where there should be neither poor nor wicked; and where, consequently, every individual is careful to guard and restrain himself. Primitive Christianity may be defined as a vast association of poor people; as a heroic struggle against egotism, founded upon the idea that no one has a right to more than is absolutely necessary for him, and that all the superfluity belongs to those who possess nothing. It will at once be seen that with such a spirit and the Roman spirit war to the death must ensue; and that Christianity, on its part, can never dominate the world without important modifications of its native tendencies and its original programme.

But the needs which it represents will always last. The communistic life during the second half of the Middle Ages, serving for the abuses of an intolerant Church, the monastery having become a mere feudal fief, or the barracks for a dangerous and fanatic military modern feeling, became bitterly opposed to the cenobitic system. We have forgotten that it was in the communistic life that the soul of man experienced its fullest joy. The song, "Oh, how good and joyful a thing it is for brethren to dwell together in unity,"[30] has ceased to be our refrain. But when modern individualism shall have borne its latest fruits, when humanity, shrunken and saddened, shall also have become weak and impotent, it will return to these great institutions and stern disciplines; when our material society—I should say our world of pigmies—shall have been scourged with whips by the heroic and the idealistic, then the communistic system will regain all its force. Many great things, such as science, will be organized under a monastic form. Egotism, the essential law of civil law, of civil society, will be insufficient for great minds; all coming, from whatever point of view, will be opposed to vulgarity. The words of Jesus and the ideas of the Middle Ages in regard to poverty will again be appreciated. It will be understood that the possession of anything implies an inferiority, and that the founders of the mystic life disputed for centuries as to whether Jesus owned even that which he used for his daily wants. The Franciscan subtleties will become again great social problems. The splendid ideal devised by the author of the *Acts* will be inscribed as a prophetic revelation at the gates of the paradise of humanity: "And the multitude of them that believed were of one heart and one soul; neither said of them that aught of the things which he possessed was his own, but they had all things in common, neither was any among them that lacked: for as many as were possessors of land or houses sold them, and brought the price of the things that were sold, and laid them down at the apostles' feet, and distribution was made unto every man, according as he had need. And they continuing with one accord in the temple and breaking bread from house to house, did eat their meat with gladness and singleness of heart."[31]

Let us not anticipate events. It is now about the year 36. Tiberius at Caprea could have no more doubt that a formidable enemy to the empire was growing up. In two or three years the new sect had made surprising progress; now counted several thousands of adherents.[32] It was easy to foresee that its conquests would be chiefly among the Hellenists and proselytes. The Galilean group, which had heard the Master, though preserving its precedence, seemed almost lost in the current of new-comers who spoke Greek. At the time of which we speak, no heathen, that is to say, no man who had not held previous relations with Judaism, had entered into the Church; but proselytes performed important functions in it. The jurisdiction of the disciples had also largely extended, and was no longer simply a little college of Palestineans, but included people of Cyprus, Antioch, and Cyrene, and of almost all the points on the eastern shore of the Mediterranean where Jewish colonies had been established. Egypt alone knew nothing of the primitive Church, and for a long time remained ignorant. The Jews of that country were almost in a state of schism with those of Judea. They had customs of their own, superior in many points to those of Palestine, and were almost entirely unaffected by the great religious movement at Jerusalem.

CHAPTER VIII.

FIRST PERSECUTION.—DEATH OF STEPHEN.—DESTRUCTION OF THE FIRST CHURCH OF JERUSALEM.

IT was inevitable that the preachings of the new sect, even while they were disseminated with much reserve, should revive the animosities which had accumulated against its Founder, and had ultimately resulted in His death. The Sadducee family of Hanan, which had caused the death of Jesus, was still reigning. Joseph Caiaphas occupied, up to the year 36, the sovereign Pontificate, the effective power of which he left to his father-in-law Hanan, and to his relations, John and Alexander.[1] These arrogant and pitiless personages saw with impatience a troop of good holy men, without any official position, gaining the favor of the crowd.[2] Once or twice Peter, John, and the principal members of the apostolical college, were thrust into prison and condemned to be beaten. This was the punishment inflicted on heretics.[3] The authorization of the Romans was not necessary for its infliction. As may well be supposed, these brutalities did but excite the ardor of the apostles. They came forth from the Sanhedrim, where they had just undergone flagellation, full of joy at having been deemed worthy to undergo contumely for Him whom they loved.[4] Eternal puerility of penal repressions, applied to things of the soul! They passed, no doubt, for men of order, for models of prudence and wisdom, these blunderers, who seriously believed in the year 36 they could put down Christianity with a few whippings!

These outrages were perpetrated principally by the Sadducees,[5] that is to say by the upper clergy, who surrounded the temple, and derived thence immense profits.[6] It does not seem that the Pharisees displayed towards the sect the animosity they showed to Jesus. The new believers were people pious and strict in their manner of life, not a little like the Pharisees themselves. The rage which the latter felt against the Founder sprang from the superiority of Jesus—a superiority which He took no pains to disguise. His delicate sarcasms, His intellect, the charm there was about Him, His hatred to hypocrites, had enkindled a savage ire. The apostles, on the contrary, were destitute of wit; they never employed irony. The Pharisees were at certain moments favorable to them; many Pharisees even became Christians.[7] The terrible anathemas of Jesus against Pharisaism had not yet been written, and tradition of the words of the Master was neither general nor uniform.[8]

These first Christians were, moreover, people so inoffensive, that many persons of the Jewish aristocracy, without exactly forming part of the sect, were well disposed towards them. Nicodemus and Joseph of Arimathea, who had known Jesus, remained, no doubt, linked in bonds of brotherhood with the Church. The most celebrated Jewish Doctor of the times, Rabbi Gamaliel the Elder, grandson of Hillel, a man of broad and very tolerant ideas, gave his opinion, it is said, in the Sanhedrim in favor of the freedom of Gospel preaching.[9] The author of *The Acts* puts into his mouth some excellent reasoning, which ought to be the rule of conduct for Governments whenever they find themselves confronted with novelties in the intellectual or moral order. "If this work is frivolous, leave it alone, it will fall of itself; if it is serious, how dare you resist the work of God? In any case you will not succeed in stopping it." Gamaliel was but little heeded. Liberal minds in the midst of opposing fanaticisms have no chance of success.

A terrible excitement was provoked by the Deacon Stephen.[10] His preaching had, as it seems, great success. The crowd flocked around him, and these gatherings resulted in some lively disputes. It was mostly Hellenists, or proselytes, attendants at the synagogue of the *Libertini*,[11] as it was called—people of Cyrene, of Alexandria, of Cilicia, of Ephesus, who were active in these disputes. Stephen passionately maintained that Jesus was the Messiah; that the priests had committed a crime in putting him to death; that the Jews were rebels, sons of rebels, people that denied evidence. The authorities resolved to destroy this audacious preacher; witnesses were suborned to watch for some word in his discourses against Moses. Naturally they found what they sought for. Stephen was arrested and taken before the Sanhedrim. The word with which he was reproached was nearly the same as that which led to the condemnation of Jesus.[12] He was accused of saying that Jesus of Nazareth would destroy the temple, and change the traditions attributed to Moses. It is very possible, in fact, that Stephen had used such language. A Christian of this epoch would not have had any idea of speaking directly against the law, since all still observed it; but as to traditions, Stephen might combat them as Jesus himself had done. Now these traditions were foolishly ascribed to Moses by the orthodox, and an equal value was attributed to them as to the written law.[13]

Stephen defended himself by expounding the Christian thesis, with copious citations from the law, from the Psalms, from the prophets, and terminated by reproaching the members of the Sanhedrim with the homicide of Jesus. "O blockheads! and uncircumcised in heart," said he to them, "you will then ever resist the Holy Ghost, as your fathers also have done. Which of the prophets have not your fathers persecuted? They have slain those who announced the coming of the Just One, whom you have betrayed, and of whom you have been the murderers. This law that you had received from the mouth of angels[14] you have not kept." At these words a cry of rage interrupted him. Stephen, becoming more and more exalted, fell into one of those paroxysms of enthusiasm that are called the inspiration of the Holy Ghost. His eyes were fixed on high; he saw the glory of God and Jesus beside his Father, and cried out: "Behold, I see the heavens opened, and the Son of Man sitting on the right hand of God." All the listeners stopped their ears and threw themselves upon him, gnashing their teeth. They dragged him outside the city and stoned him. The witnesses who, according to the law,[15] had to cast the first stones, took off their garments and laid them at the feet of a young fanatic named Saul, or Paul, who was thinking with secret joy of the merits which he was acquiring in participating in the death of a blasphemer.[16]

In all this there was a literal observance of the prescriptions of Deuteronomy, Chap. 13. But looked at from the point of view of the civil law, this tumultuous execution, accomplished without the concurrence of the Romans, was not regular.[17] In the case of Jesus, we have seen that the ratification of the Procurator was needed. Perhaps his ratification was obtained in Stephens' case, and his execution may not have followed quite so closely upon his sentence as the narrator of the Acts would have it. Possibly, however, the Roman authority was then somewhat relaxed in Judea. Pilate had just been suspended from his functions, or was on the point of being so. The cause of this disgrace was simply the too great firmness he had shown in his administration. Jewish fanaticism had rendered life unbearable to him. Very likely he was tired of refusing these madmen the violence they demanded of him, and the proud family of Hanan had come to have no longer any need of permission in order to pronounce sentence of death. Lucius Vitellius (the father of him who was emperor) was then imperial legate of Syria. He sought to win the good graces of the population; and he had the pontifical vestments which, since the time of Herod the Great, had been deposited in the town of Antonia, returned to the Jews.[19] Far from sustaining Pilate in his acts of rigor, he gave ear to the complaints of the native citizens, and sent Pilate back to Rome to reply to the accusations of his subordinates (beginning of the year 36). The principal grievance of the latter was that the Procurator would not lend himself with sufficient complaisance to their desires—intolerant desires.[20] Vitellius replaced him provisionally by his friend Marcellus, who was no doubt more careful not to displease the Jews, and consequently more ready to indulge them with religious murders. The death of Tiberius (16th March in the year 37) only encouraged Vitellius in his policy. The two first years of the reign of Caligula were an epoch of general enfeeblement of the Roman authority in Syria. The policy of this prince, before he lost his wife, was to restore to the people of the East their autonomy and native chiefs. Thus he established the kingdoms or principalities of Antiochus, of Comagene, of Herod Agrippa, of Soheym, of Cotys, of Polemon II., and allowed that of Hâreth to aggrandize itself.[21] When Pilate arrived at Rome, he found the new reign already begun. It is probable that Caligula decided against him, since he confided the government of Jerusalem to a new functionary, Marcellus, who appears not to have excited on the part of the Jews the violent recriminations which overwhelmed the unfortunate Pilate with embarrassment and filled him with chagrin.

At any rate, the important remark is this: that at the epoch of which we are treating the persecutors of Christianity were not Romans; they were orthodox Jews. The Romans preserved, in the midst of this fanaticism, a principle of tolerance and of reason. If there is anything for which the imperial authority is to be reproached, it is for having been too weak, and not having cut short at the outset the civil consequences of a sanguinary law pronouncing the pain of death for religious offences. But the Roman domination had not yet become a complete power, as it was at a later day; it was a sort of protectorate or suzerainty. Its complaisance was carried even to the extent of withholding the effigy of the Emperor from the coins struck under the procurators, in order not to shock Jewish ideas.[23] Rome did not yet seek, at least not in the East, to impose on conquered peoples her laws, her gods, her manners; she left them in their local practices outside the Roman law. Their semi-independence was but another sign of their inferiority. The Imperial power in the East at this epoch pretty closely resembled the Turkish authority, and the government of the native populations that of the Rajahs. The idea of equal rights and equal guarantees for all did not exist. Each provincial group had its own jurisdiction, as at this day the various Christian churches and the Jews in the Ottoman Empire. A few years ago, in Turkey, the patriarchs of the various communities of Rajahs, provided they were on good terms with the Porte, were sovereign in regard to their subordinates, and could pronounce against them the most cruel punishments.

As the period of the death of Stephen may fluctuate between the years 36, 37, and 38, we do not know whether Caiphas ought to bear the responsibility of it. Caiphas was deposed by Lucius Vitellius in the year 36, shortly after Pilate;[24] but the change was slight. He was succeeded by his brother-in-law, Jonathan, son of Hanan. The latter in his turn was succeeded by his brother Theophilus, son of Hanan,[25] who kept the Pontificate in the house of Hanan till the year 42. Hanan was still alive, and possessor of the real power maintained in his family—the principles of pride, of severity, of hatred to innovators, which were in a manner hereditary in it.

The death of Stephen produced a great impression. The converts solemnized his funeral in the midst of tears and groans.[26] The separation between the new sectaries and Judaism was not yet absolute. The proselytes and the Hellenists, less strict in the matter of orthodoxy than the pure Jews, felt that they ought to render public homage to a man who had been an honor to their body, and whose peculiar opinions had not shut him out from the pale of the law.

Thus dawned the era of Christian martyrs. Martyrdom was not a thing entirely new. To say nothing of John Baptist and of Jesus, Judaism, at the epoch of Antiochus Epiphanus, had had its witnesses faithful unto the death. But the series of brave victims which opens with St. Stephen has exercised a peculiar influence upon the history of the human mind. It introduced into the western world an element which was wanting to it, absolute and exclusive Faith—this idea, that there is but one good and true religion. In this sense, the martyrs began the era of intolerance. It may be said, with great probability, that any one who gives his life for his faith would be intolerant if he were master. Christianity, after it had passed through three centuries of persecutions and became in its turn dominant, was more persecuting than any religion had ever been. When we have poured out our own blood for a cause, we are but too strongly led to shed the blood of others for the conservation of the treasure we have won.

The murder of Stephen was not, moreover, an isolated fact. Taking advantage of the weakness of the Roman functionaries, the Jews brought a real persecution[27] to bear down upon the Church. It seems that the vexations pressed hardest upon the Hellenists and the proselytes whose free tendencies enraged the orthodox. The Church of Jerusalem, already so strongly organized, was obliged to disperse. The apostles, according to a principle which seems to have taken strong hold of their minds,[28] did not leave the city. It was probably so with all the purely Jewish group, with those who were called the "Hebrews."[29] But the great community, with its meals in common, its diaconal services, its varied exercises, ceased thenceforth, and was never again reconstructed upon its first model. It had lasted three or four years. It was for nascent Christianity an unequalled good fortune that its first attempts at association, essentially communist, were so soon broken up. Attempts of this kind engender abuses so shocking, that communist establishments are condemned to crumble away in a very short time,[30] or very soon to ignore the principle on which they are created.[31] Thanks to the persecution of the year 37, the cenobitic Church of Jerusalem was saved from the test of time. It fell in its flower, before interior difficulties had undermined it. It remained like a splendid dream, the memory of which animated in their life of trial all those who had formed part of it, like an ideal to which Christianity will incessantly aspire to return, without ever succeeding.[32] Those who know what an inestimable treasure for the members still existing of the St. Simonian Church is the memory of Ménilmontant, what friendship it creates between them, what joy gleams from their eyes as they speak of it, will comprehend the powerful link established between the new brethren by the fact of having loved and then suffered together. Great lives have nearly always to remember a few months during which they felt God—months which, though existing only in memory, delight all the after years of their lives.

The leading part, in the persecution we have just recounted, was played by that young Saul whom we have already found contributing, as far as in him lay, to the murder of Stephen. This furious man, furnished with a permission from the priests, entered into houses suspected of concealing Christians, took violent hold of men and women, and dragged them into prison or before the tribunals.[33] Saul prided himself on there being no one of his generation so zealous as himself for the traditions.[34] Often, it is true, the mildness, the resignation of his victims astonished him; he experienced a sort of remorse; he imagined hearing these pious women, hoping for the Kingdom of God, whom he had thrown into prison, say to him during the night, with a gentle voice: "Why persecutest thou us?" The blood of Stephen, by which he was almost literally stained, sometimes disturbed his vision. Many things he had heard said of Jesus went to his heart. This superhuman being, in his ethereal life, whence he sometimes issued to reveal himself in short apparitions, haunted him like a spectre. But Saul repulsed such thoughts with horror; he confirmed himself with a sort of frenzy in the faith of his traditions, and he was dreaming of new cruelties against those who attacked them. His name had become the terror of the faithful; the fiercest outrages, the most sanguinary perfidies, were dreaded at his hands.[35]

CHAPTER IX.

FIRST MISSIONS.—PHILIP THE DEACON.

The persecution of the year 37 had for its result, as always happens, the expansion of the doctrine it was wished to arrest. Until then the Christian preaching had scarcely extended beyond Jerusalem; no mission had been undertaken; inclosed within its lofty but narrow communion, the mother Church had not radiated around itself nor formed any branches. The dispersion of the little supper-table scattered the good seed to the four winds. The members of the Church of Jerusalem, violently driven from their quarters, spread themselves throughout Judea and Samaria,[1] and preached everywhere the kingdom of God. The deacons in particular, disengaged from their administrative functions by the ruin of the Community, became excellent evangelists. They were the active young element of the sect, in opposition to the somewhat heavy element constituted by the apostles and the "Hebrews." One single circumstance, that of language, would have sufficed to create in these latter an inferiority in respect to preaching. They spoke, at least as their habitual tongue, a dialect which the Jews themselves did not use at a few leagues distance from Jerusalem. It was to the Hellenists that fell all the honor of the grand conquest, the recital of which is henceforth to be our principal object.

The theatre of the first of these missions, which was

destined soon to embrace all the basin of the Mediterranean, was the region round about Jerusalem, within a circle of two or three days' journey. Philip the Deacon [1] [2] was the hero of this first holy expedition. He evangelized Samaria with great success. The Samaritans were schismatics; but the young sect, after the example of their Master, was less susceptible than the rigorous Jews upon questions of orthodoxy. Jesus, it was said, had shown Himself on different occasions not altogether unfavorable to the Samaritans.[3]

Philip appears to have been one of the apostolical men most preöccupied with theurgy.[4] The accounts which relate to him carry us into a strange and fantastic world. It is by prodigies that are explained the conversions which he made among the Samaritans, and in particular at Sebaste, their capital. This country was itself filled with superstitious ideas about magic. In the year 36, that is to say two or three years before the arrival of the Christian preachers, a fanatic had excited quite a serious emotion among the Samaritans by preaching the necessity of returning to primitive Mosaism, of which he pretended to have found the sacred utensils.[5] A certain Simon, of the village of Gitta, or Gitton,[6] who afterwards rose to a great reputation, began about that time to make himself known by his wonderful operations.[7] It is painful to see the Gospel finding a preparation and a support in such chimeras. Quite a large multitude were baptized in the name of Jesus. Philip had the power of baptizing, but not that of conferring the Holy Ghost. This privilege was reserved to the apostles. When the tidings came to Jerusalem of the formation of a group of believers at Sebaste, it was resolved to send Peter and John to complete their initiation. The two apostles came, laid their hands upon the new converts, prayed over their heads; the latter were immediately endowed with marvellous powers attached to the conferring of the Holy Ghost. Miracles, prophecy, all the phenomena of illuminism, were produced, and the Church of Sebaste had nothing on this score to envy that of Jerusalem.[8]

If we are to believe tradition about it, Simon of Gitton was thenceforth in relations with the Christians. Converted according to their reports by the preaching and the miracles of Philip, he was baptized and attached himself to this evangelist. Then, when the apostles Peter and John had come, and he saw the supernatural powers procured by the laying on of hands, he came, it is said, to offer them money in order that they should give him also the faculty of conferring the Holy Ghost. Peter then made him this admirable reply: "Thy money perish with thee, because thou hast thought that the gift of God may be bought! Thou hast neither part nor lot in this matter, for thy heart is not right in the sight of God."[9]

Whether these words were pronounced or not, they seem to trace exactly the situation of Simon in regard to the nascent sect. We shall see, in fact, that according to all appearances, Simon of Gitton was the chief of a religious movement parallel to that of Christianity, one which may be regarded as a sort of Samaritan counterfeit of the work of Jesus. Had Simon already begun to dogmatize and to work wonders when Philip arrived at Sebaste? Did he thenceforward enter into relations with the Christian Church? Is there any reality in the anecdote which makes of him the father of all "simony?" Must we admit that the world one day saw face to face two thaumaturgists, one a charlatan and the other the "corner-stone," which became the foundation of the faith of humanity? Was a conjuror able to balance himself against the destinies of Christianity? We know not, for want of documents; for the account of the *Acts* is here of feeble authority; and from the first century Simon became for the Christian Church a subject of legends. In history the general idea alone is pure. It would be unjust to dwell on anything we may see to be shocked at in this sad page of the origin of Christianity. For vulgar hearers the miracle proves the doctrine; for us the doctrine causes the miracle to be forgotten. When a belief has consoled and ameliorated humanity, it is excusable for having employed proofs proportioned to the weakness of the public whom it addressed. But when one has proved error by error, what excuse is there to allege? This is not a condemnation we here pronounce against Simon of Gitton. We shall have to explain further on this doctrine, and the part he had to play, which only made itself clear under the reign of Claudius.[10] It is necessary only to remark here, that an important principle seems to have been introduced through him into the Christian theurgy. Obliged to admit that impostors also worked miracles, orthodox theology attributed these miracles to the devil. In order to retain some demonstrative value in prodigies, rules had to be imagined for distinguishing true from false miracles. Orthodoxy descended for this purpose to an order of ideas exceedingly puerile.

Peter and John, after having confirmed the Church

of Sebaste, set out again for Jerusalem, on their return evangelizing the villages of the country of the Samaritans.[12] Philip the Deacon continued his evangelizing travels, bending his steps towards the south, towards the ancient country of the Philistines.[13] This country, since the advent of the Maccabees, had received a strong infusion of the Jewish element;[14] although Judaism was still by no means dominant there. During this journey Philip accomplished a conversion which made some noise, and which was much talked about on account of a particular circumstance. One day as he was going along the road from Jerusalem to Gaza, quite a deserted road,[15] he met a rich traveller, evidently a foreigner, for he was riding in a chariot, a mode of locomotion which was at all times almost unknown to the inhabitants of Syria and Palestine. He was returning from Jerusalem, and gravely seated, he was reading the Bible aloud, according to a custom then quite common.[16] Philip, who thought that in everything his actions were guided by an inspiration from on high, felt himself drawn towards his chariot. He placed himself alongside of it, and quietly entered into conversation with the opulent personage, offering to explain to him the passages which he did not understand. This was a fine occasion for the evangelist to develop the Christian thesis upon the figures of the Old Testament. He proved that in the prophetic books everything related to Jesus; that Jesus was the solution of the great enigma; that it was of Him in particular that the All-Seeing had spoken in this fine passage: "He was led as a sheep to the slaughter; as a lamb that is dumb before its shearers, he opened not his mouth."[17] The traveller believed him, and at the first water that they met, "Behold, here is water," said he, "why could I not be baptized?" The chariot was stopped; Philip and the traveller descended into the water, and the latter was baptized.

Now the traveller was a powerful personage. He was a eunuch of the Candace of Ethiopia, her Minister of Finance, and guardian of her treasures, who had come to worship at Jerusalem, and was now returning to Napata[18] by way of Egypt. *Candace*, or *Candaoce*, was the title of feminine royalty in Ethiopia towards the period in which we now are.[19] Judaism had consequently penetrated into Nubia and Abyssinia.[20] Many natives were converted, or at least counted among these proselytes who, without being circumcised, adored the one only God.[21] The eunuch was perhaps of this latter class, a simple, pious pagan, like the centurion Cornelius, who will shortly figure in this history. It is impossible in any case to suppose that he was completely initiated into Judaism.[22] After this we hear nothing more said about the eunuch. But Philip related the incident, and further on much importance was attached to it. When the question of the admission of pagans into the Christian Church became the leading business, there was found here a precedent of great weight. Philip was deemed to have acted in all this affair by Divine inspiration.[23] This baptism, given by order of the Holy Ghost, to a man scarcely a Jew, notoriously uncircumcised, who had believed in Christianity only for a few hours, had an eminent dogmatic value. It was an argument for those who thought that the doors of the new Church ought to be open to all.[24]

Philip after this adventure, made his appearance at Ashdod, or Azote. Such was the state of artless enthusiasm in which these missionaries lived, that at each step they believed they heard voices from Heaven and received directions from the Spirit.[25] Each of their steps seemed to them regulated by a superior force; and when they went from one city to another, they thought they were obeying a supernatural inspiration. Sometimes they imagined they made aërial voyages. Philip was in this respect one of the most exalted. It was on the indication of an angel, as he believed, that he came from Samaria to the place where he met the eunuch; after the baptism of the latter, he was persuaded that the Spirit lifted him up and carried him direct to Azote.[26]

Azote and the Gaza road were the limit of the first Gospel preaching towards the south. Beyond were the desert and the nomadic life upon which Christianity has ever taken but very slight hold. From Azote, Philip the Deacon hurried towards the north, and evangelized all the coast as far as Cesarea. Perhaps the Churches of Joppa and of Lydda, which we shall soon find flourishing,[27] were founded by him. At Cesarea he settled and founded an important church.[28] We shall meet him there again twenty years later.[29] Cesarea was a new city, and the most considerable in Judea.[30] It had been built on the site of a Sidonian fortress called "Abdastarte's or Strato's Tower," by Herod the Great, who gave to it, in honor of Augustus, the name which its ruins bear even to this day. Cesarea was by much the best port in all Palestine, and tended from day to day to become its capital. Tired of living at Jerusalem, the Procurators of Judea were soon going to make it their habitual residence.[31] It was peopled chiefly by pagans;[32] the Jews, however, were quite numerous there, and severe disputes often took place between the two classes of the population.[33] The Greek language was alone spoken there, and the Jews themselves had come to recite certain parts of their liturgy in Greek.[34] The austere Rabbis of Jerusalem looked upon Cesarea as a profane and dangerous abode, in which one became very nearly a pagan.[35] From all the reasons which have just been cited, this city will be of much importance in the sequel of our history. It was in a manner the port of Christianity, the point by which the Church of Jerusalem communicated with all the Mediterranean.

Many other missions, the history of which is unknown to us, were conducted side by side with that of Philip.[36] The very rapidity with which this first preaching was accomplished was the cause of its success. In the year 38, five years after the death of Jesus, and one perhaps after the death of Stephen, all Palestine on the higher side of Jordan had heard the glad tidings from the mouth of missionaries sent out from Jerusalem. Galilee, on its side, kept the holy seed and probably spread it around, although we know nothing of any missions issuing from this country. Perhaps the city of Damascus, which, from the epoch at which we have arrived, also had its Christians,[37] received the faith from Galilean preachers.

CHAPTER X.

CONVERSION OF ST. PAUL.

BUT the year 38 is marked in the history of the nascent Church by a new and important conquest. It was during that year[1] that we may safely place the conversion of that saint whom we saw a participant in the stoning of Stephen, and a principal agent in the persecution of 37, and who now, by a mysterious act of grace, becomes the most ardent of the disciples of Jesus.

Saul was born at Tarsus, in Cilicia,[2] in the year 10 or 12 of our era.[3] According to the manner of that day, his name was Latinized into that of Paul;[4] yet he did not regularly adopt this last name until he became the apostle of the Gentiles.[5] Paul was of the purest Jewish blood.[6] His family, probably originally from the town of Gischala, in Galilee,[7] professed to belong to the tribe of Benjamin;[8] and his father enjoyed the title of Roman citizen,[6] no doubt inherited from ancestors who had obtained that honor either through purchase or through services rendered to the state. Perhaps his grandfather had obtained it for aid given to Pompey during the Roman conquest (63 B.C.). His family, like most of the old and solid Jewish houses, belonged to the sect of Pharisees.[10] Paul was reared according to the strictest principles of this sect,[11] and though he subsequently repudiated its narrow dogmas, he always retained its asperity, its exaltation, and its ardent faith.

During the epoch of Augustus, Tarsus was a very flourishing city. The population, though chiefly of the Greek and Aramaic races, included, as was common in all the commercial towns,[12] a large number of Jews. The taste for letters and the sciences was a marked characteristic of the place; and no city in the world, not even excepting Athens and Alexandria, was so rich in scientific institutions and schools.[13] The number of learned men which Tarsus produced, or who pursued their studies there, was truly extraordinary;[14] but it should not therefore be imagined that Paul received a careful Greek education. The Jews rarely frequented the institutions of secular instruction.[15] The most celebrated schools of Tarsus were those of rhetoric,[16] where the Greek classics received the first attention. It is hardly probable that a man who had taken even elementary lessons in grammar and rhetoric would have written in the incorrect non-Hellenistic style of the Epistles of St. Paul. He talked habitually and fluently in Greek,[17] and he wrote or rather dictated[18] in that language; but his Greek was that of the Hellenistic Jews, a Greek replete with Hebraisms and Syriacisms, scarcely intelligible to a lettered man of that period, and which can only be accounted for by his Syriac turn of mind. He himself recognised the common and defective character of his style.[19] Whenever it was possible he spoke Hebrew—that is to say, the Syro-Chaldaic of his time.[20] It was in this language that he thought, and it was in this language that he was addressed by the mysterious voice on the road to Damascus.[21]

Nor did his doctrine show any direct adaptation made from Greek philosophy. The verse quoted from the Thais of Menander, that occurs in his writings,[22] is one of those versified proverbs which were familiar to the public, and could easily have been quoted by one who had not read the original. Two other quotations—one from Epimenides, the other from Aratus—which appear under his name,[23] although it is not certain that he used them, may also be explained as having been borrowed at second-hand.[24] The literary training of Paul was almost exclusively Jewish,[25] and it is in the Talmud rather than in the Greek classics that the analogies of his ideas must be sought. A few general ideas of wide-spread philosophy, which one could learn without opening a single book of the philosophers,[26] alone reached him. His manner of reasoning was very curious. He certainly knew nothing of the peripatetic logic. His syllogism was not at all that of Aristotle; but on the contrary his dialectics greatly resembled those of the Talmud. Paul, as a general thing, was influenced by words rather than by ideas. When a word took possession of his mind it suggested a train of thought singularly irrelevant to the subject in question. His transitions were sudden, his developments interrupted, his conclusions frequently suspended. Never was a writer more unequal. One may seek in vain throughout the realm of literature for a phenomenon as *bizarre* as that of a sublime passage like the thirteenth chapter of the First Epistle to the Corinthians by the side of feeble arguments, laborious repetitions, and fastidious subtleties.

His father early intended that he should be a Rabbi; but, according to the general custom,[27] gave him a trade. Paul was an upholsterer, [28] or rather a manufacturer of the heavy cloths of Cilicia, which were called *Cilicium* At various times he worked at this trade,[29] for he had no patrimonial fortune. It seems quite certain that he had a sister whose son lived at Jerusalem.[30] In regard to a brother[31] and other relatives,[32] who it is said had embraced Christianity, the indications are very vague and uncertain. Refinement of manners being, according to some modern ideas, in direct relation to personal wealth, it might be imagined from what has just been said, that Paul was a man of the people, badly educated and without dignity. This opinion would, however, be thoroughly erroneous. His politeness was often extreme, and his manners were exquisite. Notwithstanding the defects in his style, his letters show that he was a man of rare intelligence,[33] who formed for his lofty sentiments expressions of rare felicity; and no correspondence exhibits more careful attentions, finer shades of meaning, and more amiable hesitancies and timidity. One or two of his pleasantries shock us.[34] But what animation! What a wealth of charming sayings! What simplicity! It is easy to see that his character, at the times when his passions do not make him irascible and fierce, is that of a polite, earnest, and affectionate man, sometimes susceptible, and a little jealous. Inferior as such men are before the general public,[35] they possess within small sects immense advantages, through the attachments they inspire, through their practical aptitude, and through their skill in arranging difficult matters.

Paul was small in size, and his personal appearance did not correspond with the greatness of his soul. He was ugly, stout, short, and stooping, and his broad shoulders awkwardly sustained a little bald head. His sallow countenance was half hidden in a thick beard; his nose was aquiline, his eyes piercing, and his eyebrows heavy[36] and joined across his forehead. Nor was there anything imposing in his speech,[37] for his timid and embarrassed air gave but a poor idea of his eloquence.[38] He shrewdly, however, admitted his exterior defects, and even drew advantage therefrom.[39] The Jewish race possesses the peculiarity of at the same time presenting types of the greatest beauty, and the most thorough ugliness; but this Jewish ugliness is something quite apart by itself. Some of the strange visages which at first excite a smile, assume, when lighted up by emotion, a sort of deep brilliancy and grandeur.

The temperament of Paul was not less singular than his exterior. His constitution was not healthy, though at the same time its endurance was proved by the way in which he supported an existence full of fatigues and sufferings. He makes incessant allusions to his bodily weakness. He speaks of himself as a man sick and bruised, timid, without prestige, without any of those personal advantages calculated to make an effect, and altogether so uninviting that it was surprising that he did not repel people.[40] Besides this, he hints with mystery at a secret trial, "a thorn in the flesh," which he compares to a messenger of Satan sent to buffet him, "lest he should be exalted above measure."[41] Thrice he besought the Lord to deliver him, and thrice the Lord replied, "My grace is sufficient for thee." This was apparently some bodily infirmity; for it is not possible to suppose that he refers to the attractions of carnal delights, since he himself informs us elsewhere that he was insensible to them.[42] It appears that he was never married;[43] the entire coldness of his temperament, the consequence of the unequalled ardor of his brain, showed itself throughout his life, and he boasts of it with an assurance savoring, perhaps, of affectation, and which, certainly, seems to us rather unpleasant.[44]

He came to Jerusalem,[45] it is said, at an early age, and entered the school of Gamaliel the Elder.[46] This Gamaliel was the most enlightened man in Jerusalem. As the name of Pharisee was applied to every prominent Jew who was not of a priestly family, Gamaliel passed for a member of that sect. Yet he had none of its narrow and exclusive spirit, and was a liberal, intelligent man, tolerant of the heathen, and acquainted with Greek. Perhaps, indeed, the large ideas professed by Paul after he received Christianity, were a reminiscence of the teachings of his first master; it must, however, be admitted that at first he did not learn much moderation from him. An extreme fanaticism was then prevalent in Jerusalem. Paul was the leader of a young and rigorous Pharisee party, most warmly attached to the national traditions of the past.[47] He did not know Jesus,[48] nor was he present at the bloody scene of Golgotha; but we have seen him take an active part in the murder of Stephen, and among the foremost of the persecutors of the Church. He breathed only threatenings and slaughter, and furiously passed through Jerusalem bearing a mandate which authorized and legalized all his brutalities. He went from synagogue to synagogue, forcing the more timid to deny the name of Jesus, and subjecting others to scourging or imprisonment.[49] When the Church of Jerusalem was dispersed, his persecutions extended to the neighboring cities;[50] and exasperated by the progress of the new faith, and having learned that there was a group of the faithful at Damascus, he obtained from the high-priest Theophilus, son of Hanan,[51] letters to the synagogue of that city, which conferred on him the power of arresting all evil-thinking persons, and of bringing them bound in cords to Jerusalem.[52]

The disarrangement of Roman authority in Judea explains these arbitrary vexations. The half mad Caligula was in power, and the administrative service was everywhere disturbed. Fanaticism had gained all that the civil power had lost. After the dismissal of Pilate, and the concessions made to the natives by Lucius Vitellius, the country was allowed to govern itself according to its own laws. A thousand local tyrannies profited by the weakness of the decaying power. Damascus had just passed into the hands of Hartat, or Hâreth, whose capital was at Petra.[53] This bold and powerful prince, after having beaten Herod Antipas, and withstood the Roman forces commanded by the imperial legate Lucius Vitellius, had been marvellously aided by fortune. The news of the death of Tiberius had suddenly arrested the march of Vitellius.[54] Hâreth seized Damascus, and established there an ethnarch or governor.[55] The Jews at that time were a numerous party at Damascus, where they carried on an extensive system of proselytizing, especially among the females.[56] It was deemed advisable to make them contented; the best method of doing so was to allow concessions to their autonomy, and every concession was simply a permission to commit further religious violences.[57] To punish and even kill those who did not think as they did, was their idea of independence and liberty. Paul, in leaving Jerusalem, followed without doubt the usual road, and crossed the Jordan at the "Bridge of the Daughters of Jacob." His mental excitement was at its greatest height, and he was alternately troubled and depressed. Passion is not a rule of faith. The passionate man flies from one extreme creed to another, but always retains the same impetuosity. Now, like all strong minds, Paul quickly learned to love that which he had hated. Was he sure, after all, that he was not thwarting the design of God? Perhaps he remembered the calm, just views of his master Gamaliel.[58] Often these ardent souls experience terrible revulsions. He felt the charms of those whom he had tortured,[59] and the better he knew these excellent sectarians the better he liked them; and than their persecutor none had greater opportunities of knowing them well. At times he saw the sweet face of the Master who had inspired His disciples with so much patience, regarding him with an air of pity and tender reproach. He was also much impressed by the accounts of the apparitions of Jesus, describing him as an aerial being; for at the epochs and in the countries when and where there is a tendency to the marvellous, miraculous recitals influence equally each opposing party. The Mahommedans, for instance, were afraid of the miracles of Elias; and like the Christians, invoked supernatural cures in the names of St. George and St. Anthony. Having crossed Ithuria, and while in the great plain of Damascus, Paul, with several companions, all journeying on foot,[60] approached the city, and had probably already reached the beautiful gardens which surround it. The time was mid-day.[61]

The road from Jerusalem to Damascus has in nowise changed. It is that one which, leaving Damascus in a south-easterly direction, crosses the beautiful plain watered by the streams flowing into the Abana and Pharpar, and upon which are now marshalled the villages of Dareya, Kankab, and Sasa. The exact locality of which we speak, and which was the scene of one of the most important facts in the history of humanity, could not have been beyond Kankab (four hours from Damascus).[62] It is even probable that the point in question was much nearer the city, at about Dareya (an hour and a half from Damascus), or between Dareya and Meidan.[63] The great city lay before Paul, and the outlines of several of its edifices could be dimly traced beyond the thick foliage; behind him towered the majestic dome of Hermon, with its furrows of snow, making it resemble the bald head of an old man; upon his right were the Hauran, the two little parallel chains which inclose the lower course of the Pharpar,[64] and the tumuli of the region of the lakes; and upon his left were the outer spurs of the Anti-Libanus stretching out to join Mt. Hermon. The impression produced by these richly cultivated fields, by these beautiful orchards, separated the one from the other by trenches and laden with the most delicious fruits, is that of peace and happiness. Let one imagine to himself a shady road passing through the rich soil crossed at intervals by canals for irrigation, bordered by declivities and winding through forests of olives, walnuts, apricots, and prunes, these trees draped by graceful festoons of vines, and there will be presented to the mind the image of the scene of that remarkable event which has exerted so wide an influence upon the faith of the world.

In these environs of Damascus[65] you could scarcely believe yourself in the East; and above all, after leaving the arid and burning regions of the Gaulonitide and of Ithuria, it is joy indeed to meet once more the works of man and the blessings of Heaven. From the most remote antiquity until the present day there has been but one name for this zone, which surrounds Damascus with freshness and health, and that name is the "Paradise of God."

If Paul there met with terrible visions, it was because he carried them in his heart. Every step in his journey towards Damascus awaked in him afflicting perplexities. The odious part of executioner, which he was about to perform, became insupportable. The houses which he just saw through the trees, were perhaps those of his victims. This thought beset him and delayed his steps; he did not wish to advance; he seemed to be resisting a mysterious influence which pressed him back.[66] The fatigue of the journey,[67] joined to this preoccupation of the mind, overwhelmed him. He had, it would seem, inflamed eyes,[68] probably the beginning of ophthalmia. In these prolonged journeys, the last hours are the most dangerous. All the debilitating causes of the days just past accumulate, the nerves relax their power, and reaction sets in. Perhaps, also, the sudden passage from the sun-smitten plain to the cool shades of the gardens heightened his suffering condition[69] and seriously excited the fanatical traveller. Dangerous fevers, accompanied by delirium, are always sudden in these latitudes, and in a few minutes the victim is prostrated as by a thunder-stroke. When the crisis is over, the sufferer retains only the impression of a period of profound darkness, crossed at intervals by dashes of light or of images outlined against a dark background.[70] It is quite certain that a terrible stroke instantly deprived Paul of his remaining consciousness, and threw him senseless on the ground.

It is impossible, with the accounts which we have had of this singular event,[71] to say whether any exterior fact led to the crisis to which Christianity owes its most ardent apostle. In such cases, moreover, the exterior fact is of but little importance. It was the state of St. Paul's mind, it was his remorse on his approach to the city where he was to commit the most signal of his misdeeds, which were the true causes of his conversion.[72] I much prefer, for my part, the hypothesis of an affair personal to Paul, and experienced by him alone.[73] The incident, nevertheless, was not wholly unlike a sudden storm. The flanks of Mt. Hermon are the point of formation for thunder-showers unequalled in violence.[74] The most unimpressible people cannot observe without emotion these terrible showers of fire. It should be remembered that in ancient times accidents from lightning strokes were considered divine relations; that with the ideas regarding providential interference then prevalent, nothing was fortuitous; and that every man was accustomed to view the natural phenomena around him as bearing a direct relation to himself individually. The Jews in particular always considered that thunder was the voice of God, and that lightning was the fire of God. Paul at this moment was in a state of lively excitement, and it was but natural that he should interpret as the voice of the storm the thoughts really passing in his mind. That a delirious fever, resulting from a sun-stroke or an attack of ophthalmia, had suddenly seized him; that a flash of lightning blinded him for a time; that a peal of thunder had produced a cerebral commotion, temporarily depriving him of sight—nothing of this occurred to his mind. The recollections of the apostle on this point appeared to be considerably confused; he was persuaded that the incident was supernatural, and this conviction would not permit him to entertain any clear consciousness of material circumstances. Such cerebral commotions produce sometimes a sort of retroactive effect, and greatly perturb the recollections of the moments immediately preceding the crisis.[75] Paul, moreover, elsewhere informs us himself that he was subject to visions;[76] and this circumstance, insignificant as it may be to others, is sufficient to show that for the time being he was demented.

And what did he see, what did he hear, while a prey to these hallucinations? He saw the countenance which had haunted him for several days; he saw the phantom of which so much had been said. He saw Jesus Himself, who spoke to him in Hebrew, saying, "Saul, Saul, why persecutest thou me?" Impetuous natures pass immediately from one extreme to the other.[77] For them there exist solemn moments and crucial instants which change the course of a lifetime, and which colder natures never experience. Reflective men do not change, but are transformed; while ardent men, on the contrary, change and are not transformed. Dogmatism is a shirt of Nessus which they cannot tear off. They must have a pretext for loving and hating. Only our western races have been able to produce those minds—large yet delicate, strong yet flexible—which no empty affirmation can mislead, and no momentary illusion can carry away. The East has never had men of this description. Instantly, the most thrilling thoughts rushed upon the soul of Paul. Alive to the enormity of his conduct, he saw himself stained with the blood of Stephen, and this martyr appeared to him as his father, his initiator into the new faith. Touched to the quick, his sentiments experienced a revulsion as thorough as it was sudden; and yet all this was but a new order of fanaticism. His sincerity and his need of an absolute faith prevented any middle course; and it was already clear that he would one day exhibit in the cause of Jesus the same fiery zeal he had shown in persecuting Him.

With the assistance of his companions, who led him by the hand,[78] Paul entered Damascus. His friends took him to the house of a certain Judas, who lived in the street called Straight, a grand colonnaded avenue over a mile long and a hundred feet broad, which crossed the city from east to west, and the line of which yet forms, with a few deviations, the principal artery of Damascus.[79] The transport and excitement of his brain[80] had not yet subsided. For three days Paul, a prey to fever, neither ate nor drank. It is easy to imagine what passed during this crisis in that brain maddened by violent disease. Mention was made in his hearing of the Christians of Damascus, but especially of a certain Ananias who appeared to be the chief of the community.[81] Paul had often heard of the miraculous powers of new believers over maladies, and he became seized by the idea that the imposition of hands would cure him of his disease. His eyes all this time were highly inflamed, and in his delirious imaginations[82] he thought he saw Ananias enter the room and make a sign familiar to Christians. From that moment he was convinced that he should owe his recovery to Ananias. The latter, informed of this, visited the sick man, spoke kindly, addressed him as his "brother," and laid his hands upon his head; and from that hour peace returned to the soul of Paul. He believed himself cured; and as his ailment had been purely nervous, he was so. Little crusts or scales, it is said, fell from his eyes;[83] he again partook of food and recovered his strength.

Almost immediately after this he was baptized.[84] The doctrines of the Church were so simple that he had nothing new to learn, but was at once a Christian and a perfect one. And from whom else did he need instruction? Jesus Himself had appeared to him. He too, like James and Peter, had had his vision of the risen Jesus. He had learned everything by direct revelation. Here the fierce and unconquerable nature of Paul was made manifest. Smitten down on the public road, he was willing to submit, but only to Jesus, to that Jesus who had left the right hand of the Father to convert and instruct him. Such was the foundation of his faith; and such will be the starting-point of his claims. He will maintain that it was by design that he did not go to Jerusalem immediately after his conversion, and place himself in relations with those who had been apostles before him; he will maintain that he has received a special revelation, for which he is indebted to no human agency; that, like the twelve, he is an apostle by divine institution and by direct commission from Jesus; that his doctrine is the true one, although an angel from heaven should say to the contrary.[85] An immense danger finds entrance through this proud man into the little society of poor in spirit who until now had constituted Christianity. It will be a real miracle if his violence and his inflexible personality does not burst forth. But at the same time his boldness, his initiative force, his prompt decision, will be precious elements beside the narrow, timid, and indecisive spirit of the saints of Jerusalem! Certainly, if Christianity had remained confined to these good people, shut up in a conventicle of elect, leading a communistic life, it would, like Essenism, have faded away, leaving scarcely a trace. It is this ungovernable Paul who will secure its success, and who at the risk of every peril will lift on high its holy banner. By the side of the obedient faithful, accepting his creed without questioning his superior, there will be a Christian disengaged from all authority who will believe only from personal conviction. Protestantism thus existed five years after the death of Jesus, and St. Paul was its illustrious founder. Jesus had no doubt anticipated such disciples; and it was such as these who would most largely contribute to the vitality of His work and insure its eternity. Violent natures inclined to proselytism, only change the object of their passion. As ardent for the new faith as he had been for the old, St. Paul, like Omar, in one day dropped his part of persecutor for that of apostle. He did not return to Jerusalem,[86] where his position towards the twelve would have been peculiar and delicate. He tarried at Damascus and in the Hauran[87] for three years (38–41), preaching that Jesus was the Son of God.[88] Herod Agrippa I. held the sovereignty of the Hauran and the neighboring countries; but his power was at several points superseded by that of a Nabatian king, Hârath. The decay of the Roman power in Syria had delivered to the ambitious Arab the great and rich city of Damascus, besides a part of the countries beyond Jordan and Hermon, then just opening to civilization.[89] Another emir, most probably Soheym,[90] a relative or lieutenant of Hârath, had received from Caligula the command of Ithuria. It was in the midst of this great awakening of the Arab nation,[91] upon a foreign soil where an energetic race manifested its fiery activity, that Paul first showed the brilliancy of his apostolic soul.[92] Perhaps the material yet dazzling movement which revolutionized the country was prejudicial to a theory and preaching wholly idealistic, and founded on a belief of a speedy end of the world. Indeed, there exists no trace of an Arabian church founded by St. Paul. If the region of the Hauran became, towards the year 70, one of the most important centres of Christianity, it was owing to the emigration of Christians from Palestine; and it was really the Ebionites, the enemies of St. Paul, who had in this region their principal establishment.

At Damascus, where there were many Jews,[93] the teachings of Paul received more attention. In the synagogues of that city he entered into vigorous arguments to prove that Jesus was the Christ. Great indeed was the astonishment of the faithful on beholding him who had persecuted their brethren at Jerusalem, and who had come to Damascus "to bring themselves bound unto the chief-priests," now appearing as their leading defender.[94] His audacity and personal characteristics almost alarmed them. He was alone; he sought no counsel;[95] he established no school; and the emotions he excited were those of curiosity rather than of sympathy. The faithful felt that he was a brother, but a brother marked by singular peculiarities. They believed him incapable of treachery; but amiable and mediocre natures always experience sentiments of mistrust and alarm when brought in contact with powerful and original minds, whom they acknowledge as their superiors, and who they know must surpass them.

CHAPTER XI.

PEACE AND INTERIOR DEVELOPMENTS OF THE CHURCH OF JUDEA.

From the year 38 to the year 44 no persecution seems to have weighed upon the Church.[1] The faithful, no doubt, were far more prudent than before the death of Stephen, and avoided speaking in public. Perhaps, also, the troubles of the Jews who, during all the second part of the reign of Caligula, were at variance with that prince, contributed to favor the nascent sect. The Jews, in fact, were active persecutors in proportion to the good understanding they maintained with the Romans. To buy or to recompense their tranquillity, the latter were led to augment their privileges, and in particular that one to which they clung most closely—the right of killing persons whom they regarded as unfaithful to their law.[2] Now the period at which we have arrived was one of the most stormy of all in the turbulent history of this singular people.

The antipathy which the Jews, by their moral superiority, their odd customs, and also by their severity, excited in the populations among whom they lived, was at its height, especially at Alexandria.[3] This accumulated hatred took advantage, for its own satisfaction, of the coming to the imperial throne of one of the most dangerous madmen that ever wore a crown.

Caligula, at least after the malady which consummated his mental derangement (October 37), presented the frightful spectacle of a maniac governing the world with the most enormous powers ever put into the hands of any man. The disastrous law of Cæsarism rendered such horrors possible, and left them without remedy. This lasted three years and three months. One cannot without shame narrate in a serious history that which is now to follow. Before entering upon the recital of these saturnalia we cannot but exclaim with Suetonius: *Reliqua ut de monstro narranda sunt.*

The most inoffensive pastime of this madman was the care of his own divinity.[4] In this he used a sort of bitter irony, a mixture of the serious and the comic (for the monster was not wanting in wit), a sort of profound derision of the human race. The enemies of the Jews were not slow to perceive the advantage they might derive from this mania. The religious abasement of the world was such that not a protest was heard against the sacrilege of the Cæsar; every worship hastened to bestow upon him the titles and the honors which it had reserved for its gods. It is to the eternal glory of the Jews that, in the midst of this ignoble idolatry, they uttered the cry of outraged conscience. The principle of intolerance which was in them, and which led them to so many cruel acts, showed here its bright side. Alone affirming their religion to be the absolute religion, they would not bend to the odious caprice of the tyrant. This was the source of untold troubles for them. It needed only that there should be in any city some man discontented with the synagogue, spiteful, or simply mischievous, to bring about frightful consequences. At one time the people would insist on erecting an altar to Caligula in the very place where the Jews could least of all suffer it.[5] At another, a troupe of ragamuffins would collect, hooting and crying out against the Jews for alone refusing to place the statue of the emperor in their houses of prayer; then the people would run to the synagogues and the oratories; they would install there the bust of Caligula;[6] and the unfortunate Jews were placed in the alternative of either renouncing their religion, or committing treason. Thence followed frightful vexations.

Such pleasantries had been several times repeated, when a still more diabolical idea was suggested to the emperor. This was to place a colossal golden statue of himself in the sanctuary of the temple at Jerusalem, and to have the temple itself dedicated to his own divinity.[7] This odious intrigue had very nearly hastened by thirty years the revolt and the ruin of the Jewish nation. The moderation of the imperial legate, Publius Petronius, and the intervention of King Herod Agrippa, favorite of Caligula, prevented the catastrophe. But until the moment in which the sword of Chæræa delivered the earth from the most execrable tyrant it had as yet endured, the Jews lived everywhere in terror. Philo has preserved for us the unheard-of scene which occurred when the deputation of which he was the chief was admitted to see the emperor.[8] Caligula received them during a visit he was paying to the villas of Mæcenas and of Lamia, near the sea, in the environs of Pozzuoli. He was on that day in a vein of gaiety. Helicon, his favorite joker, had been relating to him all sorts of buffooneries about the Jews. "Ah, then, it is you," said he to them with a bitter smile and showing his teeth, "who alone will not recognise me for a god, and prefer to adore one whose name you cannot even utter!" He accompanied these words with a frightful blasphemy. The Jews trembled; their Alexandrian enemies were the first to take up the word: "You would still more, O Sire, detest these people and all their nation, if you knew the aversion they have for you; for they alone have refused to offer sacrifices for your health when all other people did so!"

At these words, the Jews cried out that it was a calumny, and that they had three times offered for the prosperity of the emperor the most solemn sacrifices known to their religion. "Yes," said Caligula, with a very comical seriousness, "you have sacrificed, and so far, well; but then it was not to me that you sacrificed. What advantage do I derive from it?" Thereupon, turning his back upon them, he strode through the apartments, giving orders for repairs, incessantly going up and down stairs. The unfortunate deputies, and among them Philo, eighty years of age, the most venerable man of the time, perhaps—Jesus being no longer living—followed him up and down out of breath, trembling, the object of derision to the assembled company. Caligula turning suddenly, said to them: "By the by, why will you not eat pork?" The flatterers burst into laughter; some of the officers, with a severe tone, reminded them that they offended the majesty of the emperor by immoderate laughter. The Jews stammered; one of them awkwardly said: "There are some persons who do not eat lamb." "Ah!" said the emperor, "they have good reason; lamb is insipid." Some time after, he made a show of inquiring into their business; then, when speaking had just begun, he left them and went off to give orders about the decoration of a hall which he wanted to have furnished with polished stones. He returned, affecting an air of moderation, and asked the deputation if they had anything to add; and as the latter resumed their interrupted discourse, he turned his back upon them to go and see another hall which he was ornamenting with paintings. This game of tiger sporting with its prey lasted for hours. The Jews were expecting death; but at the last moment the claws of the beast relaxed. "Well," said Caligula, while repassing, "these folks are decidedly less guilty than pitiable for not believing in my divinity." Thus could the gravest questions be treated under the horrible regimen created by the baseness of the world, cherished by a soldiery and a populace about equally vile, and maintained by the dissoluteness of nearly all.

We can easily understand how so oppressive a situation must have taken from the Jews of the time of Marcellus much of that audacity which made them speak so proudly to Pilate. Already almost entirely detached from the temple, the Christians must have been much less alarmed than the Jews at the sacrilegious projects of Caligula. They were, moreover, too little numerous for their existence to be known at Rome. The storm of the time of Caligula, like that which resulted in the taking of Jerusalem by Titus, passed over their heads, and was in many regards serviceable to them. Everything which weakened Jewish independence was favorable to them, since it was so much taken away from the power of a suspicious orthodoxy, maintaining its pretensions by severe penalties.

This period of peace was fruitful in interior developments. The nascent Church was divided into three provinces: Judea, Samaria, Galilee[9], to which Damascus was no doubt attached. The primacy of Jerusalem was uncontested. The Church of this city, which had been dispersed after the death of Stephen, was quickly reconstituted. The Apostles had never quitted the city. The brothers of the Lord continued to reside there, and to wield a great authority.[10] It does not seem that this new Church of Jerusalem was organized in so rigorous a manner as the first; the community of goods was not strictly reëstablished in it. But there was founded a large fund for the poor, to which were added the contributions sent by minor churches to the mother church, the origin and permanent source of their faith.[11]

Peter undertook frequent apostolical journeys in the environs of Jerusalem.[12] He always enjoyed a great reputation as a thaumaturgist. At Lydda[13] in particular he passed for having cured a paralytic named Æneas, a miracle which is said to have led to numerous conversions in the plain of Saron.[14] From Lydda he repaired to Joppa,[15] a city which appears to have been a centre for Christianity. Cities of workmen, of sailors, of poor people, where the orthodox Jews were not dominant, were those in which the new sect found the best dispositions. Peter made a long sojourn at Joppa, at the house of a tanner named Simon who dwelt near the sea.[16] Working in leather was an industry almost unclean, according to the Mosaic code; it was not lawful to visit too frequently those who carried it on, so that the curriers had to live in a district by themselves.[17]

Peter, in choosing such a host, gave a proof of his indifference to Jewish prejudices, and worked for that ennoblement of petty callings which constitutes a noble feature of the Christian spirit.

The organization of works of charity was soon actively pursued. The church of Joppa possessed a woman admirably named in Aramaic, *Tabitha* (gazelle), and in Greek, *Dorcas*,[18] who consecrated all her cares to the poor.[19] She was rich, it seems, and distributed her wealth in alms. This worthy lady had formed a society of pious widows, who spent their days with her in weaving clothes for the poor.[20] As the schism between Christianity and Judaism was not yet consummated, it is probable that the Jews shared in the benefit of these acts of charity. The "saints and widows"[21] were thus pious persons, doing good to all, a sort of friars and nuns, whom only the most austere devotees of a pedantic orthodoxy could suspect, *fraticelli*, loved by the people, devout, charitable, full of pity.

The germ of those associations of women, which are one of the glories of Christianity, thus existed in the first churches of Judea. At Jaffa commenced that series of the veiled women, clothed in linen, who were destined to continue through centuries the tradition of charitable acts. Tabitha was the mother of a family which will have no end as long as there are miseries to be solaced and good feminine instincts to assuage them. It is related further on, that Peter raised her from the dead. Alas! death, utterly senseless, utterly revolting as it is in such a case, is inflexible. When the most exquisite soul has evaporated, the decree is irrevocable; the most excellent woman can no more respond to the invitation of the friendly voices which would fain recall her than can the vulgar and frivolous. But ideas are not subject to the conditions of matter. Virtue and goodness escape the fangs of death. Tabitha had no need to be resuscitated. For the sake of three or four days more of this sad life, why disturb her sweet and eternal repose? Let her sleep in peace; the day of the just will come!

In these very mixed cities, the problem of the admission of pagans to baptism was propounded with much urgency. Peter was strongly preöccupied with it. One day while he was praying at Joppa, on the terrace of the tanner's house, having before him this sea that was soon going to bear the new faith to all the empire, he had a prophetic ecstasy. Plunged into a state of dreamy reverie, he thought he experienced a sensation of hunger, and asked for something to eat. Now while they were making it ready for him, he saw the heavens opened, and a cloth tied at the four corners come down thence. Looking inside the cloth he saw there all sorts of animals, and thought he heard a voice saying to him: "Kill and eat." And on his objecting that many of these animals were impure, he was answered: "Call not that unclean which God has cleansed." This, as it appears, was repeated three times. Peter was persuaded that these animals represented the mass of the Gentiles, which God Himself had just rendered fit for the holy communion of the kingdom of God.[22]

An occasion was soon presented for applying these principles. From Joppa, Peter repaired to Cesarea. There he came into relations with a centurion named Cornelius.[23] The garrison of Cesarea was formed, at least in part, of one of those cohorts composed of Italian volunteers which were called *Italicæ*.[24] The complete name for which this stood may have been *cohors prima Augustus Italica civium Romanorum*.[25] Cornelius was a centurion of this cohort, consequently an Italian and a Roman citizen. He was a man of probity, who had long felt drawn towards the aconotheistic worship of the Jews. He prayed, gave alms; practised, in a word, those precepts of natural religion which are taken for granted by Judaism; but he was not circumcised; he was not a proselyte in any degree whatever; he was a pious pagan, an Israelite in heart, nothing more.[26] All his household and some soldiers of his command were, it is said, in the same state of mind.[27] Cornelius applied for admission into the new Church. Peter, whose nature was open and benevolent, granted it to him, and the centurion was baptized.[28]

Perhaps Peter saw at first no difficulty[29] in this; but on his return to Jerusalem he was severely reproached for it. He had openly violated the law, he had gone in among the uncircumcised and had eaten with them. The question was an important one; it was no other than whether the law were abolished, whether it was permissible to violate it in proselytism, whether Gentiles could be received on an equal footing into the Church. Peter, to defend himself, related the vision he had at Joppa. Subsequently the fact of the centurion served as an argument in the great question of the baptism of the uncircumcised. To give it more force it was supposed that each phase of this important business had been marked by a revelation from Heaven. It was related that after long prayers Cornelius had seen an angel who ordered him to go and inquire for Peter at Joppa; that the symbolical vision of Peter took place at the very hour of the arrival of the messengers from Cornelius; that, moreover, God had taken it upon Himself to legitimize all that had been done, seeing that the Holy Ghost had descended upon Cornelius and upon his household, the latter having spoken strange tongues and sung psalms after the fashion of the other believers. Was it natural to refuse baptism to persons who had received the Holy Ghost?

The Church of Jerusalem was still exclusively composed of Jews and of proselytes. The Holy Ghost being shed upon the uncircumcised before baptism, appeared an extraordinary fact. It is probable that there existed thenceforth a party opposed in principle to the admission of Gentiles, and that every one did not accept the explanations of Peter. The author of the *Acts*[30] would have it that the approbation was unanimous. But in a few years we shall see the question revived with much greater intensity.[31] The fact of the good centurion was, perhaps, like that of the Ethiopian eunuch, accepted as an exceptional one, justified by a revelation and an express order from God The matter was far from being settled. This was the first controversy in the bosom of the Church; the paradise of interior peace had lasted six or seven years.

About the year 40, the great question on which hung all the future of Christianity appears thus to have been propounded. Peter and Philip took a very just view of the true solution, and baptized pagans. It is difficult, no doubt, in the two accounts given us by the author of the *Acts* on this subject, and which are partly sketched one from the other, not to recognise a system. The author of the *Acts* belongs to a party of conciliation, favorable to the introduction of pagans into the Church, and who is not willing to confess the violence of the divisions to which the affair gave rise. One feels strongly that in writing the episodes of the eunuch, of the centurion, and even of the conversion of the Samaritans, this author means not only to narrate facts, but seeks especially precedents for an opinion. On the other hand, we cannot admit that he invents the facts which he narrates. The conversions of the eunuch of Candace, and of the centurion Cornelius, are probably real facts, presented and transformed according to the needs of the thesis in view of which the book of the Acts was composed.

Paul, who was destined, some ten or eleven years later, to give to this discussion so decisive a bearing, had not yet meddled with it. He was in the Hauran, or at Damascus, preaching, refuting the Jews, placing at the service of the new faith as much ardor as he had shown in fighting against it. The fanaticism, of which he had been the instrument, was not long in pursuing him in his turn. The Jews resolved to destroy him. They obtained from the ethnarch, who governed Damascus in the name of Hârath, an order to arrest him. Paul hid himself. It was known that he had to leave the city; the ethnarch, who wanted to please the Jews, placed detachments at the gates to seize his person; but the brethren enabled him to escape by night, letting him down in a basket from the window of a house which overhung the ramparts.[33]

Having escaped this danger, Paul turned his eyes towards Jerusalem. He had been a Christian for three years,[33] and had not yet seen the apostles. His rigid, unyielding character, prone to isolation, had made him at first turn his back as it were upon the great family into which he had just entered in spite of himself, and prefer for his first apostolate a new country, in which he would find no colleague. There was awakened in him, however, a desire to see Peter.[34] He recognised his authority, and designated him, as every one did, by the name of *Cephas*, "the stone." He repaired then to Jerusalem, taking the same road, but in an opposite direction to that he had traversed three years before in a state of mind so different.

His position at Jerusalem was extremely false and embarrassing. It had been understood there, no doubt, that the persecutor had become the most zealous of evangelists, and the first defender of the faith which he had formerly sought to destroy.[35] But there remained great prejudices against him. Many feared some horrible plot on his part. They had seen him so enraged, so cruel, so zealous in entering houses and rending open family secrets in order to find victims, that he was believed capable of playing an odious farce in order to destroy those whom he hated.[36] He stayed, as it seems, in the house of Peter.[37] Many disciples remained deaf to his advances, and shrank from him.[38] A man of courage and will, Barnabas, played at this moment a decisive part. As a Cyprian and a new convert, he understood better than the Galilean disciples the position of Paul. He came to meet him, took him in a manner by the hand, introduced him to the most suspicious, and became his surety.[39] By this act of wisdom and penetration, Barnabas won at the hands of the Christian world the highest degree of merit. It was he who appreciated Paul; it was to him that the Church owes the most extraordinary of her founders. The fruitful friendship of these two apostolic men, a friendship that no cloud ever tarnished, notwithstanding many differences in opinion, afterwards led to their association in the work of missions to the Gentiles. This grand association dates, in one sense, from Paul's first sojourn at Jerusalem. Among the causes of the faith of the world we must count the generous movement of Barnabas, stretching out his hand to the suspected and forsaken Paul; the profound intuition which led him to discover the soul of an apostle under that humiliated air; the frankness with which he broke the ice and levelled the obstacles raised between the convert and his new brethren by the unfortunate antecedents of the former, and perhaps, also, by certain traits of his character.

Paul, meantime, systematically as it were, avoided seeing the apostles. It is he himself says so, and he takes the trouble to affirm it with an oath; he saw only Peter, and James the brother of the Lord.[40] His sojourn lasted only two weeks.[41] Assuredly it is possible that at the epoch in which he wrote the Epistle to the Galatians (towards 56), Paul may have found himself led, by the needs of the moment, to give some little coloring to his relations with the apostles; to represent them as more harsh, more imperious, than they were in reality. Towards 56 the essential point for him to prove was that he had received nothing from Jerusalem—that he was in no wise the mandatory of the Council of

Twelve established in this city. His attitude at Jerusalem would have been the proud and lofty bearing of a master who avoids relations with other masters in order not to have the air of subordinating himself to them, and not the humble and repentant mien of a sinner ashamed of the past, as the author of the *Acts* represents. We cannot believe that from the year 44 Paul was animated by this jealous care to preserve his own originality, which he showed at a later day. The rarity of his interviews with the apostles, and the brevity of his sojourn at Jerusalem, arose probably from his embarrassment in the presence of people of quite another nature than his own, and full of prejudices against him, rather than from a refined polity, which would have revealed to him fifteen years in advance the disadvantages there might be in his frequenting their society.

In reality, that which must have erected a sort of wall between the apostles and Paul, was chiefly the difference of their character and of their education. The apostles were all Galileans; they had not been at the great Jewish schools; they had seen Jesus; they remembered his words; they were good and pious folk, at times a little solemn and simple-hearted. Paul was a man of action, full of fire, only moderately mystical, enrolled, as by a superior force, in a sect which was not that of his first adoption. Revolt, protestation, were his habitual sentiments.[42] His Jewish education was much superior to that of all his new brethren. But not having heard Jesus, not having been appointed by him, he had, according to Christian ideas, a great inferiority. Now Paul was not made to accept any secondary place. His haughty individuality demanded a position for himself. It is probably towards this time that there sprang up in his mind the proud idea that after all he had nothing to envy those who had known Jesus and had been chosen by him, since he also had seen Jesus and had received from Jesus a direct revelation and the commission of his apostleship. Even those who had been honored by the personal appearance to them of the risen Christ, had no more than he had. Although the last, his vision had been no less remarkable. It had taken place under circumstances which gave it a peculiar mark of importance and of distinction.[43] Signal error! The echo of the voice of Jesus was found in the discourses of the humblest of His disciples. With all his Jewish science, Paul could not make up for the immense disadvantage under which he was placed by his tardy initiation. The Christ whom he had seen on the road to Damascus was not, whatever he might say, the Christ of Galilee; it was the Christ of his imagination, of his own senses. Although he may have been most attentive to gather the words of the Master,[44] it is clear that he was only a disciple at second-hand. If Paul had met Jesus during his life, it may be doubtful whether he would have attached himself to Him. His doctrine will be his own, not that of Jesus; the revelations of which he is so proud are the fruit of his own brain.

These ideas, which he dared not as yet communicate, rendered his stay at Jerusalem very disagreeable. At the end of a fortnight he took leave of Peter and went away. He had seen so few people that he ventured to say that no one in the churches of Judea knew him by sight, or knew aught of him, save by hearsay.[45] At a subsequent period he attributed this sudden departure to a revelation. He related that being one day in the temple praying, he was in an extasy, and saw Jesus in person, and received from Him the order to quit Jerusalem immediately, "because they were not inclined to receive his testimony." In exchange for these hard hearts, Jesus had promised him the apostolate of distant nations, and an auditory more docile to his voice.[46] Those who would fain hide the traces of the many ruptures caused by the coming of this insubordinate disciple into the Church, pretended that Paul passed quite a long time at Jerusalem, living with the brethren on a footing of the most complete liberty; but that, having undertaken to preach to the Hellenist Jews, he was very nearly killed by them, so that the brethren had to watch over him and protect him, and finally took him to Cesarea.[47]

It is probable, in fact, that from Jerusalem he did repair to Cesarea. But he stayed there only a short time, and then set out to traverse Syria, and afterwards Cilicia.[48] He was, no doubt, already preaching, but on his own account, and without any understanding with anybody. Tarsus, his native place, was his habitual sojourn during this period of his apostolical life, which we may reckon as having lasted about two years.[49] It is possible that the churches of Cilicia owed their origin to him.[50] Still, the life of Paul was not at this epoch that which we see it to have been subsequently. He did not assume the title of an apostle, which was then strictly reserved to the Twelve.[51] It was only from the time of his association with Barnabas (year 45) that he entered upon that career of sacred peregrinations and preachings which made of him the type of the travelling missionary.

CHAPTER XII.

ESTABLISHMENT OF THE CHURCH OF ANTIOCH

THE new faith was propagated from one neighborhood to another with astonishing rapidity. The members of the Church of Jerusalem who had been dispersed immediately after the death of Stephen, pushing their conquests along the coast of Phœnicia, reached Cyprus and Antioch. They were as yet guided by an unvarying principle of refusing to preach the gospel to the Jews.[1] Antioch, "the metropolis of the East," the third city of the world,[2] was the centre of this Christendom of northern Syria. It was a city with a population of more than 500,000 souls, almost as large as Paris before its recent extensions,[3] and the residence of the Imperial Legate of Syria. Suddenly advanced to a high degree of splendor by the Seleucidæ, it had only to profit by the Roman occupation of it. In general, the Seleucidæ had surpassed the Romans in the taste for theatrical decorations as applied to great cities. Temples, aqueducts, baths, basilicas, nothing was wanting at Antioch in what constituted a grand Syrian city of that period. The streets flanked by colonnades, with their cross-roads decorated with statues, had there more of symmetry and regularity than anywhere else.[4] A *Corso*, ornamented with four ranges of columns, forming two covered galleries with a wide avenue in the midst, crossed the city from one side to the other,[5] the length of which was thirty-six stadia (more than a league).[6] But Antioch not only possessed immense edifices of public utility,[7] she had that also which few of the Syrian cities possessed—the noblest specimens of Grecian art, wonderfully beautiful statues,[8] classical works of a delicacy of detail which the age was no longer capable of imitating. Antioch, from its foundation, had been altogether a Grecian city. The Macedonians of Antigone and Seleucus had imported into that country of the lower Orontes their most lively recollections, their worship, and the names of their country.[9] The Grecian mythology was there adopted as it were in a second home; they pretended to exhibit in the country a crowd of "holy places" forming part of this mythology. The city was full of the worship of Apollo and of the nymphs. Daphne, an enchanting place two short hours distant from the city, reminded the conquerors of the pleasantest fictions. It was a sort of plagiarism, a counterfeit of the myths of the mother country, analogous to these adventurous transportations which the primitive tribes carried with them in their travels; their mythical geography, their Berecyntha, their Arnanda, their Ida, and their Olympus. These Greek fables constituted for them a very old religion, and one scarcely more serious than the metamorphoses of Ovid. The ancient religions of the country, particularly that of Mount Cassius,[10] contributed some little gravity to it. But Syrian levity, Babylonian charlatanism, and all the impostures of Asia, mingled at this limit of the two worlds, had made Antioch the capital of lies and the sink of every description of infamy.

Besides the Greek population, indeed, which in no part of the East (with the exception of Alexandria) was as numerous as here, Antioch numbered amongst its population a considerable number of native Syrians, speaking Syriac.[11] These natives composed a low class, inhabiting the suburbs of the great city and the populous villages which formed a vast suburb[12] all around it, Charandama, Ghisira, Gaudigura, and Apate (chiefly Syrian names).[13] Marriages between the Syrians and the Greeks were common. Seleucus having formerly made naturalization a legal obligation binding on every stranger establishing himself in the city, Antioch, at the end of three centuries and a half of its existence, became one of the places in the world where race was most intermingled with race. The degradation of the people there was terrible. The peculiarity of these focuses of moral putrefaction is, to reduce all the races of mankind to the same level. The degradation of certain Levantine cities, dominated by the spirit of intrigue, delivered up entirely to low cunning, can scarce give us a conception of the degree of corruption reached by the human race at Antioch. It was an inconceivable medley of merry-andrews, quacks, buffoons,[14] magicians, miracle-mongers, sorcerers, priests, impostors; a city of races, games, dances, processions, fêtes, debauches, of unbridled luxury, of all the follies of the East, of the most unhealthy superstitions, and of the fanaticism of the orgy.[16] By turns servile and ungrateful, cowardly and insolent, the people of Antioch were the perfect model of those crowds devoted to Cæsarism, without country, without nationality, without family honor, without a name to keep. The great *Corso* which traversed the city was like a theatre, where rolled, day after day, the waves of a trifling, light-headed, changeable, insurrection-loving[17] populace—a populace sometimes *spirituel*,[18] occupied with songs, parodies, squibs, impertinence of all sorts.[19] The city was very literary,[20] but literary only in the literature of rhetoricians. The sights were strange; there were some games in which bands of naked young girls took part in all the exercises, with a mere fillet around them;[22] at the celebrated festival of Näiouma, troupes of courtezans swarmed in public in basins[23] filled with limpid water.[24] This fête was like an intoxication, like a dream of Sardanapalus, where all the pleasures, all the debaucheries, not excluding some of a more delicate kind, were unrolled pell-mell. This river of dirt, which, making its exit by the mouth of the Orontes, was about to invade Rome,[25] had here its principal sources. Two hundred decurions were employed in regulating the religious ceremonies and celebrations.[26] The municipality possessed great public domains, the rents of which the decemvirs divided between the poor citizens.[27] Like all cities of pleasure, Antioch had a lowest section of the people, living on the public or on sordid gains. The beauty of works of art and the infinite charm of nature[28] prevented this moral degradation from degenerating entirely into ugliness and vulgarity. The site of Antioch is one of the most picturesque in the world. The city occupied the interval between the Orontes and the slopes of Mount Silpius, one of the spurs of Mount Casius. Nothing could equal the abundance and beauty of the waters.[29] The fortified space, climbing up perpendicular rocks, by a real master-work of military architecture,[30] inclosed the summit of the mountains, and formed with the rocks at a tremendous height an indented crown of marvellous effect. This disposition of their ramparts, uniting the advantage of the ancient acropoles with those of the great walled cities, was in general preferred by the Generals of Alexander, as one sees in the Pierian Seleucia, in Ephesus, in Smyrna, in Thessalonica. The result was various astonishing perspectives. Antioch had within its walls mountains seven hundred feet in height, perpendicular rocks, torrents, precipices, deep ravines, cascades, inaccessible caves; in the midst of all these, delicious gardens.[31] A thick wood of myrtles, of flowering box, of laurels, of plants always green—and of the most tender green—rocks carpeted with pinks, with hyacinth, and cyclamens, give to these wild heights the aspect of gardens hung in the air. The variety of the flowers, the freshness of the turf, composed of an incredible number of minute grasses, the beauty of the plane trees which border the Orontes, inspire the gaiety, the tinge of sweet scent with which the beautiful genius of Chrysostom, Libanus, and Julian is, as it were, intoxicated. On the right bank of the river stretches a vast plain bordered on one side by the Amanus, and the oddly truncated mountains of Pieria; on the other side by the plateaus of Chyrrestica,[32] behind which is hiddden the dangerous neighborhood of the Arab and the desert. The valley of the Orontes, which opens to the west, brings this interior basin into communication with the sea, or rather with the vast world in the bosom of which the Mediterranean has constituted from all time a sort of neutral highway and federal bond.

Amongst the different colonies which the liberal ordinances of the Seleucidæ had attracted to the capital of Syria, that of the Jews was one of the most numerous;[33] it dated from the time of Seleucus Nicator, and was governed by the same laws as the Greeks.[34] Although the Jews had an ethnarch of their own, their relations with the pagans were very frequent. Here, as at Alexandria, these relations often degenerated into quarrels and aggressions.[35] On the other hand, they afforded a field for an active religious propagandism. The polytheism of the officials becoming more and more insufficient to meet the wants of serious persons, the Grecian and Jewish philosophies attracted all those whom the vain pomps of paganism could not satisfy. The number of proselytes was considerable. From the first days of Christianity, Antioch had furnished to the Church of Jerusalem one of its most influential members, viz. Nicolas, one of the deacons.[36] There existed there promising germs, which only waited for a ray of grace to burst forth into bloom and bear the most excellent fruits which had hitherto been produced.

The church of Antioch owed its foundation to some original believers from Cyprus and Cyrene, who had already been zealous in preaching.[37] Up to this time they had only addressed themselves to the Jews. But in a city where pure Jews—Jews who were proselytes, "people fearing God"—or half-Jews, half-pagans and pure pagans, lived together,[39] confined preachings, restricted to a group of houses, became impossible. That feeling of religious aristocracy on which the Jews of Jerusalem so much prided themselves, had no existence in these large cities, where civilization was altogether of the profane sort, where the atmosphere was more expanded, and where prejudices were less firmly rooted. The Cypriot and Cyrenian missionaries were then constrained to depart from their rule. They preached to the Jews and to the Greeks indifferently.

The reciprocal dispositions of the Jewish and of the pagan population appeared at this time to have been very unsatisfactory.[40] But circumstances of another kind probably subserved the new ideas. The earthquake, which had done serious damage to the city on 23d March, of the year 37, still occupied their minds. The whole city was talking about an impostor named Debborius, who pretended to prevent the recurrence of such accidents by ridiculous talismans.[41] This sufficed to direct preoccupied minds towards supernatural matters. However that may have been, great was the success of the Christian preaching. A young, innovating, and ardent Church, full of the future, because it was composed of the most diverse elements, was quickly founded. All the gifts of the Holy Spirit were there poured out, and it was then easy to perceive that this new Church, emancipated from the strict Mosaism which traced an irrefragable circle around Jerusalem, would become the second cradle of Christianity. Assuredly, Jerusalem will remain for ever the capital of the Christian world ; nevertheless, the point of departure of the church of the Gentiles, the primal focus of Christian missions, was, in truth, Antioch. It is there, for the first time, that a Christian church was established, divorced from the bonds of Judaism; it is there that the great propaganda of the Apostolic age was established; it was there that St. Paul assumed a definite character. Antioch marks the second halting-place of the progress of Christianity, and in respect of Christian nobility, neither Rome, nor Alexandria, nor Constantinople can be at all compared with it.

The topography of ancient Antioch is so effaced that we should search in vain over its site, nearly destitute as it is of any vestiges of the antique, for the point to which to attach such grand recollections. Here, as everywhere, Christianity was, doubtless, established in the poor quarters of the city and among the petty tradesfolk. The basilica, which is called "the old" and "apostolic" to the fourteenth century, was situated in the street called Singon, near the Pantheon?[43] But no one knows where this Pantheon was. Tradition and certain vague analogies induced us to search the primitive Christian quarter alongside the gate, which even to-day is still called Paul's gate, *Bâb-bolos*,[44] and at the foot of the mountain, named by Procopius *Stavrin*, which overlooks the south-west coast from the ramparts of Antioch.[45] It was one of the quarters of the town which least abounded in pagan monuments. There we saw the remains of ancient sanctuaries dedicated to St. Peter, St. Paul, and St. John. There appeared to have been the quarter where Christianity was longest maintained after the Mohammedan conquest. There too, as it appeared, was the quarter of "the saints," in opposition to the general profanity of Antioch. The rock is honeycombed like a beehive, with grottoes formerly used by the Anchorites. When one walks on these steeply cut declivities, where, about the fourth century, the good Stylites, disciples at once of India and of Galilee, of Jesus and of Cakya-Mouni, disdainfully contemplated the voluptuous city from the summit of their pillar or from their flower-adorned cavern,[46] it is probable that one is not far from the very spots where Peter and Paul dwelt. The Church of Antioch is the one whose history is most authentic and least encumbered with fables. Christian tradition, in a city where Christianity was perpetuated with so much vigor, ought to possess some value. The prevailing language of the Church of Antioch was the Greek. It is, however, quite probable that the suburbs where Syriac was spoken furnished a number of converts to the sect. In consequence, Antioch already contained the germ of two rival and, at a later period, hostile Churches, the one speaking Greek, and now represented by the Syrian Greeks, whether orthodox or Catholics; the other, whose actual representatives are the Maronites, having previously spoken Syriac and guarding it still as if it were a sacred tongue. The Maronites, who under their entirely modern Catholicism conceal a high antiquity, are probably the last descendants of those Syrians anterior to Seleucus, of those suburbans or *pagani* of Ghisra, Charandama, etc.,[47] who from the first ages became a separate Church, were persecuted by the orthodox emperors as heretics, and escaped into the Libanus,[48] or, from hatred of the Grecian Church and in consequence of deeper sympathies, allied themselves with the Latins.

As to the converted Jews at Antioch, they were also very numerous.[49] But we must believe that they accepted from the very first a fraternal alliance with the Gentiles.[50] It was then on the shores of the Orontes that the religious fusion of races, dreamed of by Jesus, or to speak more fully, by six centuries of prophets, became a reality.

CHAPTER XIII.

THE IDEA OF AN APOSTOLATE TO THE GENTILES.—SAINT BARNABAS.

GREAT was the excitement at Jerusalem[1] on hearing what had passed at Antioch. Notwithstanding the kindly wishes of a few of the principal members of the Church of Jerusalem, Peter in particular, the Apostolic College continued to be influenced by mean and unworthy ideas. On every occasion when they heard that the good news had been announced to the heathen, these veteran Christians manifested signs of disappointment. The man who this time triumphed over this miserable jealousy, and who prevented the narrow exclusiveness of the "Hebrews" from ruining the future of Christianity, was Barnabas. He was the most enlightened member of the Church at Jerusalem. He was the chief of the liberal and progressive party, and wished the Church to be open to all. Already he had powerfully contributed to remove the mistrust with which Paul was regarded; and this time, also, he excited a marked influence. Sent as a delegate of the apostolical body to Antioch, he examined and approved of all that had been done, and declared that the new Church had only to continue in the course upon which it had entered. Conversions were effected in great numbers. The vital and creative force of Christianity appeared to be concentrated at Antioch. Barnabas, whose zeal always inclined to action, resided there. Antioch thenceforth is his Church, and it is thence that he exercised his most influential and important ministry. Christianity has always done injustice to this man in not placing him in the first rank of her founders. Barnabas was the patron of all good and liberal ideas. His intelligent boldness often served to neutralize the obstinacy of the narrow-minded Jews who formed the conservative party of Jerusalem.

A magnificent idea germinated in this noble heart at Antioch. Paul was at Tarsus in a forced repose, which to an active man like him, was a perfect torture. His false position, his haughtiness, and his exaggerated pretensions, had neutralized many of his other and better qualities. He was uselessly wearing his life away; Barnabas knew how to apply to its true work that force which was corroding Paul in his unhealthy and dangerous solitude. For the second time, Barnabas took the hand of Paul, and led this savage character into the society of those brethren whom he avoided. He went himself to Tarsus, sought him out, and brought him to Antioch.[2] He did that which those obstinate old brethren of Jerusalem were never able to do. To win over this great, reticent, and susceptible soul; to accommodate oneself to the caprices and whims of a man full of fiery excitement, but very personal; to take a secondary part under him, and forgetful of oneself, to prepare the field of operations for the most favorable display of his abilities—all this is certainly the very climax of virtue; and this is what Barnabas did for Paul. Most of the glory which has accrued to the latter is really due to the modest man who led him forward, brought his merits to light, prevented more than once his faults from resulting deplorably to himself and his cause, and the illiberal views of others from exciting him to revolt; and also prevented his insignificant and unworthy personalities from interfering with the work of God.

During an entire year Barnabas and Paul cooperated actively.[3] This was without doubt a most brilliant and happy year in the life of Paul. The prolific originality of these two great men raised the Church of Antioch to a degree of grandeur to which no Christian Church had previously attained. Few places in the world had experienced more intellectual activity than the capital of Syria. During the Roman epoch, as in our time, social and religious questions were brought to the surface principally at the centres of population. A sort of reaction against the general immorality which later made Antioch the special abode of stylites and hermits[4] was already felt; and the true doctrine thus found in this city more favorable conditions for success than it had yet met.

An important circumstance proves besides, that it was at Antioch that the sect for the first time had full consciousness of its existence; for it was in this city that it received a distinct name. Hitherto its adherents had called themselves "believers," "the faithful," "saints," "brothers," or disciples; but the sect had no public and official name. It was at Antioch that the title of *Christianus* was devised.[5] The termination of the word is Latin, not Greek, which would indicate that it was selected by the Roman authority as an appellation of the police[6] like *Herodiani*, *Pompeiani*,

Cæsariani.[7] In any event it is certain that such a name was formed by the heathen population. It included a misapprehension, for it implied that *Christus*, a translation of the Hebrew *Maschiah* (the Messiah), was a proper name.[8] Not a few of those who were unfamiliar with Jewish or Christian ideas, by this name were led to believe that *Christus* or *Chrestus* was a sectarian leader yet living.[9] The vulgar pronunciation of the name indeed was *Chrestiani.*[10]

The Jews did not adopt in a regular manner, at least,[11] the name given by the Romans to their schismatic co-religionists. They continued to call the new converts "Nazarenes" or "Nazorenes,"[12] undoubtedly because they were accustomed to call Jesus Han-nasri or Hannosri, "the Nazarene;" and even unto the present day this name is still applied to them throughout the entire East.[13]

This was a most important moment. Solemn indeed was the hour when the new creation received its name, for that name is the direct symbol of its existence. It is by its name that an individual or a community really becomes itself as distinct from others. The formation of the word "Christian" also marks the precise date of the separation from Judaism of the Church of Jesus. For a long time to come the two religions will be confounded; but this confusion will only take place in those countries where the spread of Christianity is slow and backward. The sect quickly accepted the appellation which was applied to it, and viewed it as a title of honor.[14] It is really astonishing to reflect that ten years after the death of Jesus His religion had already in the capital of Syria, a name in the Greek and Latin tongues. Christianity is now completely weaned from its mother's breast; the true sentiments of Jesus have triumphed over the indecision of its first disciples; the Church of Jerusalem is left behind; the Aramaic language, in which Jesus spoke, is unknown to a portion of His followers; Christianity speaks Greek; and the new sect is finally launched into that great vortex of the Greek and Roman world, whence it will never issue.

The feverish activity of ideas manifested by this young Church was truly extraordinary. Great spiritual manifestations were frequent.[15] All believed themselves to be inspired in different ways. Some were "prophets," others "teachers."[16] Barnabas, as his name indicates,[17] was undoubtedly among the prophets. Paul had no special title. Among the leaders of the church at Antioch may also be mentioned Simeon, surnamed *Niger*, Lucius of Cirene, and Menahem, who had been the foster-brother of Herod Antipas, and was naturally quite old.[18] All these personages were Jews. Among the converted heathen was, perhaps, already that Evhode, who, at a certain period, seems to have occupied a leading place in the Church of Antioch.[19] Undoubtedly the heathen who heard the first preaching were slightly inferior, and did not shine in the public exercises of using unknown tongues, of preaching, and prophecy. In the midst of the congenial society of Antioch, Paul quickly adapted himself to the order of things. Later, he manifested opposition to the use of tongues, and it is probable that he never practised it; but he had many visions and immediate revelations.[21] It was apparently at Antioch that occurred that ecstatic trance which he describes in these terms: "I knew a man in Christ above fourteen years ago (whether in the body I cannot tell; or whether out of the body, I cannot tell—God knoweth). Such an one was caught up to the third heaven.[23] And I knew such a man (whether in the body or out of the body I cannot tell—God knoweth), how that he was caught up into paradise[24] and heard unspeakable words which it is not lawful for a man to utter."[25] Paul, though in general sober and practical, shared the prevalent ideas of the day in regard to the supernatural. Like so many others, he believed that he possessed the power of working miracles;[26] it was impossible that the gift of the Holy Spirit, which was acknowledged to be the common right of the Church,[27] should be denied to him.

But men permeated with so lively a faith cannot content themselves with merely exuberant piety, but pant for action. The idea of great missions, destined to convert the heathen, and beginning in Asia Minor, seized hold of the public mind. Had such an idea been formed at Jerusalem, it could not have been realized, because the Church there was without pecuniary resources. An extensive establishment of propagandism requires a solid capital to work on. Now, the common treasury at Jerusalem was devoted to the support of the poor, and was frequently insufficient for that purpose; and to save these noble mendicants from dying with hunger, it was necessary to obtain help from all quarters.[28] Communism had created at Jerusalem an irremediable poverty and a thorough incapacity for great enterprises. The Church at Antioch was exempt from such a calamity. The Jews in the profane cities had attained to affluence, and in some cases had accumulated vast fortunes.[29] The faithful were wealthy when they entered the Church. Antioch furnished the pecuniary capital for the founding of Christianity, and it is easy to imagine the total difference in manner and spirit which this circumstance alone would create between the two churches. Jerusalem remained the city of the poor of God, of the *ebionim* of those simple Galilean dreamers, intoxicated, as it were, with the expectation of the kingdom of Heaven.[30] Antioch, almost a stranger to the words of Jesus, which it had never heard, was the church of action and of progress. Antioch was the city of Paul; Jerusalem, the seat of the old apostolic college, wrapped up in its dreamy fantasies, and unequal to the new problems which were opening, but dazzled by its incomparable privileges, and rich in its unsurpassed recollections.

A certain circumstance soon brought all these traits into bold relief. So great was the lack of forethought in this half-starved Church of Jerusalem, that the least accident threw the community into distress. Now in a country, destitute of economic organization, where commerce is almost without development, and where the sources of welfare are limited, famines are inevitable. A terrible one occurred in the reign of Claudius, in the year 44.[31] When its threatening symptoms appeared, the veterans at Jerusalem decided to seek succor from the members of the richer churches of Syria. An embassy of prophets was sent from Jerusalem to Antioch.[32] One of them, named Agab, who was in high reputation for his prophetic powers, was suddenly inspired, and announced that the famine was now at hand. The faithful were deeply moved at the evils which menaced the mother Church, to which they still deemed themselves tributary. A collection was made, at which every one gave according to his means, and Barnabas was selected to carry the funds obtained to the brethren in Judea.[33] Jerusalem for a long time remained the capital of Christianity. There were centred the objects peculiar to the faith, and there only were the apostles.[34] But a great forward step had been taken. For several years there had been only one completely organized Church, that of Jerusalem—the absolute centre of the faith, the heart from which all life proceeded and through which it circulated; but it no longer maintained this monopoly. The church at Antioch was now a perfect church. It possessed all the hierarchy of the gifts of the Holy Ghost. It was the starting-point of the missions,[35] and their head-quarters.[36] It was a second capital, or rather a second heart, which had its own proper action, exercising its force and influence in every direction.

It is easy to foresee that the second capital must soon eclipse the first. The decay of the church at Jerusalem was, indeed, rapid. It is natural that institutions founded on communism should enjoy at the beginning a period of brilliancy, for communism involves high mental exaltation; and it is equally natural that such institutions should very quickly degenerate, because communism is contrary to the instincts of human nature. During a moment of great religious excitement, a man readily believes that he can entirely sacrifice his selfish individuality and his peculiar interests; but egotism has its revenge, in proving that absolute disinterestedness engenders evils more serious than by the suppression of individual rights in property it had hoped to avoid.

CHAPTER XIV.

PERSECUTION OF HEROD AGRIPPA THE FIRST.

BARNABAS found the Church of Jerusalem in great trouble. The year 44 was perilous to it. Besides the famine, the fires of persecution which had been smothered since the death of Stephen were rekindled.

Herod Agrippa, grandson of Herod the Great, had succeeded, since the year 41, in reconstituting the kingdom of his grandfather. Thanks to the favor of Caligula, he had reunited under his domination Batania, Trachonites, a part of the Hauran, Cibilene, Galilee, and the Persea.[1] The ignoble part which he played in the tragicomedy which raised Claudius to the empire,[2] completed his fortune. This vile Oriental, in return for the lessons of baseness and perfidy he had given to Rome, obtained for himself Samaria and Judea, and for his brother Herod the kingdom of Chalcis.[3] He had left at Rome the worst memories, and the cruelties of Caligula were attributed in part to his counsels.[4] The army and the pagan cities of Sebaste and Cesarea, which he sacrificed to Jerusalem, were averse to him.[5] But the Jews found him to be generous, munificent, and sympathetic. He sought to render himself popular with them, and affected a polity quite different from that of Herod the Great. The latter was much more regardful of the Greek and Roman world than of the Jewish. Herod Agrippa, on the contrary, loved Jerusalem, rigorously observed the Jewish religion, affected scrupulousness, and never let a day pass without attending to his devotions.[6] He went so far as to receive with mildness the advice of the rigorists, and took the trouble to justify himself from their reproaches.[7] He returned to the Hierosolymites the tribute which each house owed to him.[8] The orthodox, in a word, had in him a king according to their own heart.

It was inevitable that a prince of this character should persecute the Christians. Sincere or not, Herod Agrippa was, in the most thorough sense of the word, a Jewish Sovereign.[9] The house of Herod, as it became weaker, took to devotion. It was no longer that broad profane idea of the founder of the dynasty, seeking to make the most diverse religions live together under the common empire of civilization. When Herod Agrippa, for the first time after he had become king, set foot in Alexandria, it was as a King of the Jews that he was received; it was this title which irritated the population and gave rise to endless buffooneries.[10] Now what could a King of the Jews be, if not the guardian of the laws and the traditions, a sovereign theocrat and persecutor? From the time of Herod the Great, under whom fanaticism was entirely repressed, until the breaking out of the war which led to the ruin of Jerusalem, there was thus a constantly augmenting progress of religious ardor. The death of Caligula (24th Jan., 41) had produced a reaction favorable to the Jews. Claudius was generally benevolent towards them,[11] as a result of the favorable ear he lent to Herod Agrippa and Herod King of Chalcis. Not only did he decide in favor of the Jews of Alexandria in their quarrels with the inhabitants and allow them the right of choosing an ethnarch, but he published, it is said, an edict by which he granted to the Jews throughout the whole empire that which he had granted to those of Alexandria; that is to say, the freedom to live according to their own laws, on the sole condition of not outraging other worships. Some attempts at vexations analogous to those which were inflicted under Caligula were repressed.[12] Jerusalem was greatly enlarged; the quarter of Bezetha was added to the city.[13] The Roman authority scarcely made itself felt, although Vibius Marsus, a prudent man, of wide public experience, and of a very cultivated mind,[14] who had succeeded Publius Petronius in the function of imperial legate of Syria, drew the attention of the authorities at Rome from time to time to the danger of these semi-independent Eastern Kingdoms.[15]

The species of feudality which, since the death of Tiberius, tended to establish itself in Syria and the neighboring countries,[16] was in fact an interruption in the imperial polity, and had almost uniformly injurious results. The "Kings" coming to Rome were personages, and exercised there a detestable influence. The corruption and abasement of the people, especially under Caligula, proceeded in great part from the spectacle furnished by these wretches, who were seen successively dragging their purple at the theatre, at the palace of the Cæsar, and in the prisons.[17] So far as concerns the Jews, we have seen that autonomy meant intolerance. The Sovereign Pontificate quitted for a moment the family of Hanan, only to enter that of Boethus, no less haughty and cruel. A Sovereign anxious to please the Jews could not fail to grant them what they loved best; that is to say, severities against everything which diverged from rigorous orthodoxy.[19]

Herod Agrippa, in fact, became towards the end of his reign a violent persecutor.[20] Some time before Easter of the year 44, he cut off the head of one of the principal members of the apostolical college, James son of Zebedee, brother of John. The matter was not presented as a religious one; there was no inquisitorial process before the Sanhedrim; the sentence, as in the case of John the Baptist,[21] was pronounced by virtue of the arbitrary power of the sovereign. Encouraged by the good effect which this execution produced upon the Jews,[22] Herod Agrippa was not willing to stop upon so easy a road to popularity. It was the first days of the feast of Passover, ordinarily marked by a redoubled fanaticism. Agrippa ordered the imprisonment of Peter in the tower of Antonia, and sought to have him judged and put to death with great pomp before the mass of people then assembled.

A circumstance with which we are unacquainted, and which was regarded as miraculous, opened Peter's prison. One evening, as many of the disciples were assembled in the house of Mary, mother of John-Mark, where Peter habitually dwelt, there was suddenly heard a knock at the door. The servant, named Rhoda, went to listen. She recognised Peter's voice. Transported with joy, instead of opening the door she ran back to announce that Peter was there. They regarded her as mad. She swore she spoke the truth. "It is his angel," said some of them. The knocking was heard repeatedly; it was indeed himself. Their delight was infinite. Peter immediately announced his deliverance to James, brother of the Lord, and to the other disciples. It was believed that the angel of God had entered into the prison of the apostle and made the chains fall from his hands and the bolts fly open. Peter related, in fact, all that had passed while he was in a sort of ecstasy; that after having passed the first and second guard, and overleaped the iron gate which led into the city, the angel accompanied him still the distance of a street, then quitted him; that then he came to himself again and recognised the hand of God, who had sent a celestial messenger to deliver him.[23]

Agrippa survived these violences but a short time.[24] In the course of the year 44, he went to Cesarea to celebrate games in honor of Claudius. The concourse of people was extraordinary; and many from Tyre and Sidon, who had difficulties with him, came thither to ask pardon. These festivals were very displeasing to the Jews, both because they took place in the impure city of Cesarea, and because they were held in the theatre. Already, on one occasion, the king having quitted Jerusalem under similar circumstances, a certain Rabbi Simeon had proposed to declare him an alien to Judaism, and to exclude him from the temple. Herod Agrippa had carried his condescension so far as to place the Rabbi beside him in the theatre, in order to prove to him that nothing passed there contrary to the law,[25] and thinking he had thus satisfied the most austere, he allowed himself to indulge his taste for profane pomps. The second day of the festival he entered the theatre very early in the morning, clothed in a tunic of silver fabric, with a marvellous brilliancy. The effect of this tunic, glittering in the rays of the rising sun, was extraordinary. The Phœnicians who surrounded the king lavished upon him adulations borrowed from paganism. "It is a god," they cried, "and not a man." The king did not testify his indignation, and did not blame this expression. He died five days afterwards; and Jews and Christians believed that he was struck dead for not having repelled with horror a blasphemous flattery. Christian tradition represents that he died of a vermicular malady,[26] the punishment reserved for the enemies of God. The symptoms related by Josephus would lead rather to the belief that he was poisoned; and what is said in the Acts of the equivocal conduct of the Phœnicians, and of the care they took to gain over Blastus, valet of the king, would strengthen this hypothesis.

The death of Herod Agrippa I. led to the end of all independence for Jerusalem. The administration by Procurators was resumed, and this régime lasted until the great revolt. This was fortunate for Christianity; for it is very remarkable that this religion, which was destined to sustain subsequently so terrible a struggle against the Roman empire, grew up in the shadow of the Roman principality, under its protection. It was Rome, as we have already several times remarked, which hindered Judaism from giving itself up fully to its intolerant instincts, and stifling the free instincts which were stirred within its bosom. Every diminution of Jewish authority was a benefit for the nascent sect. Cuspius Fadus, the first of this new series of Procurators, was another Pilate, full of firmness, or at least of good-will. But Claudius continued to show himself favorable to Jewish pretensions, chiefly at the instigation of the young Herod Agrippa, son of Herod Agrippa I., whom he kept near to his person, and whom he greatly loved.[27] After the short administration of Cuspius Fadus, we find the functions of Procurator confided to a Jew, to that Tiberius Alexander, nephew of Philo, and son of the *alabarque* of the Alexandrian Jews who attained to nigh functions and played a great part in the political affairs of the century. It is true that the Jews did not like him; and regarded him, and with reason, as an apostate.[28]

To cut short these incessantly renewed disputes, recourse was had to an expedient in conformity with sound principles. A sort of separation was made between the spiritual and temporal. The political power remained with the procurators; but Herod, king of Chalcis, brother of Agrippa I., was named prefect of the temple, guardian of the pontifical habits, treasurer of the sacred fund, and invested with the right of nominating the high-priests.[29] At his death (year 48), Herod Agrippa II., son of Herod Agrippa I., succeeded his uncle in his offices, which he retained until the great war. Claudius, in all this, manifested the greatest kindness. The high Roman functionaries in Syria, although not so strongly disposed as the emperor to concessions, acted with great moderation. The procurator, Ventidius Cumanus, carried condescension so far as to have a soldier beheaded in the midst of the Jews, drawn up in line, for having torn a copy of the Pentateuch.[30] It was all useless, however; Josephus, with good reason, dates from the administration of Cumanus the disorders which ended only with the destruction of Jerusalem.

Christianity played no part in these troubles.[31] But these troubles, like Christianity itself, were one of the symptoms of the extraordinary fever which devoured the Jewish people, and the Divine travail which was accomplishing in its midst. Never had the Jewish faith made such progress.[32] The temple of Jerusalem was one of the sanctuaries of the world, the reputation of which was most widely extended, and where the offerings were most liberal.[33] Judaism had become the dominant religion of various portions of Syria. The Asmonean princes had violently converted entire populations to it (Idumeans, Itureans, etc.).[34] There were many examples of circumcision having been imposed by force;[35] the ardor for making proselytes was very great.[36] The house of Herod itself powerfully served the Jewish propaganda. In order to marry princesses of this family, whose wealth was immense, the princes of the little dynasties of Emese, of Pontus, and of Cilicia, vassals of the Romans, became Jews.[37] Arabia and Ethiopia counted also a great number of converts. The royal families of Mesene and of Adiabene, tributaries of the Parthians, were gained over, especially by their women.[38] It was generally granted that happiness was found in the knowledge and practice of the law[39] Even when circumcision was not practised, religion was more or less modified in the Jewish direction; a sort of monotheism became the general spirit of religion in Syria. At Damascus, a city which was in nowise of Israelitish origin, nearly all the women had adopted the Jewish religion.[40] Behind the Pharisaical Judaism there was thus formed a sort of free Judaism, of inferior quality not knowing all the secrets of the sect;[41] bringing only its good-will and its good heart, but having a greater future. The situation was, in all respects, that of the Catholicism of our days, in which we see, on one hand, narrow and proud theologians, who alone would gain no more souls for Catholicism than the Pharisees gained for Judaism; on the other, pious laymen, very often heretics without knowing it, but full of a touching zeal, rich in good works and in poetical sentiments, altogether occupied in dissimulating or repairing by complaisant explanations the faults of their doctors.

One of the most extraordinary examples of this tendency of religious souls towards Judaism was that given by the royal family of Adiabene, upon the Tiger.[42] This house, of Persian origin and manners,[43] already partly initiated into Greek culture, [44] became entirely Jewish, and even preëminently devout; for, as we have already said, these proselytes were often more pious than the Jews by birth. Izate, chief of the family, embraced Judaism through the preaching of a Jewish merchant named Ananias, who, entering the seraglio of Abermerig, king of Mesene, for the purposes of his petty traffic, had converted all the women, and constituted himself their spiritual preceptor. The women brought Izate into communication with him. Towards the same time Helen, his mother, received instruction in the true religion from another Jew. Izate, with the zeal of a new convert, wished to be circumcised. But his mother and Ananias vehemently dissuaded him from it. Ananias proved to him that the observation of God's command ments was of more importance than circumcision, and that he might be a very good Jew without this ceremony Such a tolerance was the privilege of a small number of enlightened minds. Some time after, a Jew of Galilee, named Eleazar, finding the king occupied in reading the Pentateuch, showed him by texts that he could not observe the law without being circumcised. Izate was convinced, and submitted immediately to the operation.[45]

The conversion of Izate was followed by that of his brother, Monobaze, and of all the family. Towards the year 44, Helen came and established herself at Jerusalem, where she had built for the royal house of Adiabene a palace and family mausoleum, which still exist.[46] She rendered herself dear to the Jews by her affability and her alms. It was very edifying to see her, like a pious Jewess, frequenting the temple, consulting the doctors, reading the law, teaching it to her sons. During the plague of the year 44, this holy personage was the providence of the city. She had a large quantity of wheat bought in Egypt, and of dried figs in Cyprus. Izate, on his part, sent considerable sums to be distributed among the poor. The wealth of Adiabene was in part expended at Jerusalem. The sons of Izate came thither to learn the customs and the language of the Jews. All this family was thus the resource of this population of beggars. It acquired there a sort of citizenship; several of its members were found there at the time of the siege of Titus;[47] others figure in the Talmudic writings, presented as models of piety and devotedness.[48]

It is thus that the royal family of Adiabene belongs to the history of Christianity. Without being Christian, in fact, as certain traditions have represented,[49] this family represented under various aspects the first fruits of the Gentiles. In embracing Judaism, it obeyed a sentiment which was destined to bring over the entire pagan world to Christianity. The true Israelites according to God, were much rather these foreigners animated by so profoundly sincere a religious sentiment than the arrogant and spiteful Pharisee, for whom religion was but a pretext for hatred and disdain. These good proselytes, although they were truly saints, were in nowise fanatics. They admitted that true religion might be practised under the empire of the most widely differing civil codes. They completely separated religion from politics. The distinction between the seditious sectaries, who must presently defend Jerusalem with rage, and the devoutly pious who, at the first rumor of war, were going to flee to the mountains,[50] made itself more and more manifest.

We may see at least that the question as to proselytes was propounded in a very similar manner at once in Judaism and in Christianity. On both hands alike the void was felt for enlarging the door of entrance. For those who were placed at this point of view, circumcision was a useless or noxious custom ; the Mosaic observances were simply a mask of a race having no value but for the sons of Abraham. Before becoming the universal religion, Judaism was obliged to reduce itself to a sort of deism, imposing only the duties of natural religion. That was a sublime mission to fulfil, and to it a portion of Judaism, in the first half of the first century, lent itself in a very intelligent manner. On one side, Judaism was one of those innumerable national worships[51] of which the world is full, and the sanctity of which springs solely from the fact that the ancestors had adored in the same way; on another side, Judaism was the absolute religion, made for all, destined to be adopted by all. The terrible flood of fanaticism which spread over Judea, and which led to the war of extermination, cut short this future. It was Christianity which took upon its own account the task which the synagogue had been unable to accomplish. Laying aside ritual questions, Christianity continued the monotheistic propaganda of Judaism. That which had caused the success of Judaism with the women of Damascus in the seraglio of Abenverig, with Helen, with so many pious proselytes, became the force of Christianity throughout an entire world. In this sense the glory of Christianity is truly confounded with that of Judaism. A generation of fanatics deprived this latter of its recompense, and hindered its gathering the harvest it had prepared.

CHAPTER XV.

MOVEMENTS PARALLEL TO AND IMITATIVE OF CHRISTIANITY—SIMON OF GITTO.

We have now arrived at a period when Christianity may be said to have become established. In the history of religions it is only the earliest years during which their existence is precarious. If a creed can triumphantly pass through the severe ordeals which await every new system, its future is assured. With sounder judgment than other cotemporary sects, such as the Essenes, the Baptists, and the followers of Judas the Gaulonite, who clung to and perished with the Jewish institutions, the founders of Christianity displayed rare prevision in going forth at an early period to disseminate and root their new opinions over the broad expanse of the Gentile world. The meagreness of the allusions to Christianity which are found in Josephus, in the Talmud, and in the Greek and Latin writers, need not surprise us. Josephus is transmitted to us by Christian copyists, who have omitted everything uncomplimentary to their faith. It is possible that he wrote more at length concerning Jesus and the Christians than is preserved in the edition which has been handed down to us. The Talmud in like manner, during the Middle Age, and after its first publication, underwent much abridgment and alteration.[1] This resulted from the severe criticisms of the text by Christian writers, and from the burning of a number of unlucky Jews who were found in possession of a work containing what were considered blasphemous passages. As to the Greek and Latin writers, it is not surprising that they paid little attention to a movement which they could not comprehend, and which was going on within a narrow space foreign to them. Christianity was lost to their vision upon the dark background of Judaism. It was only a family quarrel amongst the subjects of a degraded nation; why trouble themselves about it? The two or three passages in which Tacitus and Suetonius mention the Christians show that the new sect, even if generally beyond the visual circle of full publicity, was, notwithstanding, a prominent fact, since we are enabled at intervals to catch a glimpse of it defining itself with considerable clearness of outline through the mist of public inattention.

The relief of Christianity above the general level of Jewish history in the first century has also been somewhat diminished, by the fact that it was not the only movement of the kind. At the epoch we have arrived at, Philo had finished his career, so wholly consecrated to the love of virtue. The sect of Judas the Gaulonite still existed. This agitator had left the perpetuation of his ideas to his sons, James, Simon, and Menahem. The two former were crucified by command of the renegade procurator Tiberius Alexander.[2] Menahem remained, and is destined to play an important part in the final catastrophe of the nation.[3] In the year 44, an enthusiast by the name of Theudas arose, announcing the speedy deliverance of the Jews, calling on the people to follow him to the desert, and promising like a second Joshua to cause them to pass dry-shod across the Jordan.[4] This passage was, according to him, the true baptism which should admit every believer into the kingdom of God. More than four hundred persons followed him. The procurator Cuspius Fadus sent out against him a troop of horse, which dispersed his disciples and slew him.[5] A few years before this Samaria had been stirred by the voice of a fanatic, who pretended to have had a revelation of the spot on Mount Gerizim where Moses had concealed the sacred instruments of worship. Pilate suppressed this movement with great severity.[6]

In Jerusalem, tranquillity was at an end. From the arrival of the procurator Ventidius Cumanus (A. D. 48), disturbances were incessant. The excitement reached such a point that it became almost impossible to live there; the most trifling occurrences brought about explosions.[7] People everywhere felt a strange fermentation, a kind of mysterious foreboding. Impostors sprang up on every side.[8] That fearful scourge, the society of zealots or *sicarii*, began to appear. Wretches armed with daggers mingled in the crowds, gave the fatal thrust to their victims, and were the first to cry murder. Hardly a day passed that some assassination of this kind was not told of. An extraordinary terror spread around. Josephus speaks of the crimes of the zealots as pure wickedness;[6] but it cannot be doubted that they sprang in part from fanaticism.[10] It was to defend the law and the testimony that these wretches drew the poniard. Whoever was wanting in their view in one of the requirements of the law, was judged and at once executed. They believed that in so doing they were rendering a service most meritorious and pleasing to God.

Dreams like those of Theudas occurred everywhere. Men calling themselves inspired, drew the people after them into the desert, under the pretext of showing them by manifest signs that God was about to deliver them. The Roman authorities exterminated the dupes of these agitators in crowds.[11] An Egyptian Jew who came to Jerusalem about the year 56, succeeded by his devices in drawing after him thirty thousand persons, among whom were four thousand zealots. From the desert he was going to lead them to the Mount of Olives, that they might thence behold the walls of Jerusalem crumble at his command. Felix, who was at that time procurator, marched against him, and dispersed his band. The Egyptian escaped and was seen no more.[12] But, as we see in a diseased body one malady succeed another, soon afterwards there appeared here and there troops of magicians and robbers, who openly excited the people to revolt, and threatened with death those who should continue to obey the Roman authorities. Under this pretext they murdered and pillaged the rich, burned villages, and filled all Judea with the marks of their outrages.[13] A terrible war seemed impending. A spirit of madness reigned everywhere, and the imagination of the people was kept in a state bordering on lunacy.

It is not impossible that Theudas may have had an idea of imitating the acts of Jesus and John the Baptist. At any rate such an imitation is evident in the accounts of Simon of Gitto, if we may credit the Christian traditions.[14] We have already encountered him in communication with the apostles on the first mission of Philip to Samaria. He attained his celebrity during the reign of the Emperor Claudius.[15] His miracles were unquestioned, and all Samaria regarded him as a supernatural being.[16]

Miracles were not, however, the only basis of his renown. He taught a doctrine, it seems, of which it is difficult for us to acquire a definite knowledge, in a treatise entitled "The Great Exposition," which is ascribed to him, and a few extracts from which have come down to us, being probably only a modified expression of his ideas.[17] During his sojourn at Alexandria, where he studied the Grecian philosophy, he appears to have framed a system of syncretic theology and allegorical exegesis, in many respects analogous to that of Philo.[18] His system is not without sublimity. Sometimes it reminds us of the Jewish Kabala, sometimes of the pantheistic theories of Indian philosophy; and in other respects it resembles that of the Buddhists and the Parsees.[19] The primal being is, "He who is, has been, and shall be,"[20] *i.e.* the *Jah-veh* of the Samaritans, understood according to the etymological force of the name, as the eternal and only Being, self-begotten, self-augmenting, self-seeking, and self-finding—the father, mother, sister, spouse, and son of himself.[21] In this infinite being, all things exist potentially to all eternity; and pass into action and reality through human conscience, reason, language, and science.[22] The universe is explained either upon the basis of a hierarchy of abstract principles like the Æons of Gnosticism and the Sephirotic tree of the Kabala, or upon that of an order of angels apparently borrowed from the Persian doctrine. Sometimes these abstractions are presented as representations of physical and physiological facts. Elsewhere, the "divine powers," considered as distinct substances, are realized in successive incarnations, either in the male or female form, whose end is the emancipation of those beings which are enslaved in the bonds of material existence. The highest of these "Powers" is called "the Great," which is the universal Providence, the intelligent soul of this world.[23] It is masculine. Simon passed for an incarnation of this spirit. In connexion with it is its feminine counterpart, "the Great Thought." Accustomed to clothe his theories in a strange symbolism, and to devise allegorical interpretations for the ancient writings both sacred and profane, Simon, or whoever was the author of "The Great Exposition," ascribed to this Divine existence the name of "Helena," thereby signifying that she was the object of universal pursuit, the eternal cause of dispute among men, and that she avenged herself on her enemies by depriving them of sight until the moment they consented to recant;[24]—a strange theory, and one which, imperfectly understood or designedly travestied, gave rise among the early Fathers of the Church to the most puerile legends.[25] The acquaintance with Greek literature possessed by the author of "The Great Exposition" is at all events very remarkable. He contended that, rightly understood, the heathen writings sufficed for the knowledge of all things.[26] His broad eclecticism embraced all revelations, and sought to combine them into one sole and universal system of accepted truths.

His plan was essentially quite similar to that of Valentinus, and to the doctrines in regard to the Divine Persons which are found in the fourth Gospel, in Philo, and in the Targums.[27] The "Metatronos,"[28] which the Jews placed at the side of the Deity, and almost in his bosom, strongly resembles "The Great Power." In Samaritan theology we find a Great Angel, who presides over other angels, and we find also a variety of manifestations or "Divine Virtues," analogous to those of the Kabala.[29] It appears certain, then, that Simon of Gitto was a theosophist of the type of Philo and the Kabalists. Perhaps he may have come near to Christianity, but certainly he did not attach himself to it in any defined way.

Whether he actually borrowed anything from the disciples of Jesus, is difficult to decide. If "The Great Exposition" is the expression of his ideas in any degree, it must be admitted that upon several points he is in advance of the Christian ideas, and that upon others he adopts them with much fulness.[30] He seems to have attempted an eclecticism similar to that which Mahomet afterwards adopted, and to have based his religious action upon the preliminary belief in the divine mission of John and of Jesus.[31] He professed to bear a mystic relation to them. He asserted, it is said, that it was he himself who appeared to the Samaritans as the Father, to the Jews by the visible crucifixion of the Son, and to the Gentiles by the inspiration of the Holy Ghost.[32] He also, it would seem, prepared the way for the doctrine of the "Docetæ." He claimed to have suffered in Judea in the person of Jesus, but that his suffering was only apparent.[33] These pretensions to Divinity and claims of adoration have probably been exaggerated by the Christians, who have in every way sought to cover him with odium.

The doctrine of "the Great Exposition" is that of nearly all the Gnostic writings; and if Simon really professed that doctrine, it is with good reason that the Fathers charged him with being the founder of Gnosticism.[34] It is our belief that the "Exposition" has only a relative authenticity; that it is to the doctrine of Simon very nearly what the fourth Gospel is to the ideas of Jesus; and that it dates from the earlier years of the second century, the epoch when the theosophic notions of the Logos acquired a definite ascendency. These notions, of which we shall find the germ in the Christian Church about the year 60,[35] may, however, have been known to Simon, whose career was probably prolonged until the close of the century.

The notion then that we obtain of this enigmatic personage is, that he was a kind of plagiarist of Christianity. Imitation seems to have been a constant habit of the Samaritans.[36] In the same manner as they had always been imitators of the Jewish ceremonies of Jerusalem, so these sectaries had also their copy of Christianity, their Gnosis, their theosophic speculations, and their Kabala. But we shall probably remain for ever ignorant whether Simon was a respectable imitator, who just fell short of success, or only an immoral and insincere juggler, who was working for his own profit and celebrity a doctrine stitched together out of the rags of other systems.[37] He thus assumes in history a most difficult position; he walks on a tight-rope, where no hesitation is permitted; in such a case there is no midway path between ridiculous failure and triumphant success.

We have yet to examine whether the legends relative to Simon's sojourn at Rome comprise any truth. It is at least certain that the Simonian sect continued as far down as the third century;[38] that it possessed churches as far as Antioch—perhaps even at Rome; and that Menander of Capharetes and Cleobius[39] sustained the same doctrine, or at least imitated Simon's performance as theurgist with more or less recurrence in type to the acts of Jesus and the apostles. Simon and his followers were in great esteem among their co-religionists. Sects of the same kind, parallel with Christianity,[40] and more or less tinctured with Gnosticism, continued to spring up among the Samaritans, until their almost total destruction by Justinian. It was the lot of this little religious community to receive an impression from everything that happened in its vicinity, without producing anything altogether original.

As to Christians, the memory of Simon was amongst them an abomination. Those illusions of his which so closely resembled their own, were irritating to them. To have competed with the success of the apostles was the most unpardonable of crimes. They pretended that the wonders performed by Simon and his disciples were works of the devil, and they branded the Samaritan theosophist with the title of "Sorcerer,"[41] which his believers took in high dudgeon. The entire Christian account of Simon bears the imprint of concentrated hatred. The maxims of quietism were ascribed to him, with the excesses which are generally supposed to be their consequence. He was considered the father of all error, the primitive heresiarch. They delighted in recounting his ludicrous adventures, and his defeats by the apostle Peter,[43] and attributed to the vilest motives his apparent tendency towards Christianity. They were so preoccupied with his name that they read it at random upon columns where it did not exist.[44] The symbolism in which he had clothed his ideas was interpreted in the most grotesque way. The "Helena," whom he identified with "The First Intelligence," became a girl of the town purchased by him in the streets of Tyre.[45] His very name, hated nearly as much as that of Judas, and used as a synonym of *Anti-apostle*,[46] became the grossest word of abuse and a proverbial expression to designate a professional impostor or adversary of truth whom it was desired to refer to under a disguise.[47] He was the first enemy of Christianity, or rather the first personage whom Christianity treated as such. It is sufficient to say that neither pious frauds nor calumny were spared in defaming him.[48] Criticism in such a case need not attempt a rehabilitation; it has no documents on the other side. All it can do is to show the physiognomy of the traditions and the set purpose of abuse which they display.

At least it should prevent the loading of the memory of the Samaritan theurgist with a resemblance which may be only accidental. In a story related by Josephus, a Jewish sorcerer named Simon, a native of Cyprus, plays for the procurator Felix the part of a Pandarus.[49] The circumstances of this story do not accord well enough with what is known of Simon of Gitto, to make him responsible for the acts of a person who may have had nothing in common with him but a name borne by thousands, and a pretension to supernatural powers, which was unfortunately shared by a crowd of his cotemporaries.

CHAPTER XVI.

GENERAL PROGRESS OF THE CHRISTIAN MISSIONS.

WE have seen Barnabas leaving Antioch in order to carry to the faithful at Jerusalem the contributions of their brethren in Syria, and arriving at Jerusalem in time to be present at several of the excitements occasioned there by the persecution of Herod Agrippa.[1] Let us now follow him again to Antioch, where, at this period, all the creative energy of the sect seems to have been concentrated.

Barnabas took back a zealous assistant, his cousin John-Mark, the disciple of Peter,[2] and the son of that Mary at whose house the chief apostle loved to stay. Doubtless in calling this new co-worker to his aid, he had already in view the great enterprise in which they were to embark. Perhaps he foresaw the disputes it would occasion, and was well pleased to engage in it one who was understood to be the right hand of Peter, whose influence in general matters was predominant.

The enterprise itself was no less than a series of great missions starting from Antioch and seeking the conversion of the world. Like all the great resolves of the early Church, this idea was ascribed to a direct inspiration of the Holy Ghost. A special call, a supernatural election, was believed to have been vouchsafed to the Church of Antioch while engaged in fasting and prayer. Perhaps one of the prophets of the Church, Menahem, or Lucius, uttered under the power of the gift of tongues the words intimating that Paul and Barnabas were predestined to this mission.[3] Paul was convinced that God had chosen him from his mother's womb for this task, to which thenceforth he exclusively devoted himself.[4]

The two apostles took with them, as an assistant in the details of their enterprise, the John-Mark whom Barnabas had brought from Jerusalem.[5] When the preparations were completed, after fasting and prayer, and laying on of hands as a sign of the authority conferred by the Church itself on the apostles,[6] they were commended to the grace of God, and set out.[7] Whither they should journey, and what races they should evangelize, is what we are now to learn.

The early missions were all directed westward, or in other words adopted the Roman empire for their scene of operations. Excepting some small provinces between the Tigris and the Euphrates under the rule of the Arsacides, the Parthian countries received no Christian missions during the first century.[8] Until the reigns of the Sassanides, Christianity did not pass eastward beyond the Tigris. This important fact was due to two causes, the Mediterranean sea, and the Roman empire.

For a thousand years the Mediterranean had been the great pathway of ideas and civilizations. The Romans, in extirpating its pirates, had rendered it an unequalled method of intercourse. A numerous coasting-marine made it very easy to pass from point to point on the borders of this immense lake. The comparative safety of the imperial highways, the protection afforded by the civil authority, the diffusion of the Jews around the Mediterranean coasts, the spreading of the Greek language over their eastern portion, and the unity of civilization, which first the Greeks, and then the Romans, had extended over those countries, all joined to make the map of the empire a map of the regions set apart for Christian missions, and destined to be Christianized. The Roman world became the Christian world, and in this sense the founders of the empire may be called the founders of the Christian monarchy. Every province conquered by the empire was a conquest for Christianity. Had the apostles been placed in presence of an independent Asia Minor; of a Greece or an Italy divided into a hundred little republics; of a Gaul, Spain, Africa; of Egypt with her ancient institutions—we cannot conceive of their succeeding, or even imagine that such a project could have been seriously formed. The unity of the empire was the preliminary condition of all great religious conversions which should transcend lines of nationality. This the empire saw clearly in the fourth century; it became Christian. It perceived that it had established Christianity without knowing it; a religion conterminous with the Roman territory, identified with the empire, and capable of inspiring it with new life. The Church, on the other hand, became entirely Roman, and has remained down to our own day as a fragment of the empire. Had any one told Paul that Claudius was his chief coöperator, or Claudius that the Jew just setting out from Antioch was about to found the most enduring part of the imperial structure, both would have been much astonished. Nevertheless both sayings would have been true.

Syria was the first country out of Judea in which Christianity became naturally established. This was an evident result of the vicinity of Palestine and of the great number of Jews living in Syria.[10] The apostles visited Cyprus, Asia Minor, Macedonia, Greece, and Italy next in order, and only a few years after. Southern Gaul, Spain, and the coast of Africa, although made acquainted with the Gospel at an early period, may be considered as of a more recent epoch in the building up of the new faith.

It was the same with Egypt. Egypt plays hardly any part in the apostolic history, and the missionaries seem to have systematically passed it by. Although after the third century it was the scene of such momentous events in religious history, it was at first very backward in Christian progress. Apollos was the only teacher of Christianity who ame from the Alexandrian school, and he learned it during his travels.[11] The cause of this remarkable fact will be found in the meagreness of the intercourse between the Egyptian and the Palestinian Jews; and above all in the circumstance that Jewish Egypt had a separate religious development in the teachings of Philo and the Therapeutæ, which were its special Christianity, and which indisposed it to lend an attentive ear to any other.[12] As to heathen Egypt, her religious institutions were much more tenacious than those of Greco-Roman paganism.[13] The Egyptian idolatry was yet in full vigor. It was almost the epoch when the enormous temples of Esneh and Ombos were constructed, and when the hope of finding a last Ptolemy, a national Messiah in the little Cesarion, inspired the building of Dendera and Hermonthis, which will compare with the finest works of the Pharaohs. Christianity planted itself everywhere upon the ruins of national feeling and local worships The degradation of mind in Egypt also made very rare those religious aspirations which opened so easy a road to Christianity in other regions.

A flash of light from Syria, illumining almost at once the three great peninsulas of Asia Minor, Greece, and Italy, and soon followed by a second, which extended over nearly the whole Mediterranean seaboard —such was the first apparition of Christianity. The course of the apostolic vessels was always much the same. The Christian preaching seems to have followed a road already laid out, and which is no other than that of the Jewish emigration. Like a contagion which, having its point of departure at the head of the Mediterranean, appears all at once at a number of separate points on the shore by a secret communication, Christianity had its points in a manner marked in advance. They were nearly all places where there existed colonies of Jews. The synagogue generally preceded the church. It was like a train of powder, or more correctly, an electric cord, along which the new idea ran with almost instantaneous rapidity.

During a century and a half Judaism, which had previously been confined to the East and to Egypt, had been spreading westward. Cyrene, Cyprus, Asia Minor, and certain cities of Macedonia, Greece, and Italy, contained large Jewish colonies.[14] The Jews first exemplified that species of patriotism which the Parsees, the Armenians, and in some degree the modern Greeks, have shown in later ages;—a patriotism of great warmth, though not attached to any particular locality; a patriotism of a nation of merchants wandering everywhere, and everywhere recognising each other as brothers; a patriotism which results in forming no great compact states, but small autonomic communities within other states. Closely associated among themselves, the dispersed Jews formed quasi-independent congregations within the cities, having their own magistrates and their own councils, some of whom were invested with powers approaching sovereignty itself. They dwelt in quarters by themselves, outside of the ordinary jurisdiction, despised by the other citizens, and happy enough at home. They were rather poor than rich. The epoch of the great Jewish fortunes had not yet arrived; they began in Spain under the Visigoths.[15] The monopoly of finance by the Jews resulted from the lack of administrative capacity in the barbarians, and from the hatred manifested by the Church against monetary science and her superficial notions about usury. Nothing of the kind occurred in the Roman empire. But when a Jew is not rich, he is poor; *bourgeois* comfort is not his forte. He is capable of enduring poverty; and he is still more capable of combining the fiercest religious energy with the rarest commercial skill. Theological eccentricities are not at all inconsistent with good sense in conducting business. In England, America, and Russia, the strangest sectaries, Irvingites, Latter-Day Saints, Raskolniks, are able business-men.

It has always been characteristic of unadulterated Jewish life to produce much gaiety and cordiality. In that little world of theirs they loved each other, they revered their common history, and their religious ceremonies mingled pleasantly with their daily existence. It was analogous to the separate communities which still exist in Turkish cities, such as the Greek, the Armenian, and the Hebrew quarters at Smyrna, where they are all acquainted, and live and intrigue together. In these little republics, religious affairs always control politics, or rather supply the want of the latter. Amongst them a heresy is an affair of state, and a schism always arises out of some personal difficulty. The Romans, with rare exceptions, never penetrated these secluded quarters. The synagogues published decrees, awarded honors, and acted like real municipalities.[16] Their influence was extreme. In Alexandria, it is predominant in all the internal history of the city.[17] At Rome the Jews were numerous and constituted a body, the support of which was by no means to be despised. Cicero claims the credit of courage for having resisted some of their demands.[19] Cæsar protected them, and found them faithful.[20] Tiberius was obliged, in order to control them, to resort to the severest measures.[21] Caligula, whose reign was most calamitous to them in the East, allowed them freedom of association at Rome.[22] Claudius, who favored them in Judea, found it necessary to expel them from the city.[23] They were encountered everywhere,[24] and it was even said of them as of the Greeks, that when themselves subdued, they had succeeded in imposing laws on their conquerors.[25]

The feelings of the native population towards these foreigners were very diverse. On the one hand that strong sentiment of repulsion and antipathy which the Jews have invariably inspired where sufficiently numerous and organized, by their jealous love of isolation, their revengeful nature, and their exclusive habits, manifested itself with great force.[26] When they were free they were in fact a privileged class, for they enjoyed the advantages of society, without sustaining its burdens.[27] Charlatans took advantage of the curiosity inspired by their religious rites, and under pretence of exposing their secrets, acted all sorts of impostures.[28] Violent and semi-burlesque pamphlets, like that of Apion, nourished the pagan enmity, and were too often the sources whence the profane historians derived their information.[29] The Jews seem to have been generally sullen and full of complaints. They were looked upon as a secret society, malevolent towards others, the members of which were pledged to push forward their own interests at any cost, regardless of injury to their fellow-men.[30] Their singular customs, their aversion to certain kinds of food, their filth and unpleasant odor,[31] their religious scruples, their minute observances on the Sabbath, all appeared absurd and ridiculous.[32] Placed under a social ban, it was a natural consequence that they should care nothing about refined appearances. They were met everywhere travelling with garments shiny with dirt, with an awkward air, a weary mien, a cadaverous skin, and large, sunken eyes,[33] assuming a hypocritical and obsequious manner, and herding apart with their women and children, and their bundles and hamper, which composed their whole movable possessions.[34] In the towns they exercised the meanest trades; they were beggars,[35] rag-pickers, match-venders,[36] and small peddlers. Their history and their law were alike unjustly reviled. Sometimes they were called cruel and superstitious;[37] [38] sometimes atheists and despisers of the gods.[39] Their hatred of images appeared purely impious. Above all, circumcision afforded a theme for endless raillery.[40]

But such superficial estimates were not concurred in by every one. The Jews had as many friends as detractors. Their gravity and good morals, and the simplicity of their religion, were attractive to many persons, who recognised in them something superior. A vast monotheistic and Mosaic propaganda was organized,[41] as it were a powerful vortex around this singular race. The poor Jew peddler of the Transteverine,[42] setting out in the morning with his basket of small wares, often returned at evening enriched with alms from some pious hand.[43] Women in particular were attracted towards these ragged missionaries.[44] Juvenal enumerates their leaning towards the Jewish religion as one of the vices of the ladies of his time.[45] Those who were converted, gloried in the treasure they had found and the happiness they enjoyed.[46] The old Greek and Roman mind resisted stoutly; contempt and hatred of Jews were the sure emotions of cultivated intellects, such as Cicero, Horace, Seneca, Juvenal, Tacitus, Quintilian, and Suetonius.[47] On the other side, the enormous mass of mingled populations which had become subject to the empire and to whom the old Roman intellect and Greek learning were foreign or indifferent, gladly and spontaneously welcomed a community where they observed such touching examples of concord, charity, and mutual aid,[48] of content, industry,[49] and proud poverty. The institution of mendicity, which afterwards became entirely Christian, was at that time Jewish. The mendicant by profession, "formed to it by his mother," presented himself to the minds of the poets of the day as a Jew.[50]

Exemption from some civil burdens, especially military duty, may also have contributed to cause the lot of the Jews to be regarded as desirable.[51] The State at that period demanded many sacrifices, and afforded few moral advantages or pleasures. It created an icy coldness as in a uniform and shelterless plain. Human life, which was so melancholy under the rule of paganism, regained its charm and its value in the mild atmospheres of the synagogue and the Church. There was little enough liberty there, it is true. The brethren watched each other and tormented each other unceasingly. But although the internal life of these communities was anything but tranquil, it was very enjoyable, and people did not abandon it; it had no apostates. The poor enjoyed content within its circle; and dwelling in the quiet of an untroubled conscience, regarded riches without envy.[52] The truly democratic idea of the folly of worldly things, and the vanity of riches and profane honors, was there completely embodied. They were but little acquainted with the pagan world, and judged it with intemperate severity. Roman civilization appeared to them a mass of hateful vices and iniquities,[53] just as an honest *ouvrier* of our day, imbued with socialistic declamation, pictures the "aristocrat" to himself in the blackest colors. But there was abundance of life, gaiety, and interest amongst these people, and is to this moment in the poorest synagogues of Poland and Galicia. Their lack of refinement and elegance in habits was compensated for by a warm family attachment and patriarchal hospitality. In high circles, on the contrary, egotism and self-seeking had arrived at their fullest growth.

The words of Zachariah were being verified, that

men of all nations should "take hold of the skirt of him that is a Jew" and cry, bring us to Jerusalem![54] There was not a large city where were not observed the Sabbath, the fast, and the other ceremonies of the Hebrew faith.[55] Josephus ventured to challenge all who doubted this to look around in their own neighborhood or even their own houses, and see if they would not find his assertion confirmed.[56] The residence at Rome and access to the emperor permitted to several members of the family of Herod, who performed their own rites openly, contributed much to the impunity enjoyed by their religion.[57] Besides, the Sabbath prevailed as it were of necessity in localities where Jews resided. Their persistence in keeping their shops closed on that day, forced many of their neighbors to modify their own habits accordingly. Thus at Salonica it may be said that the Sabbath is observed to this day, the Jewish population being rich and numerous enough to make the law, and by the cessation of their own business to prescribe a day of repose.

Almost as much as the Jew, and often in company with him, was the Syrian an active instrument in the conquest of the West by the East.[58] They were sometimes confounded together, and Cicero thought he had discovered their common trait when he called them "nations born to be slaves."[59] It was that which insured to them the control of the future, for the future then belonged to the slaves of the earth. Not less characteristic of the Syrian, was his readiness, quickness, and the superficial clearness of his thought. The Syrian nature is like the passing imagery of the clouds. We see every moment certain outlines of graceful form, but they never become united into a complete design. In the darkness, by the flickering light of a lamp, the Syrian woman with her veil, her wistful eyes, and her infinite languor, causes a brief illusion. Afterwards, when we would analyse her beauty, it disappears; it cannot endure examination, and it lasts only three or four years. What is most charming in the Syrian race is the child of five or six years old, contrary to Greece, where the child was nothing, the youth inferior to the man, and the man to the ancient.[60] Syrian intelligence attracts us at first with its air of promptness and vivacity, but it lacks fixedness and solidity, something like that "golden wine" of Libanus which causes an agreeable excitement, but soon palls on the taste. The true gifts of God have something about them at once fine and strong, exciting and enduring. Greece is more appreciated to-day than ever before, and will be more and more continually.

Many of the Syrian emigrants who were attracted westward in the pursuit of fortune were more or less attached to Judaism. Others remained faithful to the worship of their own village,[61] that is, to the memory of some temple dedicated to a local "Jupiter"[62] who was ordinarily the Supreme Deity designated by some special title;[63] and they thus carried with them a kind of monotheism under the disguise of their strange divinities. At least in comparison with the perfectly distinct divine personalities of the Greek and Roman polytheism, the Syrian gods being mostly synonymes of the sun, were almost the brothers of the one Deity.[64] Like their long and enervating chants, these Syrian rites appeared less dry than the Latin and less empty than the Greek. The women acquired from them a mixture of ecstasy and voluptuousness. Those Syrian women were always strange creatures, disputed for by God and Satan, and oscillating between the saint and the demon. The saint of serious virtues, of heroic self-denial, of accomplished vows, belongs to other races and climes. The saint of vivid imaginings, of absolute entrancements, and of sudden devotion, is the saint of Syria. The demoniac of our Middle Age became the slave of Satan through baseness or crime; that of Syria was distracted by the ideal—the woman of wounded affections, who avenges herself by madness or refusal to speak, and who needs only a gentle word and kind look to restore her. Transported to the western world, the Syrian women acquired influence, sometimes by evil feminine arts, but oftener by real capacity and moral superiority. This happened in a special degree about a hundred and fifty years later, when the most important personages of Rome married Syrian wives, who at once acquired a great ascendency over affairs. The Mussulman woman of the present time, a noisy scold and foolish fanatic, existing for scarce anything but evil, and almost incapable of virtue, ought not to make us forget such as Julia Domna, Julia Mæsa, Julia Mamæa, and Julia Sœmia, who introduced into Rome a spirit of toleration and a mystical feeling in religion which were till then unknown. What is also well worthy of remark is, that the Syrian dynasty thus established was friendly to Christianity, and that Mamæa, and afterwards the Emperor Philip the Arabian,[65] passed for Christians. In the third and fourth centuries

Christianity was the predominant religion of Syria, and next to Palestine, Syria played the greatest part in its establishment.

It was especially at Rome that the Syrian in the first century exercised his penetrating activity. Intrusted with almost every kind of ordinary duty, guide, messenger, and letter-bearer, the *Syrus*[67] was admitted everywhere, bringing with him the language and manners of his own land.[68] He possessed neither the pride nor the philosophic loftiness of Europeans, much less their bodily vigor. Of weak frame, pale and often feverish, and not knowing how to eat or sleep at stated hours, after the fashion of our slower races; consuming little meat, and subsisting on onions and pumpkins; sleeping little and uneasily—the Syrian was habitually ailing and died young.[69] What did belong to him was humility, mildness, affability, and good-nature; no solidity of mind, but much that was agreeable; little sound sense, unless in driving a bargain; but an astonishing warmth and zeal, and a truly feminine seductiveness. Having never exercised any political functions, he was specially apt for religious movements. The poor Maronite, effeminate, humble, and destitute, has brought about the greatest of revolutions. His ancestor, the *Syrus* of Rome, was the most zealous messenger of the good news to all afflicted souls. Every year colonies of Syrians arrived in Greece, Italy, and Gaul, impelled by their natural taste for trade and small employments.[70] They could be recognised on board of the vessels by their numerous families, by the troops of pretty children nearly alike in age, and the mother with the childish air of a girl of fourteen keeping close to her husband's side, submissive and smiling, and scarcely superior to her oldest offspring.[71] The heads of this peaceful group are not very strongly marked. There is no Archimedes there, no Plato or Phidias. But this Syrian trader, now arrived at Rome, will be a kind and merciful man, charitable to his countrymen, and a friend to the poor. He will talk with the slaves, and reveal to them an asylum where those miserable beings, condemned by Roman severity to a most dreary solitude, may find some solace. The Greek and Latin races, made to be masters and to accomplish great actions, knew not how to make any advantage of an humble position.[72] The slave of those races passed his life in revolt and in plotting evil. The ideal slave of antiquity has every fault; he is gluttonous, mendacious, mischievous, and the natural enemy of his master.[73] He thus, as it were, proved his nobility of race; he was a constant protest against an unnatural position. The easy, good-natured Syrian did not trouble himself to protest; he accepted his degradation and sought to do the best he could with it. He conciliated the kind feelings of his master, ventured to converse with him, and studied how to please his mistress. This great agent of democracy was thus gnawing apart, mesh by mesh, the net of the ancient civilization. The old institutions based upon pride, inequality of races, and military valor, were lost. Weakness and humble condition were about to become advantageous, and helps to virtue.[74] The Roman nobility, the Greek wisdom, will struggle for three centuries more. Tacitus will approve the deportation of some thousands of these wretches—"small loss if they had perished!"[75] The Roman aristocracy will fret, will be provoked that this *canaille* should have its gods and institutions. But the victory is written in advance. The Syrian, the poor man who loves his fellows, who shares with them and associates with them, will carry the day. The Roman aristocracy must perish, and perish without pity.

To explain the revolution which is about to take place, we must take note of the political, social, moral, intellectual, and religious condition of the countries through which Jewish proselytism has thus opened furrows for the Christian preaching to sow the seed. Such an examination will show convincingly, I hope, that the conversion of the world to the Jewish and Christian ideas was inevitable, and will leave us astonished at only one thing—namely, that that conversion proceeded so slowly and commenced so late.

CHAPTER XVII.

STATE OF THE WORLD IN THE FIRST CENTURY.

THE political condition of the world was most melancholy. All power was concentrated at Rome and in the legions. The most shameful and degrading scenes were daily enacted. The Roman aristocracy, which had conquered the world, and which alone of all the people had any voice in public business under the Cæsars, had abandoned itself to a Saturnalia of the most outrageous wickedness the human race ever witnessed. Cæsar and Augustus, in establishing the imperial power, saw perfectly the necessities of the age. The world was so low in its political relations, that no other form of government was possible. Now that Rome had conquered numberless provinces, the ancient constitution, which was based upon the existence of a privileged patrician class, a kind of obstinate and malevolent *Tories*, could not continue.[1] But Augustus had signally neglected every suggestion of true policy, by leaving the future to chance. Destitute of any canon of hereditary succession, of any settled rules concerning adoption, and of any law regulating election, Cæsarism was like an enormous load on the deck of a vessel without ballast. The most terrible shocks were inevitable. Three times in a century, under Caligula, Nero, and Domitian, the greatest power that was ever united in one person fell into the hands of most extravagant and execrable men. Horrors were enacted which have hardly been surpassed by the monsters of the Mongol dynasties. In that fatal list of monarchs, one is reduced to apologizing for a Tiberius, who only attained thorough detestableness towards the close of his life; and for a Claudius, who was only eccentric, blundering, and badly advised. Rome became a school of vice and cruelty. It should be added that the vice came, in a great degree, from the East, from those parasites of low rank and those infamous men whom Egypt and Syria sent to Rome,[2] and who, profiting by the oppression of the true Romans, succeeded in attaining great influence over the wretches who governed. The most disgusting ignominies of the empire, such as the apotheosis of the emperors and their deification during life, came from the East, and particularly from Egypt, which was at that period one of the most corrupt countries on the face of the earth.[3]

However, the veritable Roman nature still survived, and nobility of soul was far from extinct. The lofty traditions of pride and virtue, which were preserved in a few families, attained the imperial throne with Nerva, and gave its splendor to the age of the Antonines, of which Tacitus is the elegant historian. An age in which such true and noble natures as those of Quintilian, Tacitus, and Pliny the Younger were produced, need not be wholly despaired of. The corruption of the surface did not extend to the great mass of seriousness and honor which existed in the better Roman society, and many examples are yet preserved of devotion to order, duty, peace, and solid integrity. There were in the noble houses admirable wives and sisters.[4] Was there ever a more touching fate than that of the young and chaste Octavia, the daughter of Claudius, and wife of Nero, remaining pure in the midst of infamy, and slain at twenty two years of age, without having known a single joy? The epithets "*castissimæ, univiræ*," are not at all rare in the inscriptions.[5] Some wives accompanied their husbands into exile,[6] and others shared their noble deaths.[7] The ancient Roman simplicity was not lost. The children were soberly and carefully brought up. The most noble ladies worked with their own hands at woollen fabrics,[8] and the excesses of the toilet were almost unknown in the higher families.[9]

The excellent statesmen who, so to speak, sprang from the earth under Trajan, were not improvised. They had served in preceding reigns; but they had enjoyed but little influence, and had been cast into the shade by the freedmen and favorite slaves of the Emperor. Thus we find men of the first ability occupying high posts under Nero. The framework was good. The accession of bad emperors, disastrous as it was, could not change at once the general tendency of affairs, and the principles of the government. The empire, far from being in its decay, was in the full strength of vigorous youth. Decay will come, but two centuries later; and, strange to say, under much more worthy monarchs. In its political phase, the situation was analogous to that of France, which, deprived by the Revolution of any established rule for the succession-has yet passed through so many perilous changes without greatly injuring its internal organization or its national strength. In its moral aspect, the period under consideration may be compared to the eighteenth century, an epoch entirely corrupt, if we form our judgment from the memoirs, manuscripts, literature, and anecdotes of the time, but in which, nevertheless, some families maintained the greatest austerity of morals.[10]

Philosophy joined hands with the better families of Rome, and resisted nobly. The Stoic school produced the lofty characters of Cremutius Cordus, Thraseas, Arria, Helvidius Priscus, Annæus Cornutus, and Musonius Rufus, admirable masters of aristocratic virtue. The rigidity and exaggeration of this school arose from the horrible cruelty of the Cæsars. The continual thought of a good man was how to inure himself to suffering, and prepare himself for death.[11] Lucan, in bad taste, and Persius with superior talent, both gave utterance to the loftiest sentiments of a great soul. Seneca the philosopher, Pliny the Elder, and Papirius Fabianus, kept up a high standard of science and philosophy. Every one did not yield; there were a few wise men left. Too often, however, they had no resource but death. The ignoble portions of humanity at times got the upper hand. Then madness and cruelty ruled the hour, and made of Rome a veritable hell.[12]

The government, although so fearfully unstable at Rome, was much better in the provinces. At a distance the shocks which agitated the capital were hardly felt. In spite of its defects, the Roman administration was far superior to the kingdoms and commonwealths it had supplanted. The time for sovereign municipalities had long gone by. Those little States had destroyed themselves by their egotism, their jealousies, and their ignorance or neglect of individual freedom. The ancient life of Greece, all struggle, all external, no longer satisfied any one. It had been glorious in its day, but that brilliant democratic Olympus of demi-gods had lost its freshness, and become dry, cold, unmeaning, vain superficial, and lacking in both head and heart. Hence the success of the Macedonian rule, and afterwards of the Roman. The empire had not yet fallen into the error of excessive centralization. Until the time of Diocletian, the provinces and cities enjoyed much liberty. Kingdoms almost independent existed in Palestine, Syria, Asia Minor, Lesser Armenia, and Thrace, under the protection of Rome. These kingdoms became factious after Caligula, only because the profound policy of Augustus concerning them was diverged from in succeeding reigns.[13] The numerous free cities were governed according to their own laws, and had the legislative power and magistracy of autonomic States. Until the third century their municipal decrees commenced with the formula, "The Senate and People of ———".[14] The theatres were not simply places for scenic amusement, but were foci of opinion and discussion. Most of the towns were, in different ways, little commonwealths. The municipal spirit was very strong.[15] They had lost only the power to declare war, a fatal power which made the world a field of carnage. "The benefits conferred by Rome upon mankind," were the theme of adulatory addresses everywhere, to which, however, it would be unjust to deny some sincerity.[16] The doctrine of "the Peace of Rome,"[17] the idea of a vast democracy organized under Roman protection, lay at the bottom of all political speculations.[18] A Greek rhetorician displays vast erudition in proving that Roman glory should be claimed by all the branches of the Hellenic race as a common patrimony.[19] In regard to Syria, Asia Minor, and Egypt, we may say that the Roman conquest did not destroy any of their liberties. Those nations had either been already long dead to political life, or had never enjoyed it.

Finally, in spite of the extortions of governors and of the violence which is inseparable from despotic sway, the world had in many respects never been so well off. An administration coming from a remote centre was so great an advantage, that even the rapacious Prætors of the latter days of the Republic had failed to render it unpopular. The Julian law had also narrowed down the scope of abuses and peculations. The follies or cruelties of the emperor, except under Nero, reached only the Roman aristocracy and the immediate followers of the prince. Never had men who did not care to busy themselves about politics been able to live more at ease. The ancient republics, in which every one was compelled to take part in the factions, were very uncomfortable places of residence.[20] There was continually going on some disorganization or proscription. But under the empire the time seemed made expressly for great proselytisms which should overrule both the quarrels of neighborhoods and the rivalry of dynasties. Attacks on liberty were much more frequently owing to the remnants of the provincial or communal authority than to the Roman administration.[21] Of this truth we have had and shall have many occasions to take note.

For those of the conquered countries where political privileges had been unknown for ages, and which lost nothing but the right of destroying themselves by continual wars, the empire was such an era of prosperity and well-being as they had never before experienced; and we may add, without being paradoxical, that it was also for them an era of liberty.[22] On the one hand, a freedom of commerce and industry, of which the Grecian States had no conception, became possible. On the other hand, the new *régime* could not but be favorable to freedom of thought. This freedom is always greater under a monarchy than under the rule of jealous and narrow-minded citizens, and it was unknown in the ancient republics. The Greeks accomplished great things without it, thanks to the incomparable force of their genius; but we must not forget that Athens had a complete inquisition.[23] The Chief Inquisitor was represented by the archon, and the Holy Office by the royal portico whence issued the accusations of "impiety." These were numerous, and it is in this kind of causes that we find the Attic orators most frequently engaged. Not only philosophic heresies, such as the denial of a God or of Providence, but the slightest infractions of the rules of municipal worship, the preaching of foreign religions, and the most puerile departures from the absurdly strict legislation concerning the mysteries, were crimes punishable by death. The gods at whom Aristophanes scoffed on the stage, could sometimes slay. They slew Socrates, and almost Alcibiades; and they persecuted Anaxagoras, Protagoras, Theodorus, Diagoras of Melos, Prodicus of Ceos, Stilpo, Aristotle, Theophrastus, Aspasia, and Euripides.[24] Liberty of thought was, in fact, the fruit of the kingdoms which arose out of the Macedonian conquests. An Attalus and a Ptolemy first allowed the thinker those liberties which none of the old republics had permitted. The Roman empire continued the same policy. There was, indeed, under the empire more than one arbitrary decree against the philosophers, but it was always called forth by their entering into political schemes.[25] We may search in vain the Roman law before Constantine for a single passage against freedom of thought; and the history of the imperial government furnishes no instance of a prosecution for entertaining an abstract doctrine. No scientific man was molested. Men like Galen, Lucan, and Plotinus, who would have gone to the stake in the Middle Age, lived tranquilly under the protection of the law. The empire inaugurated liberty in this respect; it extinguished the despotic sovereignty of the family, the town, and the tribe, and replaced or tempered it by that of the State. But despotic power is the more vexatious the narrower its sphere of action. The old republics and the Feudal system oppressed individuals much more than did the state. The empire at times persecuted Christianity most severely, but at least it did not arrest its progress.[26] Republics, however, would have overcome the new faith. Even Judaism would have smothered it, but for the pressure of Roman authority. The Roman magistrates were all that hindered the Pharisees from destroying Christianity at the outset.[27]

Expanded ideas of universal brotherhood and a sympathy with humanity at large, derived for the most part from the Stoic philosophy,[28] were the results of the broader system of authority and the less confined education which had now assumed control.[29] Men dreamed of a new era and of new worlds.[30] The public wealth was great, and notwithstanding the imperfect economic doctrines of the day, was considerably diffused. Morals were not what is often imagined. At Rome, it is true, every kind of vice paraded itself with revolting cynicism,[31] and the public shows in particular had introduced a frightful degree of corruption. Some countries, Egypt for example, had sounded the lowest depths of infamy. But in most of the provinces there was a middle class in which good-nature, conjugal fidelity, probity, and the domestic virtues, were generally practised.[32] Is there anywhere an ideal of domestic life among the honest citizens of small towns more charming than that presented to us by Plutarch? What kindness, what gentle manners, what chaste and amiable simplicity![33] Chæronea was evidently not the only place where life was so pure and innocent.

The popular tendencies were yet somewhat cruel even outside of Rome; perhaps as the remnant of antique manners, which were everywhere sanguinary, perhaps as the special effect of Roman severity. But a marked improvement in this respect was taking place. What pure or gentle sentiment, what impression of melancholy tenderness had not received its finest expression from the pens of Virgil and Tibullus? The world was losing its ancient rigidity and acquiring softness and sensibility. Maxims of common humanity became current,[34] and the Stoics earnestly taught the abstract notions of equality and the rights of man.[35] Woman, under the dotal system of Roman law, was becoming more and more her own mistress. The treatment of slaves was improving;[36]

Seneca admitted his to his own table.[37] The slave was no longer that grotesque and malignant creature which Latin comedy introduced to excite laughter, and which Cato recommended to be treated as a beast of burden.[38] The times had changed. The slave was now morally equal to his master, and was admitted to be capable of virtue, fidelity, and devotion, of which he had given abundant proofs.[39] Prejudices of birth were becoming effaced.[40] Many just and humane laws were enacted, even under the worst emperors.[41] Tiberius was a skilful financier, and established upon an excellent basis a system of public credit.[42] Nero introduced into the taxation, which had previously been unequal and barbarous some improvements which throw discredit even on our own times.[43] The progress of the theory of legislation was also considerable, although the death-penalty was still absurdly general. Charity to the poor, and sympathy for all, became virtues.[44]

The theatre was a most insupportable scandal to decent citizens, and one of the chief causes which excited the antipathy of Jews and Judaized people of every kind against the profane civilization of the age. To their eyes, those vast inclosures were gigantic *cloacæ* in which all the vices were collected. While the lower benches applauded, in the upper were often displayed disgust and horror. The gladiatorial spectacles established themselves with difficulty in the provinces. At least the Hellenic provinces repelled them, and generally adhered to the ancient Grecian games.[45] Bloody sports always retained in the East distinct marks of Roman origin.[46]

The Athenians having one day debated the introduction of these barbarous sports in imitation of Corinth,[47] a philosopher arose and moved that they should first raze to the ground the altar of Pity.[48] Thus it happened that one of the most profound sentiments of the primitive Christians, and one, too, which produced the most extended results, was detestation of the theatre, the stadium, the gymnasium ; that is to say, of all the public resorts which gave its distinctive character to a Grecian or Roman city. Ancient civilization was a public civilization. Its affairs were transacted in the open air in presence of the assembled citizens. It was the inversion of our system, in which life is private, and is inclosed within the walls of our dwellings. The theatre was the offspring of the *agora* and the *forum*. The anathema against the theatre rebounded against society in general. A bitter rivalry grew up between the Church and the public games. The slave, driven away from the latter, betook himself to the former. I have never seated myself in those melancholy arenas, which are always the best-preserved relics of an ancient city, without seeing in imagination the struggle of the two systems. Here, the honest and humble citizen, already half a Christian, sitting in the first row, covering his face and going away ashamed; there, the philosopher, rising suddenly and openly reproaching the assemblage with its baseness.[49] These examples were rare in the first century, but the protest was beginning to make itself heard,[50] and the theatre was receiving more and more reprobation.[51]

The laws and administrative regulations of the empire were as yet a veritable chaos. Central despotism, municipal and provincial franchises, administrative caprice and the self-will of commonalties, jostled each other in the strangest manner. But religious liberty was a gainer by these conflicts. The complete unity of administration, which was established at about the time of Trajan, proved much more fatal to the rising faith than the irregular, careless, and poorly-policed system of the Cæsars.

Institutions of public charity, founded on the doctrine that the State owes paternal duties to its subjects, were not much developed until after the reigns of Nerva and Trajan.[52] A few traces of them, however, are found in the first century.[53] There were already charities for children,[54] distributions of food to the poor, fixed rates for the sale of bread with indemnity provided for the tradesmen, precautions in regard to supply of provisions, assurance against pirates, and orders enabling persons to buy grain at reduced prices.[55] All the emperors, without exception, manifested the greatest solicitude on these topics, which may indeed be called subordinate, but which at certain times rule everything else. In remote antiquity there was not much need of public charity. The world was young and strong, and required no hospital. The good and simple Homeric morality, according to which the guest and the beggar are sent by Jove, is the morality of strong and cheerful youth.[56] Greece, in her classic age, enounced the most touching maxims of pity and benevolence, without connecting with them any conception of sadness or social misfortune.[57] Man was yet at that epoch healthy and happy; how could he look forward and provide against evil days!

But in respect to institutions for mutual assistance, the Greeks were far in advance of the Romans.[58] Not a solitary liberal or benevolent arrangement was ever devised by that cruel aristocracy which, as long as the republic endured, wielded such an oppressive authority.

At the epoch we are now considering, the colossal fortunes and luxury of the nobility, the vast agglomerations of people at certain points, and above all the peculiar and implacable hard-heartedness of the Romans, had caused the rise of pauperism.[59] The indulgence of some of the emperors to the Roman mob had aggravated this evil. The public distributions of corn encouraged idleness and vice, and provided no remedy for misery. In this, as in many other things, the Oriental world was superior. The Jews possessed real institutions of charity. The Egyptian temples seem to have sometimes had a fund for the poor.[60] The male and female colleges of the Serapeum at Memphis were also to some extent charitable establishments.[61] The terrible crisis through which humanity was passing in the capital was scarcely perceived in distant provinces where the mode of life remained simple. The reproach of having poisoned the whole earth, the likening of Rome to a harlot who had made the earth drunk with the wine of her fornication, was in many respects just.[62] The provinces were better than Rome; or more properly, the impure elements which gathered together from all quarters into the metropolis, made her a sink of iniquity, in which the old Roman virtues were smothered, and the good seed brought from elsewhere grew with difficulty.

The intellectual condition of the different parts of the empire was quite unsatisfactory. In this respect there had been a real decline. High mental culture is not as independent of political circumstances as is private morality. Besides, the progress of high mental culture and that of morality are not exactly parallel. Marcus Aurelius was certainly a better man than all the old Greek philosophers. Yet his positive notions in regard to the realities of the universe were inferior to those of Aristotle and Epicurus; for he believed at times in dreams and omens, and in the gods as complete and distinct personalities. The world was then undergoing a moral improvement and an intellectual decline. From Tiberius to Nerva this decline is very perceptible. The Greek genius, with a force, originality, and copiousness which have never been equalled, had in the course of several centuries created the rational encyclopædia, the normal discipline of the mind. This wonderful movement commenced with Thales, and the earliest Ionian schools (600 years before Christ), and was stopped about B.C. 120. The last survivors of these five centuries of intellectual progress, Apollonius of Perga, Eratosthenes, Aristarchus, Hero, Archimedes, Hipparchus, Chrysippus, Carneades, and Panetius, had departed, leaving no successors. Only Posidonius and a few astronomers kept up the ancient reputation of Alexandria, Rhodes, and Pergamus. Greece, however fertile in creative genius, had not extracted from her science and philosophy any system of popular instruction or remedy against superstition. Possessing admirable scientific institutes, Egypt, Asia Minor, and Greece herself were at the same time given over to the most senseless credulity. But if science does not succeed in getting the upper hand over superstition, superstition will extinguish science. Between these two opposing forces, the combat is to the death.

Italy, while adopting Greek science, had for a time inspired it with a new sentiment. Lucretius had furnished the model of the great philosophic poem, at once a hymn and a blasphemy, by turns imparting serenity and despair, and imbued with that profound view of human destiny which was always wanting in the Greeks, who, childlike as they were, took life so gaily that they never dreamed of cursing the Gods, or of accusing nature of injustice and treachery towards man. Graver thoughts occurred to the Latin philosophers. But Rome as well as Greece failed to make science the basis of popular education. While Cicero, with exquisite taste, was transferring into a polished form the ideas he borrowed from the Greeks; while Lucretius was composing his wonderful poem; while Horace was avowing his frank infidelity in the ear of Augustus, who expressed no surprise; while Ovid, one of the most pleasing poets of the time, was treating venerable traditions after the manner of an elegant free-thinker; and while the great Stoics were developing the practical results of Greek philosophy, the silliest chimeras met with full credence, and the belief in the marvellous was unbounded. Never were people more ready for prophecies and prodigies.[63] The eclectic deism of Cicero,[64] perfected by Seneca,[65] remained the creed of a few cultivated minds, but exercised no influence on the age.

Down to Vespasian, the empire had nothing which can be called public instruction.[66] What it afterwards possessed was confined to a few dry grammatical exercises, and the general decline became rather accelerated than retarded. The last days of the republic and the reign of Augustus, witnessed one of the most brilliant literary epochs that has ever occurred. But after the death of the great emperor, the decline may as properly be called sudden as rapid. The intelligent and cultivated society in which had moved Cicero, Atticus, Cæsar, Mæcenas, Agrippa, and Pollio, had vanished like a dream. Doubtless enlightened men remained; men familiar with the learning of their day, and occupying high positions, such as Lucilius, Pliny, Gallio, and the Senecas, with the literary circle which gathered around them. The body of Roman law, which is codified philosophy, which is Greek rationalism reduced to practice, continued its majestic growth. The noble Roman families had preserved a basis of purer religion and a horror of what they called "superstition."[67] The geographers, Strabo and Pomponius Mela; the physician and encyclopædist, Celsus; the botanist, Dioscorides; the jurist, Sempronius Proculus—were able and liberal men. But these were exceptions; leaving out a few thousand enlightened persons, the world was immersed in profound ignorance of the laws of nature.[68] Credulity was a universal malady.[69] Literary culture was dwindling into a mere rhetorical shell, which contained no kernel. The essentially moral and practical turn which philosophy had taken, banished profound speculation. Human knowledge, if we except geography, made no advances. The schooled and lettered amateur replaced the creative and original student. Here was felt the fatal influence of the great defect in Roman character. That race, so mighty to command, was secondary in genius. The most cultivated Romans, Lucretius, Vitruvius, Celsus, Pliny, Seneca, were, so far as regards positive knowledge, the pupils of the Greeks. Too often, indeed, it was second rate Greek learning which they reproduced in a second-rate style.[70] Rome never possessed a great scientific school. Charlatanism reigned there almost supreme. Finally the Latin literature, which certainly displayed some admirable qualities, flourished during only a brief period, and never made its way beyond the occidental world.[71]

Greece fortunately continued faithful to her genius. The prodigious splendor of Roman power had dazzled and stunned, but not annihilated it. In fifty years more we shall find her reconquering the world, giving again her laws to thought, and sharing the throne of the Antonines. But at this period Greece herself was passing through one of her intervals of lassitude. Genius was scarce, and original science inferior to what it had been in preceding ages, and to what it would be in the following. The Alexandrian school, which had been declining for nearly two centuries, but still at Cæsar's era could furnish a Sosigenes, was now dumb.

The space from the death of Augustus to the accession of Trajan must, then, be classed as a period of temporary degradation for the human intellect. The ancient world had by no means uttered its last word, but the bitter trials through which it was passing took from it both voice and courage. When brighter days return, and genius shall be delivered from the terrible sway of the Cæsars, she will take heart again. Epictetus, Plutarch, Dionysius the golden-mouthed, Quintilian, Tacitus, Pliny the Younger, Juvenal, Rufus of Ephesus, Aretæus, Galen, Ptolemy, Hypsicles, Theon, and Lucan, will renew the palmy days of Greece; not that inimitable Greece which existed but once for the simultaneous delight and despair of all who love the beautiful, but a

Greece still fruitful and abounding, which will mingle her own gifts with the Roman genius, and produce works of novelty and originality yet able to charm the world.

The general taste was bad. Great Greek writers were wanting; and the Latin writers extant, except the satirist Persius, are of an ordinary type. Excessive declamation spoiled everything. The rule by which the public judged intellectual productions was nearly the same as it is now. Only brilliancy was looked for. Language ceased to be the simple vestment of thought, deriving all its elegance from its perfect adaptation to the idea sought to be expressed. Language began to be cultivated for its own sake. The aim of an author in his writings was to display his own talent. The excellence of a recitation or public reading was measured by the number of passages which excited applause. The cardinal principle that in art everything should serve as ornament, but that anything inserted expressly as ornament is bad, was entirely forgotten. It was a very literary period, as they say. Hardly anything was talked of but eloquence and style; and after all, nearly everybody wrote incorrectly, and there was not a solitary orator. The true orator and writer are not those who make speaking or writing their trade. At the theatre, the principal actor absorbed attention, and dramas were suppressed in order that brilliant passages might be recited. The literary fashion of the day was a silly *dilettantism*, a foolish vanity which led everybody to affect talent, and which did not stop short of the imperial throne. Hence extreme insipidity and interminable "Theseids," or dramas written to be read in literary circles; and hence a dreary desert of poetical commonplace, which can be compared only to the epics and classic tragedies of sixty years ago.

Stoicism itself could not escape this disease, or at least it did not before Epictetus and Marcus Aurelius succeeded in clothing its doctrines in an elegant vesture. What strange productions are those tragedies of Seneca, in which the loftiest sentiments are expressed in the most wearisome style of literary quackery! indices at once of moral advancement and of an irremediable decline of taste. We are compelled to say the same of Lucan. The tension of mind which resulted naturally from the eminently tragic character of the epoch, gave rise to a species of inflation, in which state the only anxiety was to win applause by brilliant sentences. Something analogous to this happened amongst us during the Revolution; and the most terrible crisis which ever existed produced scarcely anything but a schoolmaster's literature, crammed with declamation. We must not, however, stop at this point. New ideas are sometimes expressed with much ostentation. The style of Seneca is sober, simple, and pure, in comparison with that of St. Augustine. But we forgive the latter his detestable style and insipid conceits, in return for his noble sentiments.

At all events this cultivation, which was in many respects noble and superior, did not extend to the people. This would have been a minor deprivation, if the people had had at least some religious nourishment, something similar to that which the Church provides for the lowest grades of modern society. But religion was at a very low ebb in all parts of the empire. The wise policy of Rome had left unmolested the ancient forms of worship, prohibiting only those observances which were inhuman,[72] seditious, or injurious to others.[73] She had spread over them all a sort of official varnish, which gave them some general resemblance, and blended them, good and bad, together. Unfortunately these old creeds, though very diverse in origin, had one common characteristic. It was equally impossible for any and all of them to provide theological instruction, applied morality, edifying preaching, or a pastoral ministry productive of good among the people. The pagan temple was never what the synagogue and the Church were in their best days—that is, a common home, school, inn, hospital, and refuge for the poor.[74] It was only a chilly cell which the people seldom entered, and where they never learned anything.

The Roman worship was perhaps the least objectionable of those which were yet practised. In it, purity of soul and body was considered a part of religion.[75] By its gravity, its decency, and its austerity, this form of worship, leaving out a few extravagances similar to our Carnival, was far superior to the grotesque and sometimes absurd ceremonies which were secretly introduced by those seized with the mania for Oriental customs. Still, the affectation with which the Roman patricians distinguished "*religion*"—that is, their own rites—from those of foreigners, which they called "*superstition*," cannot but appear to us puerile enough.[76] All the pagan forms of worship were essentially superstitious The peasant who, in modern times, drops his penny into the contribution-box of a holy chapel, who invokes his saint in behalf of his oxen or his horses, or who drinks certain waters to cure certain diseases, is so far forth a pagan.

Nearly all our superstitions are the remains of a religion anterior to Christianity, and which it has not yet succeeded in completely rooting out. If one would find at this day the image of paganism, he may seek it in some secluded village lying hid in the recesses of some unfrequented province.

The heathen religions, having no guardians but the varying traditions of the people and a few greedy sacristans, could not fail to degenerate into adulation.[77] Augustus, although with some reserve, permitted worship of himself in some of the provinces during his lifetime.[78] Tiberius allowed the decision in his own presence, of the ignoble competition of the cities of Asia, which disputed among themselves the honor of building a temple to him.[79] The extravagant impieties of Caligula produced no reaction.[80] Outside of Juda ism there did not seem to be a single priest manly enough to resist such follies. Sprung for the most part from a primitive worship of the forces of nature, transformed over and over again by mixtures of all sorts, and by popular imagination, the pagan religions were confined by their antecedents. They could not afford what they never contained—the idea of real divinity, or popular instruction. The fathers of the Church occasion a smile when they animadvert upon the misdeeds of Saturn as a father, and of Jupiter as a husband. But it was certainly much more absurd to erect Jupiter (*i.e.* the atmosphere) into a moral divinity, who commanded, forbade, rewarded, and punished. In a state of society which was aspiring to possess a catechism, what could be done with a worship like that of Venus, which arose out of a social necessity of the early

Phœnician navigation in the Mediterranean sea, but became in time an outrage on what was becoming more and more regarded as the essence of religion.

On every side, in fact, an energetic tendency was manifested towards a monotheistic religion, which should provide divine command as a foundation of morality. There occurs in this manner a crisis when the naturalistic religions have become reduced to mere childishness and the grimaces of jugglers, and can no longer answer the wants of society. Then humanity requires a moral and philosophical religion. Buddhism and Zoroasterism responded to this requirement in India and Persia. Orphism and the Mysteries had attempted the same thing in the Grecian world without achieving a lasting success. At the period we are considering, the problem presented itself to the entire world with solemn universality and imposing grandeur.

Greece, it is true, formed an exception in this respect. Hellenism was much less worn out than the other religions of the empire. Plutarch, in his little Bœotian town, lived in the practice of Hellenism—tranquil, happy, and contented as a child, and with a religious conscience entirely undisturbed. In him we see no trace of a crisis; of distraction, uneasiness, or fear of impending revolution. But it was only the Greek mind which was capable of such childlike serenity. Always pleased with herself, proud of her past and of that brilliant mythology, all of whose sacred places lay within her borders, Greece did not participate in the internal disquiet of the world. She alone did not invite Christianity; she alone would have preferred to do without it, and she alone made pretensions of doing better.[81]

This was the result of the everlasting youthfulness, patriotic feeling, and unconquerable gaiety which always marked the genuine son of Hellas, and which to this day render the Greek a stranger to the profound anxieties which prey upon us. Hellenism was thus in a condition to attempt a *renaissance*, which no other religion existing at the time could hope for. In the second, third, and fourth centuries of our era, Hellenism had formed itself into an organized system of religion, by means of a welding, as it were, of the old mythology and the Grecian philosophy; and what with its miracle-working sages, its old writers elevated to the ranks of prophets, and its legends about Pythagoras and Apollonius, set up a competition with Christianity, which, though it ultimately failed, was yet one of the most dangerous obstacles that the religion of Jesus found in its way.

This attempt had not yet been made in the time of the Cæsars. The first philosophers who endeavored to bring about the alliance between philosophy and paganism, were Euphrates of Tyre, Apollonius of Tyana, and Plutarch, at the close of the century. Euphrates of Tyre is but little known to us. Legend has so completely disguised the plot of the real life of Apollonius, that it is impossible to say whether he should be considered the founder of a religion, a sage, or a charlatan. As to Plutarch, he was not so much an original thinker and innovator as a moderate reformer, who wished to bring the world to one mind by rendering philosophy a little timid and religion at least one-half rational. He has nothing of the character of Porphyry or Julian.

The attempts of the Stoics at allegorical exegesis were

very feeble.[82] Mysteries like those of Bacchus, in which the immortality of the soul was taught through graceful symbols,[83] were confined to certain localities and had no extended influence. Disbelief in the official religion was general in the enlightened class[84] Those public men who made the greatest pretension of upholding it, expended their wit upon it freely in moments of leisure.[85] The immoral doctrine was openly propounded, that the religious fables were only of use in governing the people, and ought to be maintained for that purpose.[86] The precaution was useless, for the faith of the people themselves was shaken to the foundation.[87]

After the accession of Tiberius, a religious reaction was perceptible. It would seem that society was shocked at the avowed infidelity of the Augustan age. The way was prepared for the unlucky attempt of Julian, and all the superstitions were reinstated for reasons of state-policy.[88] Valerius Maximus affords the first example of a writer of low rank coming to the relief of cornered theologians; of a dirty, venal pen put to the service of religion.

But the foreign rites profited the most by this reaction. The serious movement in favor of the rehabilitation of the Greco-Roman worship did not develop itself until the second century. At first, the classes troubled by religious misgivings were attracted towards the Oriental forms.[89] Isis and Serapis were more in favor than ever.[90] Impostors of all sorts thaumaturgists and magicians, profited by the popular mood, and, as ordinarily takes place when the state-religion is enfeebled, swarmed on every side.[91] We need only refer to the real or fictitious systems of Apollonius of Tyana, Alexander of Abonoticus, Perigrinus, and Simon of Gitto.[92] Even these errors and chimeræ were the cry of a world in labor; were the fruitless essays of human society in search ot the truth, and sometimes in its convulsive efforts unearthing monstrous deformities destined to speedy oblivion.

On the whole, the middle of the first century was one of the worst epochs of ancient history. Grecian and Roman society had declined from its former condition, and was far behind the ages which were to follow. The greatness of the crisis revealed a strange and secret process going on. Life seemed to have lost its motives; suicide became common.[93] Never had an age presented so dire a struggle between good and evil. The powers of evil were a terrible despotism which delivered the world to the hands of monsters and madmen, corruption of morals arising from the importation of Oriental vices, and the want of a pure religion and decent public instruction. The powers ot good were on the one side, philosophy fighting with bared breast against tyranny, defying the monsters ot oppression, and three or four times proscribed in half a century (under Nero, Vespasian, and Domitian);[94] on the other side, the struggles of popular virtue, the legitimate longings for a better religion, the tendency towards confraternities and monotheistic creeds, and the recognition of the lower classes which occurred chiefly under cover of Judaism and Christianity. These two great protests were far from being accordant. The philosophic party and the Christian party were not acquainted with each other, and had so little perception of their common interest that when the philo sophers came into power by the accession of Nerva, they were far from being favorable to Christianity. In truth, the aim of the Christians was much more radical. The Stoics, when they became masters of the empire, reformed it, and presided over a hundred of the happiest years in the history of man. The Christians, when they became masters of the empire, ended by destroying it. The heroism of the latter ought not to make us unmindful of that of the former. Christianity was always unjust towards pagan virtues, and made it her business to decry the very men who had fought against the same common enemy. There was as much grandeur in the struggle of philosophy in the first century as in that of Christianity; but how unequal has been the recompense. The martyr who overturned idols with his foot lives in pious legend. Why are not the statues of Annæus Cornutus, who declared in presence of Nero that the emperor's writings would never be worth those of Chrysippus[95]—of Helvidius Priscus, who told Vespasian to his face, "It is thine to murder—it is mine to die!"—[96] of Demetrius the Cynic, who answered an enraged Nero, "You may menace me with death; but nature threatens you"[97]—placed amongst those of the world's heroes whom all love and to whom every one pays homage? Is humanity so strong in her battle with vice and depravity, that any school of virtue can repel the aid of others, and maintain that itself alone has the right to be brave, lofty, and resigned?

CHAPTER XVIII.

RELIGIOUS LEGISLATION OF THE PERIOD.

During the first century of the Christian era, the empire, while manifesting more or less hostility to the religious innovations which were imported from the East, did not declare open war against them. The doctrine of a state-religion was not clearly defined or vigorously upheld. At different epochs under the republic, foreign rites had been proscribed, especially those of Sabazius, Isis, and Serapis.[1] But those mysterious systems presented such irresistible attractions to the common people, that the proscription proved unavailing.[2]

When (A. U. C. 535) the demolition of the temple of Isis and Serapis was decreed, not a workman could be found to commence it, and the consul himself had to set the example by breaking down the doors with an axe.[3] It is evident that the Latin creed was no longer satisfying to the masses; and we may suppose with good reason that it was for the purpose of gratifying the popular instincts that the rites of Isis and Serapis were reëstablished by Cæsar.[4]

That great man, with the profound and liberal intuition which characterized him, had shown himself favorable to entire freedom of conscience.[5] Augustus was more attached to the national religion.[6] He had an antipathy to the Oriental creeds,[7] and prohibited the spread of even the Egyptian rites in Italy;[8] but he allowed every system, and the Jewish in particular, to enjoy freedom and supremacy in its own country.[9] He exempted the Jews from all observances conflicting with their conscience, especially from civil duties on the Sabbath.[10] Some of his officers manifested a less tolerant spirit, and would willingly have prevailed on him to become a persecutor in the interest of the Latin form of worship;[11] but he does not appear to have yielded to their mischievous counsel. Josephus, whom we may, however, suspect of some exaggeration, declares that Augustus even went so far as to present a gift of consecrated vases to the service of the temple at Jerusalem.[12]

Tiberius Cæsar was the first of the emperors who definitely adopted the principle of a state-religion, and who enforced strict precautions against the Jewish and Oriental propaganda.[13] It must be borne in mind that the emperor was also "*Pontifex Maximus*," and that in protecting the ancient Roman worship he was performing an official duty. Caligula revoked the Tiberian edicts,[14] but his supervening lunacy prevented any further results. Claudius seems to have carried out the Augustan policy. At Rome he strengthened the Latin ceremonies, showed considerable dislike to the advance of foreign religions,[15] enforced rigorous measures against the Jews,[16] and implacably persecuted the religious confraternities.[17] In Judea, on the contrary, he treated the natives of the country liberally.[18] The favor enjoyed at Rome by the family of Agrippa under the two reigns just mentioned, secured to their co-religionists a powerful protection in all cases not coming within the regulations of the Roman police.

The emperor Nero troubled himself but little about religion.[19] His cruelties towards the Christians were the mere outcrops of his natural ferocity, not the results of legislative policy.[20] The instances of persecution cited in the Roman annals of this period emanated rather from the authority of the family than from that of the Government,[21] and happened only in some noble houses of Rome, where the ancient traditions of domestic rule had been preserved.[22] The provinces were entirely free to adhere to their own rites, on the sole condition of not interfering with those of others.[23] Provincials residing at Rome were allowed the same privileges so long as they avoided anything which occasioned public scandal.[24] The only two religions against which the empire made war in the first century, were Druidism and Judaism; and each of these was, in truth, a fortress wherein was entrenched a distinct and turbulent nationality. Most men were convinced that the profession of Judaism implied hatred of the civil institutions of the empire and indifference to the welfare of the state.[25] When Judaism assumed the condition of a mere individual or private system of religious belief, it was not persecuted.[26] The rigorous measures which were put in force against the worship of Serapis, were perhaps suggested by the monotheistic character[27] which caused it sometimes to be confounded in public estimation with the Jewish and the Christian religions.[28]

It appears, then, that no established legislation prohibited in the apostolic age the profession of monotheistic creeds.[29] The sectaries were always under *surveillance* down to the accession of the Syrian emperors; but it was not until Trajan's time that they were systematically persecuted, as being intolerant and hostile towards other sects, and as impliedly denying the authority of the state. In a word, the only phase of religious belief against which the Roman empire declared war was theocracy. Its own principle was that of a purely secular organization. It did not admit that religion could have any civil or political connexions or consequences. Above all it would not admit of any association within the state and independent of the state. This point it is essential to remember. It was in truth the root from which sprang all the persecutions. The law concerning the confraternities was in a much greater degree than religious intolerance, the fatal cause of the cruelties which disgraced the reigns of the most liberal emperors.

The Greeks had led the way for the Romans, as well in matters relating to private associations as in all other results of thought and refinement. The Greek ηρκνοι or θιατοι of Athens, Rhodes, and the Islands of the Archipelago were useful societies for mutual assistance in the way of loans, fire assurance, common religious observances, and harmless amusement.[30] Each society had its rules carved on a *stela*, its archives, its common fund, provided by both voluntary contributions and assessments. The members met together to celebrate the festivals and to hold banquets, where cordiality reigned supreme.[31] A brother needing money could borrow from the treasury. Women were admitted into these associations, and had a president for themselves. The meetings were held in secret, and under strict rules for the preservation of order. They took place, it seems, in inclosed gardens, surrounded by porticoes or small buildings, and in the centre was erected an altar for the sacrifices.[32] Each association had its officers,[33] selected by lot for one year, according to the usage of the ancient Greek democracies, and from which the Christian "clergy" may have derived its name.[34] The presiding officer only was elected by vote. These officers passed the candidate through a kind of examination, and were required to certify that he was "*holy, pious, and good.*"[35]

There occurred in the two or three centuries which preceded the Christian era, a movement in favor of these little religious clubs, almost as marked as that which in the middle age produced so many religious orders and subdivisions of orders. In the island of Rhodes alone there is record of nineteen, many of which bore the names of their founders, or reformers.[36] Some of them, particularly those of *Bacchus*, inculcated lofty doctrines, and sought in good faith to administer consolation to man.[37] If there yet remained in Greek society a little charity, piety, or good morals, it was due to the existence and freedom of these private devotional assemblies. They acted as it were concurrently with the public and official religion, the neglect of which was becoming more and more apparent day by day. At Rome associations of this nature met with more opposition, and found no less favor among the poorer classes.[38] The rules of Roman policy in regard to secret confraternities were first promulgated under the republic (B.C. 186) in the case of the Bacchanals. The Romans were by natural taste much inclined to associations,[39] and in particular to those of a religious character;[40] but these permanent congregations were displeasing to the patrician order, who controlled the municipal power,[41] and whose narrow conceptions of life admitted no other social group besides the family and the State. The most minute precautions were taken, such as the requirement of a preliminary authorization, the limiting of the number of members, and the prohibition against having a permanent *Magister sacrorum*, and a common fund raised by subscription.[42] The same anxiety was manifested on several occasions under the empire. The body of public law contained clauses authorizing all kinds of repression;[43] but it depended on the administrative power whether they should be enforced or not, and the proscribed religions often reappeared in a very few years after their proscription.[44] Foreign immigration, especially from Syria, unceasingly renewed the soil in which flourished the creeds so vainly doomed to extirpation.

It is astonishing to observe to what an extent a subject, seemingly so unimportant, occupied the greatest minds of that age. It was one of the chief tasks of Cæsar and Augustus to prevent the formation of new clubs, and to destroy those already established.[45] A decree published under Augustus attempts to define positively the limits of the right of association, and whose limits were extremely narrow. The clubs (*collegia*) were to be merely for the purpose of celebrating funeral rites. They were permitted to meet no oftener than once a month; they were to attend only to the obsequies of deceased members, and under no pretext could they obtain an extension of their privileges.[46] The Empire resolved on performing the impossible. In logical sequence to its exaggerated notion of the state, it attempted to isolate the individual, to destroy every moral bond of fellowship among men, and to combat that legitimate longing of the poor to press closer together in some little refuge, as it were to keep each other warm. In ancient Greece the "*city*" was tyrannical, but it offered in exchange for its oppression so much amusement, enlightenment, and glory, that none thought of complaining. The citizen submitted quietly to its wildest caprices, and went to death for it with rapture. But the Roman empire was too vast to be one's country. It offered to every one great material advantages, but it gave no one anything to love. The insupportable melancholy of such a life appeared worse than death.

Accordingly, in spite of the efforts of statesmen, the confraternities multiplied immensely. They were precisely analogous to our confraternities of the middle age, with their patron saint and their common refectory. The great families might centre their pride in their ancient name, their country, and their traditions; but the humble and the poor had nothing but the *collegium*, and there they fastened all their affections. The text of the law shows us that all these clubs were composed of slaves,[47] veterans,[48] or obscure persons.[49] Within their precincts the free-born man, the freedman, and the slave, were equal.[50] They contained also many women.[51] At the risk of innumerable taunts and annoyances, and sometimes of severer penalties, men persisted in entering the *collegium*, where they lived in the bonds of a pleasant brotherhood, where they found mutual succor in time of need, and where they contracted obligations which endured even after death.[52]

The place of meeting usually had a *tetrastyle* (portico with four fronts), where were set up the rules of the club near the altar of its protecting divinity, and where stood a *triclinium* for the repasts.[53] These repasts indeed were looked forward to with impatience; they took place on the day sacred to the patron divinity, or on the birthdays of members who had contributed endowments.[54] Every one brought his little portion; one of the brotherhood furnished in turn the accessories of the feast, such as couches, table-furniture, bread wine, sardines, and hot water.[55] A slave, newly emancipated, owed his comrades an *amphora* of good wine.[56] A quiet air of enjoyment animated the repast; it was a positive rule that none of the business of the society should be discussed, in order that nothing might disturb the brief interval of enjoyment and repose which these poor souls were thus providing for themselves.[57] Every violent act or rude remark was punished by a fine.[58]

In appearance these clubs were simply associations for burial of the members.[59] But that object alone would have been enough to invest them with a moral character. In the Roman, as in our own time, and as in all ages when the religious sentiment is weakened, reverence for the tomb is nearly all that the masses retain. The poor man loved to believe that his body would not be cast into those horrible common trenches;[60] that his club would provide for his decent obsequies; that the brethren who should follow him on foot to the funeral pile would receive each a little *honorarium*[61] (about four cents) in testimony of respect for the departed.[62] The slave especially felt the need of an assurance that if his master denied him the privilege of the ordinary rites of sepulture, there would be a little band of friends who would perform "imaginary obsequies."[63] Hardly any was so humble or destitute as not to contribute a penny per month to the common fund to procure after his death a little urn in a *Columbarium*, with a slab of marble on which his name should be carved. Sepulture among the Romans was of extreme importance, being closely connected with the *sacra gentilitia*, or family rites. Persons interred together even contracted a sort of intimate fraternity or relationship.[64]

These facts show why Christianity for a long time presented itself at Rome as a kind of funeral association, and why the earliest Christian sanctuaries were the tombs of the martyrs.[65] If Christianity had been nothing more, it would not have provoked so much hostility. But it was much more. It provided a common treasury;[66] it considered itself a complete municipality; it believed in its own assured permanency and continuity. When one enters on a Saturday night one of the Greek churches in Turkey, for example that of St. Photinus at Smyrna, he is struck with the power of those associated religious memberships existing in the midst of a persecuting or hostile community. That irregular collection of buildings (church, presbytery, school, prison); these brethren passing to and fro in their little inclosed city of refuge; these newly-opened tombs, with the lighted lamps within; this odor of dampness, decay, and mould; this murmur of prayer; these appeals for alms—create a deadened and subdued atmosphere which may, to a stranger, appear sufficiently monotonous or repulsive, but which must be full of attraction to the affiliated members.

The societies, when once provided with a special authorization, possessed at Rome all the rights and privileges of civil persons.[67] This authorization was, however, granted only with many restrictions whenever the society possessed a treasury and sought to concern itself with anything but sepulture.[68] The pretext of religious observances, or the performance of vows in common, was guarded against by law, and formally declared to be one of the circumstances which attached to an assembly the character of crime;[69] and the crime was nothing less than high treason, at least as regards the person who called the meeting together.[70] Claudius even closed the taverns where the brethren met, and the small eating-houses where the poor were furnished cheaply with hot water and boiled meat.[71] Trajan and the more liberal monarchs continued to view all these societies with distrust.[72] Low rank was an essential condition without which the privilege of religious assemblage was never accorded, and even then it was granted most sparingly.[73] The lawyers who built up the Roman jurisprudence, so eminent in legal science, displayed their ignorance of human nature by opposing in every way, even with the menace of death, and by hedging in with all sorts of odious and puerile restrictions an everlasting need of the soul of man.[74] Like the authors of the "*Code Civil*," they regarded life with a wintry glance. If man's life consisted in amusing himself under the orders of his superiors, in munching his crust and tasting his puny pleasures in his rank under the eye of a taskmaster, all this would be well devised. But the retribution awarded to social systems which follow this false and contracted view, is first a melancholy disgust, and next a violent triumph of religious partisans. Never will man consent to breathe that icy air. He needs the little circle, the brotherhood where he may live and die amongst his fellows. Our vast abstract social organizations are not sufficient to supply all the social instincts which exist in man. Let him alone to attach his heart to something, to seek consolation where it may be found, to make brothers to himself, and to draw closer the ties of affection. Let not the cold arm of the state break into this kingdom of the soul, which is also the realm of liberty. True life and happiness will not spring up again in this world until that sad heritage left us by Roman law, our inveterate distrust of the *private assembly* (*collegium*), shall have disappeared. Association independent of the state, without injury to the state, is the great question of the future. The laws to be made in regard to associations will determine whether or not modern society will tend to the same destiny as ancient. One example should suffice. The Roman empire bound its own existence to the law relating to unlawful assemblages. Christians and barbarians, accomplishing in this respect the task of human conscience, broke down that law, and the empire having planted itself thereon, went down with it.

The Greek and Roman world, a secular and profane world, which possessed not the true conception of a minister of religion, which had neither divine law nor a revealed word, had here stumbled upon a problem which it was unable to solve. And we may add that if it had possessed a body of consecrated priests, a severe theology, and a strongly organized system of religion, it would not have created the secular state, or inaugurated the idea of a social system founded merely on reason, and on the human wants and natural relations of individuals.

The religious inferiority of the Greeks and Romans was the result of their political and intellectual superiority. The religious superiority of the Jews, on the contrary, has proved the cause of their political and philosophical inferiority. Judaism and primitive Christianity comprised the negation of the civil authority, or perhaps we may more accurately say the putting it under guardianship. Like the system of Mahomet, they established social order upon the basis of religion. When human affairs are controlled from that direction, great and universal proselytisms are made, apostles traverse the world from end to end, reforming and converting it; but in that manner are not constructed political institutions, national independence, a dynasty, a code, or a homogeneous people.

CHAPTER XIX.

THE FUTURE OF MISSIONS.

SUCH was the world which the Christian missionaries undertook to convert. It may now be readily perceived, it seems to me, that the enterprise was nothing impossible, and that its success was no miracle. The world was fermenting with moral longings to which the new religion answered admirably. Manners were losing their rudeness; a purer religion was looked for; and the notions of human rights and social improvement were everywhere gaining ground. On the other hand, credulity was extreme, and the number of educated persons very limited. To such a world, a few earnest apostles had only to present themselves, believing in one God and, as disciples of Jesus, imbued with the most beneficent moral doctrine the ears of men ever listened to, and they could not fail to be heard. The imaginary miracles which they mingled with their teaching would not hinder their success; for the number of those who would refuse to believe in the supernatural or miraculous was very small. If the apostles were humble and poor, so much the better. Humanity, in the condition it had then arrived at, could not be saved but by an effort springing from the masses. The ancient heathen religions were not susceptible of reform. The Roman state was what the state always will be—rigid, dry, and unyielding. In such a world perishing for want of love, the future is the property of him who can touch the living spring of popular devotion, to do which, Greek liberalism and the old Roman gravity were alike impotent.

The founding of Christianity is in this view the mightiest work which the men of the people have ever accomplished. At an early day, it is true, we find men and women of high rank at Rome joining themselves to the Church; and about the end of the first century, the examples of Flavius Clemens and Flavia Domitilla show that Christianity was penetrating almost within the palace of the Cæsars.[1] From the time of the first Antonines there were some rich men in the Christian communities; and near the close of the second century we find in them a few of the most distinguished persons of the empire.[2] But at the commencement, all or nearly all were of humble condition.[3] The noble and powerful of the earth were found in the earliest churches no more than in Galilee, following the footsteps of Jesus. Now in these great movements the beginning is the decisive moment. The glory of a religion belongs entirely to its founders. Religion, in fact, is an affair of faith, and to exercise faith is an easy thing; the master-work is to inspire it.

When we try to become acquainted with the marvellous origin of Christianity, we ordinarily regard matters by the standards of our own day, and are thus led into grave errors. The man of the people in the first century, especially in the Greek and Oriental countries, was in no wise similar to what he is amongst us, and at this day. Education had not then separated classes as widely as a present. The Mediterranean races, excepting the Latin tribes, which had lost all importance since the empire by the conquest of the world had become a mixture of vanquished nations, were less solid than moderns, and were more vivacious, excitable, imaginative, and quick of apprehension. The heavy materialism of our lower classes, and their apparent melancholy and dulness, which are in part the result of climate, and in part the sad legacy of the Dark Ages, and which stamp our poor with so distressful a physiognomy, did not operate upon the same classes in the early times. Although they were indeed very ignorant and credulous, they were not much more so than the rich and powerful of their day.

The establishment of Christianity cannot then be considered analogous to a popular movement in the present age, starting from the common people and at last commanding the assent of the educated class. This would with us be simply impossible. The founders of Christianity belonged to the common people in a certain sense, it is true. They were clothed in the same manner, lived poorly and frugally, and spoke without polish, or rather sought only to express their thoughts with energy. But they were inferior in intelligence to only a very small and constantly diminishing class of men, the survivors of the refined age of Cæsar and Augustus. In comparison with the philosophers who flourished from the time of Augustus to that of the Antonines, the first Christians were of course illiterate. In comparison with the great mass of their fellow-subjects, they were enlightened men. At times they were even looked on as free-thinkers, and the cry of the populace arose, "Down with the Atheists!"[4] This need not surprise us. The world was making startling progress in credulity. The two earliest strongholds of Gentile Christianity, Antioch and Ephesus, were of all the cities in the empire the most superstitious. The second and third centuries carried the love of the marvellous close to the borders of folly and madness.

Christianity arose outside of the official world, but not entirely beneath it. It was only in appearance, and as viewed according to worldly prejudices, that the disciples of Jesus were of an insignificant class. The worldling admires pride and strength, and wastes no affability on inferiors. Honor in his view consists in repelling insult. He despises the spirit which is meek, long suffering, humble, which yields its cloak also, and turns its cheek to the smiter. He is wrong; the meekness which he disdains is the mark of a loftier soul than his own; and the highest virtues dwell more contentedly with those who obey and serve than with those who command and enjoy. And this accords with reason; for power and pleasure, so far from aiding us in the practice of virtue, are hindrances in the way.

Jesus knew well that the heart of the common people was the great reservoir of the self-devotion and resignation by which alone the world could be saved. Hence he called the poor blessed, deeming it easier for them to be good than for others. The primitive Christians were essentially "poor;" it was their rightful title.[5] Even if a Christian possessed riches in the second and third centuries, he was poor in spirit, and classed himself among the poor, and was saved from persecution by claiming the privilege of the law concerning the "*collegia tenuiorum*."[6] It is true that all the Christians were not slaves or persons of low rank; but the social equivalent of a Christian was a slave, and the same terms were applied to both; while the cardinal virtues of the servile condition—gentleness, humility, and resignation—were aimed at by both alike. The heathen writers are unanimous on this point. All of them without exception recognise in the Christian the traits of servile character, such as indifference to public affairs, a subdued and melancholy air, a severe estimate of the vices of the age, and a settled aversion to the theatres, baths, gymnasia, and public games.[7]

In a word, the heathen were the world; the Christians were not of the world. They were a little flock apart, hated of the world, reproving its iniquities,[8] seeking to keep themselves "unspotted from the world."[9] The ideal of the Christian was wholly opposed to that of the worldling.[10] The sincere Christian loved to be humble, and cultivated the virtues of the poor and simple and self-abasing. He had also the defects which accompany these virtues. He considered as vain and frivolous many things which are not so. He belittled the universe, looking on beauty and art with a hostile or contemptuous eye. A system under which the Venus of Milo is only a stone idol is erroneous, or at the least partial; for beauty is almost the equivalent of goodness and of truth. When such ideas prevailed, the decay of art was inevitable. The Christian set no store by architecture, sculpture, or painting; he was too much of an idealist. He cared little for the advancement of science, for it was to him nothing but idle curiosity. Confounding the higher enjoyments of the soul, by which we touch upon the infinite, with vulgar pleasures, he denied himself all amusement. He pushed his virtues to excess.

Another law demands our attention at this period, which will not fail to have its influence upon the history we are to recount. The establishment of Christianity corresponds in time with the suppression of political life in the Mediterranean world. The subjects of the imperial sway had ceased to have a country. If any one sentiment was wholly wanting in the founders of the Church, it was patriotism. They were not even cosmopolites, citizens of the world; for the planet was to them only a place of exile, and they were idealists in the most absolute sense. The country is a composite object; it has body and soul. The soul is its recollections, customs, legends, misfortunes, hopes, and common regrets; the body its soil, race, language, mountains, rivers, characteristic productions. But never were any people so regardless of all this as the primitive Christians. Judea could not retain their affection. A few years passed, and they had forgotten the walks of Galilee. The glories of Greece and Rome were foolishness to them. The regions in which Christianity first rooted itself—Syria, Cyprus, and Asia Minor—could not recall the period when they had been free. Greece and Rome still possessed much national pride. But at Rome the patriotism was hardly felt outside of the army and a few families; while in Greece, Christianity flourished only at Corinth, a city which, after its destruction by Mummius and its rebuilding by Cæsar, was a mixture of men from every land. The true Greek tribes were then, as now, very exclusive in their notions, absorbed in the memory of their past; and paid little heed to the new doctrine. They proved but half-way Christians. On the other hand, the gay, luxurious, and pleasure-loving inhabitants of Asia and Syria, accustomed to a life of enjoyment, of easy manners, and used to accept the customs and laws of every new conqueror, had nothing in the shape of national pride or cherished traditions to lose. The early centres of Christianity—Antioch, Ephesus, Thessalonica, Corinth, and Rome—were, if I may so express it, public cities; cities like modern Alexandria, whither all races gather, and where that union and tie of affection between the citizen and the soil which constitutes a nation, were entirely unknown.

The interest of the public in social questions is always in inverse ratio to its preoccupation with politics. Socialism advances when patriotism becomes weak. Christianity was an explosion of social and religious ideas which could not have had free scope until Augustus had suppressed political contests. It was destined, like Islamism, to become in essence an enemy of the tendency to separate nationality. Many ages and many schisms would be necessary before national established churches could be derived out of a religion which started with the negation of the idea of any earthly home or country; which arose at an epoch when the distinctive *city* and *citizen* of early Greece and Italy had ceased to exist; and when the stern and vigorous republican spirit of a former period had been carefully sifted out as deadly poison to the state.

Here then is one of the causes of the grandeur of the new religion. Humanity is diverse and changeable in feeling, and constantly agitated by contradictory desires. Great is the love of country and sacred are the heroes of Marathon, Thermopylæ, Valmy, and Fleurus One's country, however, is not everything here below Man is a man and a child of God before he is a Frenchman or a German. The kingdom of God, that eternal vision which cannot be torn out of the heart of man, is the protest of his nature against the exclusiveness of patriotism. The idea of a great and universal organization of the race to bring about its greatest welfare and its moral improvement, is both legitimate and Christian. The state knows and can know only one thing, the organization of self-interest. This is something, for self-interest is the strongest and most engrossing of human motives. But it is not enough. Governments founded on the theory that man is composed of selfish wants and desires alone, have proved greatly mistaken. Devotion is as natural as egotism to the race, and religion is organized devotion. Let none expect, then, to do without religion or religious associations. Every forward step of modern society will render the need of religion more imperious.

We can now see how these recitals of strange events may prove illustrative and instructive. We need not reject the lesson because of certain traits which the difference of times and manners has invested with an odd or unusual aspect. In regard to popular convictions, there is always an immense disproportion between the greatness of the ideal aimed at by the system of belief, and the trifling nature of the actual facts which have given rise to it. Hence the particularity with which religious history mingles common details and actions approaching folly with its most sublime events and doctrines. The monk who contrived the "holy vial" was one of the founders of the French monarchy. Who would not willingly efface from the life of Jesus the story of the demoniacs of Gadara? What man of cool blood and common sense would have acted like Francis of Assisi, Joan of Arc, Peter the Hermit, or Ignatius Loyola. Terms attributing folly or fanaticism to the actions of past ages must of necessity be deemed merely relative. If our ideas are to be taken as the standard, there was never a prophet, apostle, or saint, who ought not to have been confined as a lunatic. Conscience is very unstable in periods when reflection is not mature, and then good becomes evil, and evil good, by insensible stages. Unless we admit this, it is impossible to form a just estimate of the past. The same divine breath vitalizes all history and gives to it wonderful unity, but human faculties have produced an infinite variety of combinations. The apostles differed less in character from us than did the founders of Buddhism, although the latter were allied more nearly to us in language and probably in race. Our own age has witnessed religious movements quite as extraordinary as those of former times; movements attended with as much enthusiasm, which have already had in proportion more martyrs, and the future of which is still undetermined.

I do not refer to the Mormons, a sect in some respects so degraded and absurd that one hesitates to seriously consider it. There is much to suggest reflection, however, in seeing thousands of men of our own race living in the miraculous in the middle of the nineteenth century, and blindly believing in the wonders which they profess to have seen and touched. A literature has already arisen pretending to reconcile Mormonism and science. But, what is of more importance, this religion, founded upon silly impostures, has inspired prodigies of patience and self-denial. Five hundred years hence, learned professors will seek to prove its divine origin by the miracle of its establishment.

Bab-ism in Persia was a phenomenon much more astonishing.[11] A mild and unassuming man, in character and opinion a sort of pious and modest Spinoza, was suddenly and almost in spite of himself raised to the rank of a worker of miracles and a divine incarnation; and became the head of a numerous, ardent, and fanatical sect, which came near accomplishing a revolution like that of Mahomet. Thousands of martyrs rushed to death for him with joyful alacrity. The great butchery of his followers at Teheran was a scene perhaps unparalleled in history. "That day in the streets and *bazaars* of Teheran," says an eye-witness, "the residents will never forget.[12] To this moment when it is talked of, the mingled wonder and horror which the citizens then experienced appears unabated by the lapse of years. They saw women and children walking forward between their executioners, with great gashes all over their bodies and burning matches thrust into the wounds. The victims were dragged along by ropes, and hurried on by strokes of the whip. Children and women went singing a verse to this effect, 'Verily we came from God, and to him shall we return!' Their shrill voices rose loud and clear in the profound silence of the multitude. If one of these poor wretches fell down, and the guards forced him up again with blows or bayonet-thrusts, as he staggered on with the blood trickling down every limb, he would spend his remaining energy in dancing and crying in an access of zeal, 'Verily we are God's, and to him we return!' Some of the children expired on the way. The executioners threw their corpses in front of their fathers and their sisters, who yet marched proudly on, giving hardly a second glance. At the place of execution life was offered them if they would abjure, but to no purpose. One of the condemned was informed that unless he recanted, the throats of his two sons should be cut upon his own bosom. The eldest of these little boys was fourteen years old, and they stood red with their own blood and with their flesh burned and blistered, calmly listening to the dialogue. The father, stretching himself upon the earth, answered that he was ready; and the oldest boy, eagerly claiming his birthright, asked to be murdered first.[18] At length all was over; night closed in upon heaps of mangled carcasses; the heads were suspended in bunches on the scaffold, and the dogs of the *faubourgs* gathered in troops from every side as darkness veiled the awful scene."

This happened in 1852. In the reign of Chosroes Nouschirvan, the sect of Masdak was smothered in blood in the same way. Absolute devotion is to simple natures the most exquisite of enjoyments, and, in fact, a necessity. In the Bab persecution, people who had hardly joined the sect came and denounced themselves, that they might suffer with the rest. It is so sweet to mankind to suffer for something, that the allurement of martyrdom is itself often enough to inspire faith. A disciple who shared the tortures of Bab, hanging by his side on the ramparts of Tabriz and awaiting a lingering death, had only one word to say—"Master, have I done well?"

Those who regard as either miraculous or chimerical everything in history which transcends the ordinary calculations of common sense, will find such facts as these inexplicable. The fundamental condition of criticism is to be able to comprehend the diverse states of the human soul. Absolute faith is a thing entirely foreign to us. Beyond the positive sciences which possess a material certainty, all opinion is in our view only an approximation to the truth, and necessarily implies some error. The amount of error may be as small as you please, but is never zero in regard to moral subjects. Such is not the method of narrow and bigoted minds, like the Oriental for example. The mental vision of those races is not like ours; theirs is dull and fixed like the enamelled eyes of figures in mosaic. They see only one thing at a time, and that takes entire possession of them. They are not their own masters whether to believe or not. There is no room for an after-thought with them. People who embrace an opinion after this fashion will die for it. The martyr is in religion what the partisan is in politics. There have not been many very intelligent martyrs. The Christians who confessed their faith under Diocletian, would have been, after peace was gained for the Church, rather unpleasant and impracticable personages. One is never very tolerant when he believes himself entirely in the right, and his opponents entirely in the wrong.

Great religious movements, being thus the results of

a confined method of viewing moral subjects, are enigmas to an age like the present, in which the strength of conviction is enfeebled. Among us, the man of sincerity is continually modifying his opinions, because both the world around him and his own nature are changing. We believe in many things at once. We love justice and the truth, and would expose our lives in their cause; but we do not admit that justice and truth can be the peculiar property of any sect or party. We are good Frenchmen, but we confess that the Germans and the English excel us in many respects. Not so in epochs and countries where every man belongs with his whole nature to his own community, race, or school of politics. Hence all the great religious developments have occurred in states of society when the general mind was more or less analogous to the oriental. In fact, it is only absolute faith that has hitherto succeeded in conquering souls. A pious servant-girl of Lyons named Blandina, who suffered for her religion 1700 years ago; a rough chieftain, Clovis, who saw fit some fourteen centuries back to embrace Catholicism—are still giving law to us.

Who is there who has not at some time while wandering through our old cities, now so rapidly being modernized, paused at the foot of one of the gigantic monuments of the faith of the Middle Age! Everything around is becoming new; not a vestige of ancient customs remains; the cathedral alone stands, a little lowered perhaps by men's violence, but firmly rooted in the soil. *Mole sua stat!* Its strength is its right. It has withstood the flood which has washed away its surroundings. Not one of the men of old, should here visit the spots which once knew him, could find his former home. Of all the dwellers there, the rooks alone who built their nests in the lofty niches of the consecrated edifice, have never seen the hammer of destruction raised against their abode. Strange destiny! Those simple martyrs, those rude converts, those pirate church-builders, rule us still. We are Christians because it pleased them to be so. As in politics, it is only systems founded by barbarians which have endured; so in religion it is only the spontaneous, and, if I may so express it, fanatical movements, which are contagious. Their success depends not on the more or less satisfactory proofs they furnish of their divine origin, but is proportioned to what they have to say to the hearts of the people.

Are we then to conclude that religion is destined gradually to die away like the popular fallacies concerning magic, sorcery, and ghosts? By no means. Religion is not a popular fallacy; it is a great intuitive truth, felt and expressed by the people. All the symbols which serve to give shape to the religious sentiment are imperfect, and their fate is to be one after another rejected. But nothing is more remote from the truth than the dream of those who seek to imagine a perfected humanity without religion. The contrary idea is the truth. The Chinese, a very inferior branch of humanity, have hardly any religious sentiment. But if we suppose a planet inhabited by a race whose intellectual, moral, and physical force were the double of our own, that race would be at least twice as religious as we. I say "at least," for it is likely that the religious sentiment would increase more rapidly than the intellectual capacity, and not in merely direct proportion. Let us suppose a humanity ten times as powerful as we are; it would be infinitely more religious. It is even probable that at this degree of sublime elevation, being freed from material cares and egotism, endowed with perfect judgment and appreciation, and perceiving clearly the baseness and nothingness of all that is not true, good, or beautiful, man would be wholly a religious being, and would spend his days in ceaseless adoration, passing from ecstasy to ecstasy of religious rapture, and living and dying in the loftiest delight of the soul. Egotism is the measure of inferiority, and decreases as we recede from the animal nature. A perfected being would no longer be selfish, but purely religious. The progress of humanity, then, cannot destroy or weaken religion, but will develop and increase it.

But it is time that we return to the three missionaries, Paul, Barnabas, and Mark, whom we left as they sallied forth from Antioch by the Seleucian gate. In my third book I shall attempt to trace the footsteps of these messengers of good report, by land and sea, in calm and storm, through good and evil days. I long to recount that unequalled epic; to depict those tossing waves so often traversed, and those endless journeyings in Asia and Europe, during which the Gospel-seed was sown. The great Christian Odyssey begins. Already the apostolic bark has spread its sails, and the freshening breeze rejoices to bear upon its wings the words of Jesus.

FINIS.

NOTES.

NOTES TO THE INTRODUCTION.

1. The author of the *Acts* does not directly give to St. Paul the title of apostle. This title is, in general, reserved by him for the members of the central college, at Jerusalem.
2. Hom. Pseudo-Clem., xvii. 13–19.
3. Justin, Apol. i. 39. In the Acts also is seen the idea that Peter was the Apostle of the Gentiles. See especially Chap. x., comp. Petri i. 1.
4. I Cor. iii 6, 10; iv. 14, 15; ix. 1, 2. II. Cor., xi. 2, etc.
5. Letter of Denys of Corinth in Euseb. *Hist. Eccl.* ii. 25.
6. French readers, for ample details upon the discussion and comparison of the four narratives, may see Strauss, Vie de Jésus, 3d sect., chapters iv. and v. (traduction Littré); *Nouvelle Vie de Jésus*, l. i., § 46, &c.; l, ii. § 97, &c. (translation Nefftzer and Dollfus).
7. The Church early admitted this. See the canon of Muratori (*Antiq. Ital.* iii. 854), (Neutestamentliche Studien, Gotha, 1866), lines 33, &c.
8. Luke i. 1–4; *Acts* i. 1.
9. See especially *Acts*, xvi. 12.
10. The paucity of language in the New Testament writers is so great that each one has his own dictionary; so that the writers of even very short manuscripts can be easily recognised.
11. The use of this word, *Acts* xiv. 4, 14, is very indirect.
12. Comp. for example, *Acts* xvii. 14–16; xviii. 5, with I. Thess. iii. 1–2.
13. I. Cor. xv. 32; II. Cor. i. 8; xi. 23, &c.; Rom. xv. 19; xvi. 3, &c.
14. *Acts* xvi 6; xviii. 22–23, compared with the Epistle to the Galatians.
15. For instance, the sojourn at Cesarea is left in obscurity.
16. Mabillon, *Museum Italicum*, i. 1 pars, p. 109.
17. Col. iv. 14.
18. See above, p. xii.
19. Almost all the inscriptions are Latin, as at Naples (Cavala), the port of Philippi. See Heuzey, *Mission de Macédoine*, p. 11, &c. The remarkable familiarity with nautical subjects of the author of the

Acts (see especially chapters xxvii–xxviii), would give rise to the belief that he was a Neapolitan.

20. For example, *Acts* x. 28.

21. *Acts* v. 36–37.

22. The Hebraisms of his style may arise from careful reading of Greek translations of the Old Testament, and above all, from reading the manuscripts of his co-religionists of Palestine, whom he often copied word for word. His quotations from the Old Testament are made without any acquaintance with the original text (for example, xv. 16, &c.).

23. *Acts* xvii. 22, &c.

24. Luke i. 26; iv. 31; xxiv. 13.

25. Luke i. 31, compared with Matthew i. 21. The name of *Jeanne*, known only to Luke, is dubious. See, however, Talm. de Bab. Sota, 22 a.

26. *Acts* ii. 47; iv. 33; v. 13, 26.

27. *Acts* ix. 22, 23; xii. 3, 11; xiii. 45, 50, and many other passages. It is the same with the fourth gospel also compiled out of Syria.

28. Luke x. 33, &c.; xvii. 16; *Acts* viii. 5, &c. The same in the fourth gospel: John iv. 5, &c.

29. *Acts* xxviii. 30.

30. See *Vie de Jésus.*

31. Luke xxiv. 50. Mark xvi. 19, shows a similar arrangement.

32. *Acts* i. 3, 9.

33. See especially Luke i. 1, the expression τῶν πεπληροφορημένων ἐν ἡμῖν πραγμάτων.

34. Ch. x. xxii. xxvi.

35. The centurion Cornélius, the proconsul Sergius Paulus.

36. *Acts* xiii. 7, &c.; xviii. 12, &c.; xix. 35, &c.· xxiv. 7, 17; xxv. 9, 16, 25; xxvii 2; xxviii. 17–18.

37. Ibid. xvi. 37, &c.; xxii. 26, &c.

38. Similar precautions were by no means rare. In the Apocalypse and the Epistle of Peter, Rome is alluded to in disguised language.

39. Luke i. 4.

40. *Acts* i. 22.

41. See *Vie de Jésus*, p. xxxix. &c.

42. This is obvious, especially in the history of the centurion Cornelius.

43. *Acts* ii. 47; iv. 33; v. 13, 26. Cf. Luke, xxiv. 19–20.

44. *Acts* ii. 44–45; iv. 34, &c.; v. 1, &c.

45. I. Cor. xii–xiv. Comp. Mark xvi. 17, and *Acts* ii. 4–13; x. 46 xi. 15; xix. 6.

46. Comp. *Acts* iii. 2, &c., to xiv. 8, &c.; ix. 36, &c., to xx. 9, &c; v.

1, &c., with xiii. 9, &c ; v. 15–16, to xix. 12 ; xii. 7, &c., with xvi. 26, &c. ; x. 44, with xix. 6.

47. In a speech attributed by the author to Gamaliel, about the year 36, Theudas is spoken of as anterior to Judas of Galilee (*Acts* v. 36–37) Now the revolt of Theudas was in the year 44 (Jos. *Ant.* xx. v. 1), and certainly after that of the Galilean (Jos. *Ant.*, xviii. i. 1; B. J., II., viii. 1.

48. Those who cannot refer to the German works of Baur, Schneckenburger, Wette, Schwegler, Zeller, where critical questions relative to the *Acts* are brought to almost a definite solution, may consult *Etudes Historiques et Critiques sur les Origines du Christianisme*, by A. Stap (Paris, Lacroix, 1864), p. 116, &c.; Michel Nicolas *Etudes Critiques sur la Bible; Nouveau Testament* (Paris, Lévy, 1864), p. 223, &c.); Reuss, *Histoire de la Th'ologie Chretienneau siècle Apostolique* I. vi. ch. v.; other works of MM. Kayser, Scherer, Reuss, in the *Revue de Th'ologie* of Strasburg, 1st series, vol. ii. and iii.; 2d series, vol. ii. and iii.

49 For the exact meaning of οὐ προσανεθέμην σαρκὶ καὶ αἵματι, comp. Matt. xvi. 17.

50. He declares it on oath. See chapters i. and ii. of the Epistle to the Galatians.

51. *Acts* xii. 1.

52. Jos. Ant. XIX. viii. 2; B. J. II. xii. 6.

53. The quotation from Amos (xv. 16–17), made by James according to the Greek version, and in non-accordance with the Hebrew, also shows that this speech is a fiction of the author.

54. We shall show later that this is the true sense. Any way, the question of the circumcision of Titus is of no importance here.

55. Comp. *Acts* xv. 1; Gal. i. 7; ii. 12.

56. I. Cor. viii. 4, 9; x. 25, 29.

57. *Acts*, xxi. 20, &c.

58. Above all, the Ebionites. See the Homilies Pseudo-Clem. Irenæus. Adv. hær. I. xxvi. 2; Epiphanius, Adv. hær., hær. xxx; St. Jerome. *In* Matt. xii.

59. I would nevertheless willingly lose Ananias and Sapphira.

60. *De Divinatione*, ii. 57.

61. Preface to the *Etudes d'Histoire Religieuse.*

CHAPTER I.

1. Mark xvi. 11; Luke xviii. 34; xxiv. 44; John xx. 9, 24, and following verses. The contrary opinion in Matt. xii. 40; xxi. 4, 24; xvii. 9, 23; xx. 19; xxxi. 32; Mark viii. 34; ix. 9, 10—31; x. 34; Luke ix. 22; xi. 29, 30; xviii. 31 et seq.; xxiv. 6–8. Justin, *Dial. cum*

Tryph. 106, proceeds from a source on which, beginning from a certain epoch, considerable reliance may be placed as to the announcements which Jesus had made in reference to his resurrection. The synopticals acknowledge, moreover, that if Jesus spake of it at all, his disciples understood nothing of it (Mark ix. 10, 32; Luke xviii. 34: compare Luke xxiv. 8, and John ii. 21, 22).

2 Mark xiii. 10; Luke xxiv. 17, 21.

3 Preceding passages, especially Luke xvii. 24, 25; xviii. 31–34.

4. Talmud of Babylon, *Baba, Bathra*, 58, a, and the Arabic extract given by the Abbé Bargès, in the *Bulletin de l' Œuvre des Pèlerinages en terre Sainte*, February 1863.

5. Ibn. Hischam, *Sirot Errasoul*, édit. Wüsdenfeld, 1012, and following pages.

6. Ps. xvi. 10. The sense of the original is a little different. But the received versions thus translate the passage.

7. I. Thess. iv. 12, et seq.; I. Cor. xv., entire; Revelation xx.–xxii.

8. Matt. xvi. 21, et seq.; Mark viii. 31, et seq.

9. Josephus, *Ant.* XVIII., iii. 3.

10. Carefully reperuse the four stories of the Gospels, and the passage I. Cor. xv. 4, 8.

11. Matt. xxviii. 1; Mark xvi. 1; Luke xxiv. 1; John xx. 1.

12. John xx. 2, seems to suppose even that Mary was not always alone.

13. John xx. 1, et seq.; and Mark xvi. 9, et seq. It must be observed that the Gospel of Mark has, in our printed versions of the New Testament, two conclusions: Mark xvi. 1–8; Mark xvi. 9–20, to say nothing of two other conclusions, one of which has been handed down to us in the manuscript L. of Paris, and the margin of the Philoxenian version (*Nov. Test.*, edit. Griesbach, Schultz, 1, page 291 note); the other by St. Jerome, *Adv. Pelag.* l. ii. (vol. iv., 2d part, col. 250, edit. Martianay.) The conclusion in the sixteenth chapter, 9th and following verses, are wanting in the *Codex Sinaïticus* and in the most important Greek manuscripts. But, in any case, it is of great antiquity, and its harmony with the fourth Gospel is a striking coincidence.

14. Matt. xxvii. 60; Mark xv. 46; Luke xxiii. 53.

15. John xix. 41, 42.

16. See "*Life of Jesus*" p. 38.

17. The Gospel of the Hebrews contained, perhaps, some analogous circumstance (vide St. Jerome, *de Viris Illustribus*, 2).

18. M. de Vogue, *The Churches of the Holy Land*, pp. 125, 126. The verb ἀποκυλίω (Matt. xxviii. 2; Mark xvi. 3, 4; Luke xxvi. 2) clearly proves that such was the situation of the tomb of Jesus.

19. In all this, the recital of the fourth Gospel is vastly superior. It is our principal guide. In Luke xxiv. 12, Peter alone goes to the tomb. In the conclusion of Mark given in manuscript L, and in the margin of the Philoxenian version (Griesbach, *loc. citat.*) occur τοῖς

περὶ τὸν Πέτρον. St. Paul (I. Cor. xv. 5) similarly introduces Peter only in this first vision. Further, Luke (xxiv. 24) supposes that many disciples went to the tomb, which observation probably applies to successive visits. It is possible that John has here yielded to the after-thought which betrays him more than once in his Gospel, of showing that he had, in the history of Jesus, a first-rate rôle, equal even to that of Peter. Perhaps, also, the repeated declarations of John, that he was an eye-witness of the fundamental facts of the Christian faith (Gospel i. 14; xxi. 24; I. John i. 1–3; iv. 14), should be applied to this visit.

20. John xx. 1, 10; compare Luke xxiv. 12, 34; I. Cor. xv. 5, and the conclusion of Mark in the manuscript L.

21. Matt. xxviii. 9; in observing that Matt. xxviii. 9, 10, replies to John xx. 16. 17.

22. John xx. 11–17, in harmony with Mark xvi. 9, 10; compare the parallel, but far less satisfactory account of Matt. xxviii. 1–10; Luke xxiv. 1, 10.

23. John xx. 18.

24. Compare Mark xvi. 9; Luke viii. 2.

25. Luke xxiv. 11.

26. Ibid. xxiv. 24.

27. Ibid. xxiv. 34; I. Cor. xv. 5; the conclusion of Mark in the manuscript L. The fragment of the Gospel of the Hebrews in St. Ignatius, *Epist. ad Smyrn.*, and in St. Jerome, *de Viris Ill.*, 16, seem to place "the vision of Peter" in the evening, and to confound it with that of the assembled Apostles. But St. Paul expressly distinguishes between the two visions.

28. Luke xxiv. 23, 24. It results from these passages that the tidings were separately proclaimed.

29. Mark xvi. 1–8; Matthew xxviii. 9, 10, contradict this. But this is at variance with the synoptical system, where the women only see an angel. It seems that the first Gospel was intended to reconcile the synoptical system with that of the fourth, wherein one woman only saw Jesus.

30. Matt. xxxviii. 2, et seq.; Mark xvi. 5, et seq.; Luke xxiv. 4, et seq., 23. This apparition of angels is even introduced into the story of the fourth Gospel (xx. 12, 13), which it completely deranges, being applied to Mary of Magdala. The author was unwilling to abandon this traditionary feature.

31. Mark xvi. 8.

32. Luke xxiv. 4, 7; John xx. 12, 13.

33. Matt. xviii. 1, et seq. The story of Matthew is that in which the circumstances have suffered the greatest exaggeration. The earthquake and the feature of the guards are probably late additions.

34. The six or seven accounts which we have of this scene on Sunday morning (Mark having two or three, and Paul having also his own,

to say nothing of the Gospel of the Hebrews), are in complete disagreement with each other.

35. Matt. xxvi. 31; Mark xiv. 27; John xvi. 32; Justin, *Apol.* i. 50; *Dial cum Tryph.*, 53, 106. The theory of Justin is that immediately on the death of Jesus, there was a complete apostasy on the part of His disciples.

36. Matt. xxviii. 17; Mark xvi. 11; Luke xxiv. 11.

37. Mark xvi. 9; Luke viii. 2.

38. Consult, for example, Calmeil, *De la Folie au Point de Vue Pathologique, Historique et Judiciaire.* Paris, 1845. 2 vols. in 8vo.

39. See the *Pastoral Letters* of Jurieu, 1st year, 7th letter; Misson, *The Sacred Theatre of Cevennes* (London, 1707), pp. 28, 34, 38, 102, 103, 104, 107; Memoirs of Court in Sayons, *History of French Literature*, seventeenth century, i. p. 303. *Bulletin of the French Protestant Historical Society*, 1862, p. 174.

40. Matt. xiv 26; Mark vi. 49; Luke xxiv. 37; John iv. 19.

41. Mark xvi. 12–13; Luke xxiv. 13–33.

42. Compare Josephus, B. J., vii. vi. 6. Luke places this village at 60 stadia, and Josephus at 30 stadia from Jerusalem. Ἑξήκοντα, which is found in certain manuscripts and editions of Josephus, is a correction made by some Christian. Consult the edition of G. Pindorf. The most probable locality of Emmaus is Kullouvé, a beautiful place at the bottom of a valley, on the road from Jerusalem to Jaffa. Consult Sepp. *Jerusalem and the Holy Land* (1863), I. p. 56; Bourquenoud in the *Studies of Religious History and Literature*, by the Priests of the Society of Jesus, 1863, No. 9; and for the exact distances, H. Zschokke. *The Emmaus of the New Testament* (Schaffouse, 1865).

43. Mark xvi. 14; Luke xxiv. 33, et seq.: John xx. 19, et seq.: Gospel of the Hebrews in St. Ignatius, *Epist. ad Smyrn.*, 3, and in St. Jerome, *De Viris Ill.*. 16; I. Cor. xv. 5; Justin, *Dial. cum Tryph.* 106.

44. Luke xxiv. 34

45. In an island opposite Rotterdam, where the people have remained attached to the most austere Calvinism, the peasants are persuaded that Jesus comes to their death-beds to assure the elect of their justification; many, in fact, see Him

46. In order to conceive the possibility of similar illusions, it is sufficient to remember the scenes of our own days, when a number of persons assembled together unanimously acknowledged that they heard unreal voices, and that in perfectly good faith. The expectation, the effort of the imagination, the desire to believe, sometimes compliances accorded with perfect innocence, explain such of the phenomena as are not produced by direct fraud. These compliances proceed, in general, from persons who are convinced, and who, actuated by a kindly feeling, are unwilling that the party should break up unpleasantly, and are desirous of relieving the masters of the house from embarrassment. When a person believes in a miracle, he always

unwillingly assists in its propagation. Doubt and denial are impossible in this sort of assemblage. You would only cause pain to those who do believe, and to those whom you have invited. And thus it is that these experiences which succeed so well before small committees, are usually failures before a paying public, and always so when handled by scientific commissions.

47. John xx. 22, 23, echoed by Luke xxiv. 4, 9.

48. Matt. xxviii. 17; Mark xvi. 14; Luke xxiv. 39, 40.

49. John xx. 24, 29; compare Mark xvi. 14; and the conclusion of Mark preserved by St. Jerome, *Adv. Pelag.* ii. (v. above at page).

50. John xx. 29.

51. It is very remarkable indeed that John, under whose name the above dictum has been transmitted, had no particular vision for himself alone. Cf. I. Cor. xv. 5, 8.

52. John xx. 26. The passage xxi. 14 supposes it is true that there were only two apparitions at Jerusalem before the assembled disciples. But the passages xx. 30, and xxi. 25, give us far more latitude. Compare *Acts* 1, 3.

53. Luke xxiv. 41, 43; Gospel of the Hebrews, in St. Jerome, *De Viris Illustribus*, 2; conclusion of Mark, in St. Jerome, *Adv. Pelag.*, ii.

CHAPTER II.

1. Matt. xxviii. 7; Mark xvi. 7.

2. Matt. xxviii. 10.

3. Ibid. xxvi. 32.

4. Matt. xxviii. 16; John xxi.; Luke xxiv. 49, 50, 52, and the *Acts* i. 3, 4, are here in flagrant contradiction to Mark xvi. 1–8, and Matthew. The second conclusion of Mark (xvi. 9, et seq.), and even of the two others which are not a part of the received text, appeared to be included in the system of Luke. But this cannot avail in opposition to the harmony of a portion of the synoptical tradition with the fourth Gospel, and even indirectly with Paul (I. Cor. xv. 5–8), on this point.

5. Matt. xxviii. 16.

6. Ibid. xxviii. 7; Mark xvi. 7.

7. Conclusion of Mark, in St. Jerome, *Adv. Pelag.* ii.

8. Matt. xxviii. 16.

9. John xxi. 2, et seq.

10. The author of the *Acts* i. 14, makes them remain at Jerusalem until the Ascension. But this agrees with his systematic determination (Luke xxiv. 49; *Acts* i. 4), not to allow of a journey into Galilee after the resurrection (a theory contradicted by Matthew and by John). To be consistent in this theory he is compelled to place the

Ascension at Bethany, in which he is contradicted by all the other traditions.

11. I. Cor. xv. 5, et seq.

12. John xxxi. 1, et seq. This chapter has been added to the already completed Gospel, as a postscript. But it is from the same pen as the rest.

13. John xxi. 9–14; compare Luke xxiv. 41–43. John combines in one the two scenes of the fishing and the meal. But Luke arranges the matter differently. At all events, if we consider with attention the verses of John xxi. 14, 15, we shall come to the conclusion that these harmonics of John are somewhat artificial. Hallucinations, at the moment of their conception, are always isolated. It is later that consistent anecdotes are formed out of them. This habit of coupling together as consecutive events facts which are separated by months and weeks, is seen, in a very striking manner, by comparing together two passages of the same writer, Luke, Gospel, xxiv. end, and *Acts* i. at the beginning. According to the former passage, Jesus should have ascended into heaven on the same day as the resurrection; whilst, according to the latter, there was an interval of forty days. Again, if we rigorously interpret Mark xvi. 9–20, the Ascension must have taken place on the evening of the resurrection. Nothing more fully proves than the contradiction of Luke in these two passages, how little the editors of the evangelical writings observed consistency in their stories.

14. John xxi. 15, et seq.

15. Ibid. xxi. 18, et seq.

16. I. Cor. xv. 6.

17. The Transfiguration.

18. Matt. xxviii. 16–20; I. Cor. xv. 6. Compare Mark xvi. 15, et seq. Luke xxiv. 44, et seq.

19. I. Cor. xv. 6.

20. John affixes no limit to the resuscitated life of Jesus. He appears to suppose it somewhat protracted. According to Matthew, it could only have lasted during the time which was necessary to complete the journey to Galilee and to rendezvous at the mountain pointed out by Jesus. According to the first incomplete conclusion of Mark (xvi. 1–8), the incidents would seem to have transpired as found in Matthew. According to the second conclusion (xvi. 9, 20), according to others; and, according to the Gospel of Luke, the disentombed life would appear to have lasted only one day. Paul (I. Cor. xv. 5–8), agreeing with the fourth Gospel, prolongs it for two years, since he gives his vision, which occurred five or six years at least after the death of Jesus, as the last of the apparitions. The circumstance of "five hundred brethren" conduces to the same conclusion; for it does not appear that on the morning after the death of Jesus, the group of his friends was compact enough to furnish such a gathering (*Acts* i. 15). Many of the Gnostic sects, especially the Valentinians and the Sethians, esti

mated the continuance of the apparitions at eighteen months, and even founded mystic theories on that notion (Irenæus *Adv. hær.*, i. iii. 2; xxx. 14). The author of the *Acts* alone (i. 3) fixes the duration of the disentombed life of Jesus at forty days. But this is very poor authority; above all, if we remark that it is connected with an erroneous system (Luke xxiv. 49, 50, 52; *Acts* i. 4, 12), according to which the whole disentombed life of Jesus would have been passed at Jerusalem or in its vicinity. The number forty is symbolic (the people spend forty years in the desert; Moses, forty days on Mount Sinai; Elijah and Jesus fast forty days, &c.). As to the formula of the narrative adopted by the author of the last twelve verses of the second Gospel, and by the author of the third Gospel, a formula according to which the events are confined to one day, the authority of Paul, the most ancient and the strongest of all, corroborating that of the fourth Gospel, which affords the most connected and authentic record of this portion of the evangelic history, appears to us to furnish a conclusive argument.

21. Luke xxiv. 34.

22. John xx. 19, 26.

23. Matt. xxviii. 9; Luke xxiv. 37, et seq.; John xx. 27, et seq.; Gospel of the Hebrews, in St. Ignatius, the Epistle to the Smyrniotes 3, and in St. Jerome, *De Viris Illustribus,* 16.

24. John vi. 64.

25. Matt. xxviii. 11–15; Justin, *Dial. cum Tryph.* 17, 108.

26. Matt xxvii. 62–66; xxviii. 4, 11–15.

27. Ibid. xxviii. 9, et seq.

28. The Jews are enraged, Matt. xxvii. 63, when they hear that Jesus had predicted his resurrection. But even the disciples of Jesus had no precise ideas in this respect.

29. A vague idea of this sort may be found in Matthew xxvi. 32; xxviii. 7, 10; Mark xiv. 28; xvi. 7.

30. This is plainly seen in the miracles of Salette and Sourdes. One of the most usual ways in which a miraculous legend is invented is the following. A person of holy life pretends to heal diseases. A sick person is brought to him or her, and in consequence of the excitement finds himself relieved. Next day it is bruited abroad in a circle of ten miles that there has been a miracle. The sick person dies five or six days afterwards; no one mentions the fact; so that at the hour of the burial of the deceased, people at a distance of forty miles are relating with admiration his wondrous cure. The word loaned to the Grecian philosophy before the *ex votos* of Samothrace (Diog. Läert. VI. ii. 59,) is also perfectly appropriate.

A phenomenon of this kind, and one of the most striking, takes place annually at Jerusalem. The orthodox Greeks pretend that the fire which is spontaneously lighted at the holy sepulchre on the Saturday of the holy week preceding their Easter, takes away the sins of those whose faces it touches without burning them. Millions of pilgrims have tried it and know full well that this fire does burn (the contortions which they make, joined to the smell, are a sufficient proof). Nevertheless, no one has ever been found to contradict the belief of the orthodox Church. This would be to avow that they were deficient in faith, that they were unworthy of the miracle, and to acknowledge, oh, heavens! that the Latins were the true Church; for this miracle is considered by the Greeks as the most convincing proof that theirs is the only good church.

32. The affair of Salette before the civil tribunal of Grenoble (decree of 2d May. 1855), and before the court of Grenoble (decree of 6th May, 1857), pleadings of MM. Jules Favre and Bethmont, &c., collected by J. Sabbatier (Grenoble Vellot. 1857.)
33. John xx. 15. Could it include a glimmering of this?
34. See above.
35. John expressly says so, xix. 41, 42.
36. John xx. 6, 7.
37. One cannot help thinking of Mary of Bethany, who in fact is not represented as taking any part in the event of the Sunday morning. See "*Life of Jesus*" p. 341, et seq.; 359, et seq.
38. Celsus has already delivered some excellent critical observations on this subject (in Origen). *Contra Celsum*, ii. 55.
39. Mark xvi. 9; Luke viii. 2.

CHAPTER III.

1. Luke xxiv. 47.
2. Respecting the name of "Galileans" given to the Christians, see below.
3. Matthew is exclusively Galilean; Luke and the second Mark, xvi. 9–22, are exclusively Jerusalemitish. John unites the two traditions. Paul (i. Cor. xv. 5–8) also admits the occurrence of visions at widely separated places. It is possible that the vision of "the five hundred brethren" of Paul, which we have conjecturally identified with that "of the mountain of Galilee" of Matthew, was a Jerusalemite vision.
4. I. Cor. xv 7. One cannot explain the silence of the four canonical Evangelists respecting this vision in any other way than by referring it to an epoch placed on this side of the scheme of their recital. The chronological order of the visions, on which St. Paul insists with so much precision, leads to the same result.
5. Gospel of the Hebrews, cited by St. Jerome *De Viris Illustribus*, 2. Compare Luke xxiv. 41–43.
6. Gospel of the Hebrews, cited above.
7. John vii. 5.

8. Could there be an allusion to this abrupt change in Gal. ii. 6?
9. Acts i. 14, weak authority indeed. One already perceives in Luke a tendency to magnify the part of Mary. Luke, chap. i. and ii.
10. John xix. 25, 27.
11. The tradition respecting his sojourn at Ephesus is modern and valueless. See Epiphanius. *Adv. heret.* lxxviii. 11.
12. See *Life of Jesus.*
13. Gospel of the Hebrews, passage cited above.
14. Acts viii. 1; Galat. i 17–19; ii. 1, et seq.
15. Luke xxiv. 49. *Acts* i. 4.
16. This idea indeed is not developed until we come to the fourth Gospel (chap. xiv., xv., xvi.). But it is indicated in Matt. iii. 11, Mark i. 8; Luke iii. 16; xii. 11, 12, xxiv. 49.
17. John xx. 22–23.
18. Ibid. xvi. 7.
19. Luke xxiv. 49; *Acts* i. 4, et seq.
20. Acts i. 5–8.
21. I. Cor xv. 7; Luke xxiv. 50, et seq. *Acts* i. 2, et seq. Certainly it might with propriety be admitted that the vision of Bethany related by Luke was parallel to the vision of the mountain in Matthew xxviii. 16, et seq. transposing the place where it occurred. And yet this vision of Matthew is not followed by the Ascension. In the second conclusion of Mark, the vision with the final instructions, followed by the Ascension, takes place at Jerusalem. Lastly Paul relates the vision "to all the Apostles," as distinct from that seen by "the five hundred brethren."
22. Other traditions referred the conferring of this power to anterior visions. (John xx. 23.)
23. Luke xxiv. 23; Acts xxv. 19.
24. *Acts* i. 11.
25. 1 Cor. xv. 8.
26. Matt. xxviii. 20.
27. John iii. 13; vi. 62: xvi. 7; xx. 77; Ephes. iv. 10; I. Peter iii. 22. Neither Matthew nor John gives the recital of the Ascension. Paul (1 Cor. xv. 7–8) excludes even the very idea.
28. Mark xvi. 19; Luke xxiv. 50–52. *Acts* 2–12. *Apol.* i. 50. *Ascension of Isaiah*, Ethiopic version, xi. 22; Latin version (Venice, 1522), sub fin.
29. Compare the account of the Transfiguration.
30. Jos *Antiq.* iv., viii. 58.
31. II. Kings, ii. 11, et seq.
32. Luke, last chapter of the Gospel, and the first chapter of the *Acts.*
33. Luke xxiii. 52.

CHAPTER IV.

1. Matt. xviii. 20.
2. *Acts* i. 15. The greater part of these "five hundred brethren" doubtless remained in Galilee. That which is told in *Acts* ii. 41, is surely an exaggeration, or at least an anticipation.
3. Luke xxiv. 53; *Acts* ii. 46; compare Luke ii. 37; Hegesippus in Eusebius, *Hist. Eccles.* ii. 23.
4. Deuteron. x. 18; I. Tim. vi. 8.
5. Read the *Wars of the Jews* of Josephus.
6. John xx. 22.
7. I. Kings xix. 11–12.
8. This work appears to have been written at the commencement of the second century of our era.
9. *The Ascension of Isaiah*, vi. 6, et seq. (Ethiopic version.)
10. Matt. iii. 11; Mark i. 8; Luke iii. 16; *Acts* i. 5; xi. 16; xix. 14; I. John 6, et seq.
11. Compare Misson, *The Sacred Theatre of Cevennes* (London, 1707), p. 103.
12. *Revue des Deux Mondes*, Sept. 1853, p. 96, et seq.
13. Jules Remy, *Journey to the Mormon Territory* (Paris, 1860), Books II. and III.; for example, Vol. I., p. 259-260; Vol. II. 470, et seq.
14. Astiè, *The Religious Revival of the United States* (Lausanne, 1859).
15. *Acts* ii. 1–3; Justin *Apol.* i. 50.
16. The expression "tongue of fire" means in Hebrew, simply, a flame (Isaiah v. 24). Compare Virgil's Æneid II. 682, 84.
17. Jamblicus (De Myst., sec. iii. cap. 6) exposes all this theory of the luminous descents of the Spirit.
18. Compare Talmud of Babylon, Chagiga, 14 b.; Midraschim, *Schir hasschirin Rabba*, fol. 40 b.; *Ruth Rabba*, fol. 42 a.; *Koheleth Rabba*, 87 a.
19. Matt. iii. 11; Luke iii. 16.
20. Exodus iv. 10; compare Jeremiah i. 6.
21. Isaiah vi. 5, et seq. Compare Jeremiah i. 9.
22. Luke xi. 12; John xiv. 26.
23. *Acts* ii. 5, et seq. This is the most probable sense of the narrative, although it may mean that each of the dialects was spoken separately by each of the preachers.
24. *Acts* ii. 4. Compare I. Cor. xii. 10, 28; xiv. 21, 22. For analogous imaginations, see Calmeil, *De la Folie*, i. p. 9, 262; ii. p. 357, et seq.
25. Talmud of Jerusalem, *Sota*, 21 b.
26. *Testimony of the Twelve Patriarchs*, Judah, 25.
27. Acts ii. 4; x. 34, et seq.; vi. 15; xix. 6; I. Cor. xii., xiv.

28 Mark xvi. 17. It must be remembered that in the ancient Hebrew, as in all the other ancient languages (see my *Origin of Language*, p. 177, et seq.), the words meaning "stranger," "strange language," were derived from the words which signified "to stammer," "to sob," an unknown dialect always appearing to a simple people, as it were, an indistinct stammering. See Isaiah xxviii. 11; xxxiii. 19; I. Cor. xiv. 21.

29 I. Cor. viii. 1, remembering what precedes.

30. I. Cor. xii. 28, 30; xiv. 2, et seq.

31. I. Sam. xix. 23, et seq.

32. Plutarch, *Of the Pythian Oracles*, 24. Compare the prediction of Cassandra in the Agamemnon of Æschylus.

33. I. Cor. xii. 3; xvi. 22; Rom. viii. 15.

34. Rom. viii. 23, 26, 27.

35. I. Cor. vii. 1; xiv. 7, et seq.

36. Rom. viii. 26, 27.

37. I. Cor. xiv. 13, 14, 27, et seq.

38 Jurieu, *Pastoral Letters*, 3d year, 3d letter; Misson, *The Sacred Theatre of Cevennes*, p. 10, 14, 15, 18, 19, 22, 31, 32, 36, 37, 65, 66, 68, 70, 94, 104, 109, 126, 140; Bruey's *History of Fanaticism* (Montpelier, 1709). I., pages 145, et seq.; Fléchier, *Select Letters* (Lyon, 1734), I., p. 353, et seq.

39. Karl Hase, *History of the Church*, §§ 439 and 458, 5: the Protestant Journal, *Hope*, 1st April, 1847.

40. M. Hohl, *Bruhstucke aus dem Leben und den Schriften;* Edward Irving's (Saint-Gall, 2839), p. 145, 149, et seq.; Karl Hase, *History of the Church*, §§ 458, 4. For the Mormons, see Remy, *Voyage* I., p. 176–177, note; 259, 260; II., p. 55, et seq. For the Convulsionaries of St. Medard, see, above all, Carré de Montgeron, *The Truth about Miracles*, &c. (Paris, 1737, 1744), II., p. 18, 19, 49, 54, 55, 63, 64, 80, &c.

41. *Acts* ii. 13, 15.

42. Mark iii. 21, et seq.; John x. 20, et seq.; xii. 27, et seq.

43. *Acts* xix. 6; I. Cor. xiv. 3, et seq.

44. *Acts* x. 46; I. Cor. xiv. 15, 16, 26.

45. Col. iii. 16; Eph. v. 49 (ψαλμόι ὕμνοι ᾠδαὶ πνευματικαι). See the former chapters of the Gospel of Luke. Compare in particular, Luke i. 46, with *Acts* x. 46.

46. I. Cor. xiv. 15; Col. iii. 16; Eph. v. 19.

47. Jeremiah i. 6.

48. Mark xvi. 17.

49. I. Cor. xiv. 22. Πνεῦμα in the Epistles of S. Paul, often approaches the sense of δυνάμις. The spiritual phenomena are regarded as δυνάμεις, that is to say, miracles.

50. Irenæus, *Adv. hæret.* V., vi. 1; Tertullian, *Adv. Marciom*, v. 8. *Constit. Apost.* viii. 1.

51. Luke ii. 37; II. Cor. vi. 5; xi. 27.
52. II. Cor. vii. 10.
53. *Acts* viii. 26, et seq.; x. entire; xvi. 6, 7, 9, et seq. Compare Luke ii 27, &c.
54. *Acts* xx. 19, 31. Rom. viii. 23, 26.

CHAPTER V.

1. *Acts* ii. 42–47; iv. 32, 37; v. 1, 11; vi. 1, et seq.
2. Ibid. ii. 44, 46, 47.
3. Ibid. ii. 46.
4. No literary production has ever so often repeated the word "joy" as the New Testament. See I. Thess. i. 6; v. 16; Rom. xiv. 17; xv. 13; Galat. v. 22; Philip i. 25; iii. 1; iv. 4; I. John i. 4, &c.
5. *Acts* xii. 12.
6. See *Life of Jesus*, p. xxxix., et seq.
7. *Ebionim* means "poor folk." See *Life of Jesus*, p. 182, 183.
8. To recall the year 1000. All instruments in writing commencing with: *The evening of the world being at hand* or similar expressions, are in donations to the monasteries.
9. Hodgson, in the *Journal of the Asiatic Society* of Bengal, vol. V., p. 33, et seq.; Eugéne Burnouf, *Introduction to the History of Indian Buddhism*, i. p. 278, et seq.
10. Lucian, *Death of Peregrinus*, 13.
11. Papyrus at Turin, London, and Paris, collected by Brunet de Presle, *Mem. respecting the Serapeum of Memphis* (Paris, 1852); Eggee, *Mem. of Ancient History and Philology*, p. 151, et seq., and in the *Notices and Extracts*. vol. xviii., 2d part, p. 264–359. Observe that the Christian-hermit life was first commenced in Egypt.
12. *Acts* xi. 29, 30; xxiv. 17; Galat. ii. 10; Rom. xv. 26, et seq.; I. Cor. xvi. 1–4; II. Cor. viii. and ix.
13. *Acts* v. 1–11.
14. Ibid. ii. 46; v. 12.
15. Ibid. iii. 1.
16. James, for instance, was all his life a pure Jew.
17. *Acts* ii. 47; iv. 33; v. 13, 26.
18. *Acts* ii. 46.
19. I. Cor. x. 16; Justin, *Apol.* i. 65–67.
20. Συνδεῖπνα, Joseph, *Antiq.* XIV. x. 8, 12.
21. Luke xxii. 19; I. Cor. xi. 24, et seq.; Justin, passage already cited.
22. In the year 57, the institution called the Eucharist already abounded with abuses (I. Cor. xi. 17, et seq.), and was, in consequence, ancient

23. *Acts* xx. 7; Pliny, *Epist.* x. 97. Justin, *Apol.* i. 67.
24. *Acts* xx. 7, 11.
25. Pliny, Epist. x. 97.
26. John xx. 26, does not satisfactorily prove the contrary. The Ebionites always observed the Sabbath. St. Jerome, in Matt. xii., commencement.
27. *Acts* i. 15–26.
28. See *Life of Jesus.* p. 437, et seq.
29 Compare Eusebius, *Hist. Eccl.* iii. 39 (according to Papias).
30. Justin, *Apol.* i. 39, 50.
31. Pseudo-Abdias, etc.
32. Compare I. Cor. xv. 10, with Romans xv. 19.
33. Gal. i. 17, 19.
34. *Acts* vi. 4.
35. Compare Matt. x. 2–4; Mark iii. 16–19; Luke vi. 14–16; *Acts* i. 13.
36. *Acts* i. 14; Gal. i. 19; I. Cor. ix. 5.
37. Gal. ii. 9.
38. See *Life of Jesus,* p. 307.
39. See *Life of Jesus,* p. 150. Compare Papias in Eusebius, *Hist. Eccl.*, iii. 39; Polycrates, Ibid. v. 24; Clement of Alexandria, *Strom.* iii. 6; vii. 11.
40. For instance ἐπίσκοπος, perhaps κλῆρος. See Wescher, in the *Archæological Review*, April, 1866.
41. *Acts* i. 26. See below, p.
42. *Acts* xiii. 1, et seq.; Clement of Alexandria, in Eusebius, *Hist. Eccl.*, iii. 23.
43. *Acts* v. 1–11.
44. I. Cor. v. 1, et seq.
45. I. Tim. i. 20.
46. Genesis xvii. 14, and numerous other passages in the Mosaic code; Mischna, *Kerithouth*, i. 1; Talmud of Babylon, Möed Katou, 28, a. Compare Tertullian, *De Animâ*, 57.
47. Consult the Hebrew and Rabbinical dictionaries, at the word ברת. Compare the word *to exterminate.*
48. Mischna, *Sanhedrim* ix. 6; John xvi. 2; Joseph. *B. J.*, vii, viii., 1; III. Maccab. (apocr.), vii. 8, 12–13.
49. Luke vi. 15; *Acts* i. 13. Compare Matt. x. 4; Mark iii. 18.
50. *Acts* v. 1–11. Compare *Acts* xiii. 9–11.
51. *Acts* i. 15; ii. 14, 37; v. 3, 29; Gal. i. 18; ii. 8.
52. *Acts* iii. 1, et seq.; viii. 14; Gal ii. 9. Compare John xx 2, et seq.; xxi. 20, et seq.
53. According to Matthew xxviii. 1, et seq., the keepers would have been

witnesses to the descent of the angel who removed the stone. This very embarrassed account would also lead us to conclude that the women were witnesses of the same act, but it does not expressly say so. Anyhow, whatever the keepers and the women should have seen, according to the same narrative, would not be Jesus resuscitated, but the angel. Such a story, isolated and inconsistent as it is, is evidently the most modern of all.

54. Luke xxiv. 48; *Acts* i. 22; ii. 32· iii. 15; iv. 33; v. 32; x. 41; xiii. 30, 31.

55 See above p. 1, note 1.

56. See "*Life of Jesus*," p. 275, et seq.

57. I. Cor. xvi. 22. These two words are Syro-Chaldaic.

58. Matt. x, 23.

59. *Acts* ii. 33, et seq.: x. 42.

60. Luke xxiv. 19.

61. *Acts* ii. 22.

62. The diseases were generally considered to be the work of the devil.

63. *Acts* x. 38.

64. *Acts* ii. 36; viii. 37; ix. 22; xvii. 31, &c.

65. *Acts* ii. 44, et seq.; iv. 8, et seq.; 25, et seq.; vii. 14, et seq.; v. 43 and the Epistle attributed to St. Barnabas, entire.

66. James i. 26-27.

67. Later it was called χειτουργεῖν. *Acts* xiii. 2.

68. Heb. v. 6; vi. 20; viii. 4; x. 11.

69. Revel. i. 6; v. 10; xx. 6.

70. *Acts* xiii. 2; Luke ii. 37.

71. Rom. vi. 4, et seq.

72. *Acts* viii. 12, 16; x. 48.

73. *Acts* viii. 16; x. 47.

74. Matt. ix. 18; xix. 13, 15; Mark v. 23; vi. 5; vii. 32; viii. 23–25, x. 16; Luke iv. 40; viii. 13.

75. *Acts* vi. 6; viii. 17, 19; ix. 12, 17; xiii. 3; xiv. 6; xxviii. 8; 1 Tim. iv. 14; v. 22; ii. Tim. i. 6; Heb. vi. 2; James v. 13.

76. Matt. iii. 11; Mark i. 8; Luke iii. 16; John i. 26; *Acts* i. 5; xi. 16; xix. 4.

77. Matt. xxviii. 19.

78. See the *Cholasté*, Sabeau manuscripts of the Imperial Bible, Nos. 8, 10, 11, 13.

79. Vendidad-Sadé viii. 296, et seq.; ix. 1–145; xvi. 18, 19. Spiegel, *Avesta*, ii. p. 83, et seq.

80. I. Cor. xii. 9, 28, 30.

81. Matt. ix. 2; Mark ii. 5; John v. 14; ix. 2; James v. 15; Mischna *Schabbath*, ii. 6; *Talm. of Bab. Nedarim, fol.* 41 a.

82. Matt. ix. 33; xii. 22; Mark ix. 16, 24; Luke xi. 14; *Acts* xix. 12; Tertullian *Apol.* xxii.; adv. Mark iv. 8.

83. *Acts* v. 16; xix. 12–16.

84. James v. 14–15. Mark vi. 13.

85. Luke x. 34.

86. Mark xvi. 18; *Acts* xxviii. 8.

87. I. Thess. iv. 13, et seq.; I. Cor. xv. 12, et seq.

88. Phil. i. 33, seems to be a shade different. But compare I. Thess. iv. 14–17. See, above all, Revel. xx. 4–6.

89. Paul, in previously cited passages, and Phil. iii. 11; Revel. xx. entire; Papias, in Eusebius, *Hist. Eccl.* iii. 39. Sometimes one sees a different belief springing up, above all in Luke (Gospel xvi. 22, et seq.; xxiii. 43, 46). But this is a weak authority on a point of Jewish theology. The Essenians had already adopted the Greek dogma of the immortality of the soul.

90. Compare *Acts* xxiv. 15 with I. Thess. iv. 13, et seq.; Phil. iii. 11. Compare Revel. xx. 5. See Leblant, *Christian Inscriptions in Gaul* ii. p. 81, et seq.

91. *Acts* xi. 27, et seq.; xiii. 1; xv. 32; xxi. 9, 10, et seq.; I. Cor. xii. 28, et seq.; xiv. 29–37; Eph. iii. 5; iv. 11; Revel. i. 3; xvi. 6; xviii. 20, 24; xxii. 9.

92. Luke i. 46, et seq.; 68, et seq.; ii. 29, et seq.

93. *Acts* xvi. 25; I. Cor. xiv. 15; Col. iii. 16; Eph. v. 19; James v. 13.

94. The identity of this chant in religious communities which have been separated from the earliest ages proves that it is of great antiquity.

95. Num. v. 2; Deut. xxvii. 15, et seq.; Ps. 106, 48; I. Chron. xvi. 36; Nehem. v. 13, viii. 6.

96. I. Cor. xiv. 16; Justin. *Apol.* i. 65, 67.

97. I. Cor. xiv. 7, 8, does not prove it. The use of the verb ψάλλω does not any more prove it. This verb originally implied the use of an instrument with strings, but in time it became synonymous with "to chant the Psalms."

98. Col. iii. 16; Eph. v. 19.

99. See Du Cange, at the word *Lollardi* (edit. Didot). Compare the Cantilenes of the Cevenols. *Prophetic warnings of Elijah Marion* (London, 1707), p. 10, 12, 14, &c.

100. James v. 12.

101. Matt. xvi. 28; xxiv. 34; Mark viii. 39; xiii. 30; Luke ix. 27 xxi. 32.

CHAPTER VI.

1. *Acts*, first chapters.
2. *Acts* v. 42.
3. See for example, *Acts* ii. 34, &c., and in general all the first chapters
4. I. Cor. i. 22; ii. 4–5; II. Cor. xii. 12; I. Thess. i. 5; II. Thess. ii. 9 Gal. iii. 5; Rom. xv. 18–19.
5. Rom. xv. 19; II. Cor. xii. 12; I. Thess. i. 5.
6. *Acts* v. 12–16. The *Acts* are full of miracles. That of Eutychus (*Acts* xx. 7–12) is surely related by ocular testimony. The same of *Acts* xxviii. Comp. Papias in Euseb. H. E. iii. 39.
7. Jewish and Christian exorcism were regarded as the most efficacious even for the heathen. Damascius, Vie d'Isidore, 56.
8. *Acts* v. 15.
9. I. Cor. xii. 9, &c., 28, &c.; *Constit. apost.* viii. 1.
10. Irenæus. *Adv. hær.* ii. xxxii. 4; v. vi. 1; Tertull. *Apol.* 23–43; *Ad Scapulam*, 2; *De Corona*, 11; *De Spectaculis*, 24; *DeAnima*, 57; *Constit. Apost.* chapter noted, which appeared drawn from the work of St. Hippolytus upon the *Chrismata.*
11. Miracles are of daily occurrence among the Mormons. Jules Remy, *A Visit to the Mormons*, I. p. 140, 192, 259–260; II. 53, &c.
12. *Acts* iv. 36–37. Cf. ibid. xv. 32.
13. Ibid. xiii. 1.
14. Ibid. xxi. 16.
15. Jos. *Ant.* XIII. x. 4; XVII. xii. 1, 2; Philo, *Leg. ad Caium*, § 36.
16. Hence for Barnabas his name of Hallévi and of Col. iv. 10–11. Mnason appears to be the translation of some Hebrew name from the root *zacar*, as Zacharius.
17. Col. iv. 10–11.
18. *Acts* xii. 12.
19. I. Petri, v. 13. *Acts* xii. 12; Papias in Euseb. H. E. iii. 39.
20. *Acts* xii 12–14. All this chapter, where the affairs of Peter are so minutely related, appears edited by John-Mark.
21. As the name of *Marcus* was not common at that time among the Jews, there is no reason for referring to different individuals the passages relating to a personage of that name.
22. Comp. *Acts* viii. 2, with *Acts* ii. 5.
23. Acts. vi. 5.
24. Ibid.
25. Comp. *Acts* xxi. 8–9 with Papias in Euseb. *Hist. Eccl.* iii. 39.
26. Rom. xvi. 7. It is doubtful whether Ἰουνία or Ἰουνιᾶ, = *Junianus.*
27. Paul calls them his συγγενεῖς; but it is difficult to say whether that signifies that these were Jews, of the tribe of Benjamin or of Tarsus, or really relations of Paul. The first sense is the most probable.

Comp. Rom. ix. 3; xi. 14. In any event, this word implies that they were Jews.

28. *Acts* vi. 1–5; II. Cor. xi. 22; Phil. iii. 5.
29. *Acts* ii. 9–11; vi. 9.
30. The Talmud of Jerusalem, Megilla, fol. 73 d, mentions four hundred and twenty-five synagogues. Comp. Midrasch *Eka*, 52 b, 70 d. Such a number would appear by no means improbable to those who have seen the little family mosques which are found in every Mahommedan village. But the Talmudic information about Jerusalem is of mediocre authority.
31. *Acts* vi. 1.
32. The Epistle of St. James was written in moderately pure Greek. It is true that the authenticity of this Epistle is not certain.
33. The savants wrote in ancient Hebrew, somewhat altered.
34. Jos. *Ant.* last paragraph.
35. This proves the transcriptions of Greek into Syriac. I have developed here in my *Eclaircissements sir s des Langues Sémitiques sur quelque points de la Prononciatian Grecque.* (Paris, 1849.) The language of the Greek inscriptions of Syria is very bad.
36. Jos. *Ant.* loc. cit.
37. Sat. I. v. 105.

CHAPTER VII.

1. See the accounts collected and translated by Eugene Burnouf. *Introduction to the History of Indian Buddhism*, i. p. 137, and following pages, and particularly pp. 198, 199.
2. See *Life of Jesus.*
3. *Acts* ii. 45; iv. 34, 37; v. 1.
4. *Acts* v. 1, and following verses.
5. Ibid. ii. 45; iv. 35.
6. Ibid. vi. 1, &c.
7. See chapter vi.
8. *Acts* xxi. 8.
9. Phil. i. 1; I. Timothy iii. 8, and following.
10. Romans xvi. 1, 12; I. Tim. iii. 11; v. 9, and following. Pliny Epist. x. 97. The Epistles to Timothy are most probably not from the pen of Saint Paul; but are in any event of very ancient date.
11. Rom. xvi. 1; I. Cor. ix. 5. Philemon 2.
12. I. Tim. v. 9, and following.
31. Constit. Apost. vi. 17.

14. Sap. i. 10; Eccl. xxxvii. 17; Matthew xxiii. 14; Mark xii. 40; Luke xx. 47; James 27.
15. Mischna, *Sota*, iii. 4.
16. Talmud of Babylon, Sota 22 *a*; Comp. I. Tim. v. 13.
17. *Acts* vi. 1.
18. Ibid. xii. 12.
19. I. Tim. v. 9, and following. Compare Acts ix. 39, 41.
20. I. Tim. v. 3, and following.
21. Ecclesiastes vii. 27; Ecclesiasticus vii. 26, and following; ix. 1, and following; xxv. 22, and following; xxvi. 1, and following; xlii. 9, and following.
22. For the costume of the widows of the Eastern Church, see the Greek manuscript No. 64 in the *Bibliothèque Imperiale* (old building), fol. 11. The costume to this day is very nearly the same the type, the religious female of the East, being the widow, as that of the Latin nun is the virgin.
23. Compare the "Shepherd" of Hermas, vis. ii. ch. 4.
24. Κιλογοία, the name of the roligious females or nuns of the Eastern Church. Καλός combines the significance of both "beautiful" and "good."
25. See Note 16.
26. I. Cor. xii. entire.
27. The Pietist congregations of America, who are to the Protestants what convents are to the Catholics, resemble in many points the primitive churches. Bridel, *Recits Americains.* (Lausanne, 1861.)
28. Prov. iii. 27, and following; x. 2; xi. 4; xxii. 9; xxviii. 27; Eccl. iii. 23, and following; vii. 36; xii. 1, and following; xviii. 14; xx. 13, and following; xxxi. 11; Tobit, ii. 15, 22; iv. 11; xii. 9; xiv. 11; Daniel iv. 24; Talmud of Jerusalem; *Peah.* 15, *b.*
29. Matthew vi. 2; Mischna, *Schekalim*, v. 6; Talmud of Jerusalem, *Demai*, fol. 23, *b.*
30. *Acts* x. 2, 4, 31.
31. Ps. cxxxiii.
32. *Acts* ii. 44–47; iv. 32–35.
33. Ibid. ii. 41.
34. See chapter vi.
35. *Acts* vi. 5; xi. 20.

CHAPTER VIII.

1. Acts iv. 6. See *Life of Jesus.*
2. Acts iv. 1–31; v. 47–41.
3. See *Life of Jesus.*

4. Acts v. 41.
5. Ib. iv. 5–6 v. 17. Comp. James ii. 6.
6. Γένος αρχιε, ατιχιν, in Acts i.; αρχιερεις in Josephus *Ant.* xx. viii. 8
7. Acts xv. 5; xxi. 20.
8. Let us add that the reciprocal antipathy of Jesus and the Pharisees seems to have been exaggerated by the synoptical Evangelists, perhaps on account of the events which, at the time of the great war, led to the flight of the Christians beyond the Jordan. It cannot be denied that James, brother of the Lord, was pretty nearly a Pharisee.
9. Acts v. 34, and following. See *Life of Jesus.*
10. Acts vi. 8; vii. 59.
11. Probably descendants of Jews who had been taken to Rome as slaves, and then freed. Philo, *Leg. ad Caium*, § 23; Tacitus, *Ann.* ii. 85.
12. See *Life of Jesus.*
13. Matt. xv. 2, and following; Mark vii. 3; Gal. i. 14.
14. Compare Gal. iii. 19; Heb. ii. 2; Jos. Ant. XV. v. 3. It was supposed that God Himself had not revealed Himself in the theophanies of the ancient law, but that he had substituted in his place a sort of intermediary, the *maleak Jehovah.* See the Hebrew dictionaries on the word מלאך.
15. Deut. xvii. 7.
16. Acts vii. 59; xxii. 20; xxvi. 10.
17. John xviii. 31.
18. Josephus, Ant. XVIII. iv. 2.
19. Ib., Ib., XV. xi. 4; XVIII. iv. 2. Compare XX. i. 1, 2.
20. The whole trial of Jesus proves this. Compare *Acts* xxiv. 27; xvv. 9.
21. Suetonius, *Caius*, 6; Dion Cassius lix. 8, 12; Josephus Ant. XVIII. v. 3; vi. 10; 2 Cor. xi. 32.
22. Ventidius Cumanus experienced quite similar adventures. It is true that Josephus exaggerates the misfortunes of all those who are opposed to his nation.
23. Madden, History of Jewish Coinage, p. 134, and following.
24. Jos. *Ant.* XVIII. iv. 3.
25. Ib., XVIII. v. 3.
26. *Acts* viii. 2. The words ἀνὴρ εὐλαβὴς designate a proselyte, not a pure Jew. See Acts ii. 5.
27. *Acts* viii. 1, and following; xi. 19; Acts xxvi. 10, would even lead to the belief that there were other deaths than that of Stephen. But we must not misconstrue words in our versions of a style so loose. Compare Acts ix. 1–2 with xxii. 5 and xxvi. 12.
28. Compare Acts i. 4; viii. 1, 14; Gal. i. 17, and following.

29 Acts ix. 26–30 prove, in fact, that in the mind of the author the expressions of viii. 1 had not a meaning so absolute as might be supposed. [Except that after the first panic was over some of the disciples, at first wholly scattered, may have returned by the time of Saul's arrival.—Tr.]

30. This happened in the case of the Essenians.

31. This happened to the Franciscans.

32. I. Thess. ii. 14.

33. Acts viii. 3; ix. 13, 14, 21, 26; xxii. 4, 19; xxvi. 9, and following Gal. i. 13, 23; I. Cor. xv. 9; Phil. iii. 6; I. Tim. i. 13.

34. Gal. i. 14; Acts xxvi. 5; Phil. iii. 5.

35. Acts ix. 13, 21, 26.

CHAPTER IX.

1. Acts viii. 1, 4; xi. 19.

2. Acts viii. 5, and following. That it was not the apostle is evident from a comparison of the passages, *Acts* viii. 1, 5, 12, 14, 40; xxi. 8. It is true that the verse, *Acts* xxi. 9, compared with what is said by Papias (in Eusebius His. Ecc. iii. 39), Polycrates (ib. v. 24), Clement of Alexandria (Strom. iii. 6), would identify the Apostle Philip, of whom these three ecclesiastical writers are speaking, with the Philip who plays so important a part in the *Acts*. But it is more natural to admit that the statement in the verse in question is a mistake, and that the verse was only interpolated to contradict the tradition of the churches of Asia and even of Hierapolis, whither the Philip who had daughters prophetesses retired. The particular data possessed by the author of the 4th Gospel (written, as it seems, in Asia Minor), in regard to the Apostle Philip are thus explained.

3. See *Life of Jesus*, ch. xiv. It may be, however, that the habitual tendency of the author of the *Acts* shows itself here again. See *Introd.*, and supra.

4. *Acts* viii. 5–40.

5. Jos. *Ant.* XVIII. iv. 1, 2.

6. At this day Jît, on the road from Nablous to Jaffa, an hour and a half from Nablous and from Sebastieh. See Robinson *Bib. Res.* ii. p. 308, note; iii. 134 (2d ed.), and his map.

7. The accounts relative to this personage, given by the Christian writers, are so fabulous that doubts may be raised even as to the reality of his existence. These doubts are all the more specious from the fact that in the Pseudo-Clementine literature "Simon the Magician" is often a pseudonym for St. Paul. But we cannot admit that the legend of Simon rests upon this foundation alone. How could the author of the *Acts*, so favorable to St. Paul, have admitted

a doctrine the hostile bearing of which could not have escaped him." The chronological series of the Simonian School, the writings which remain to us of it, the precise facts of topography and chronology given by St. Justin, fellow-countryman of our thaumaturgist, are inexplicable, moreover, upon the hypothesis of Simon's having been an imaginary person. (See especially Justin *Apol.* ii 15, and *Dial. cum Tryph.* 120.)

8. Acts viii. 5, and following.
9. Ib. viii. 9, and following.
10. Justin, *Apol.* i. 26, 56.
11. *Homil.* Pseudo-Clem. xvii. 15, 17; Quadratus, in Eusebius *Hist. Ecc* iv. 3.
12. *Acts* viii. 25.
13. Ib. viii. 26–40.
14. I. Macc. x. 86, 89; xi. 60, and following. Jos. *Ant.* XIII., xiii. 3; XV. vii. 3; XVIII. xi. 5; *B. J.*, I. iv. 2.
15. Robinson *Bib. Res.*, II. p. 41 and 514, 515 (2d ed).
16. Talm. of Bab. *Erubin* 53 b and 54 a; *Sota*, 46 b.
17. Isaiah liii. 7.
18. At this day Mérawi, near to Gebel-Barkal (Lepsius, *Denkmæler* i. pl. 1 and 2 *bis.*) Strabo XVII., i. 54.
19. Strabo, XVII., i. 54; Pliny VI., xxxv. 8; Dion Cassius liv. 5; Eusebius *Hist. Ecc.* ii. 1.
20. The descendants of these Jews still exist under the name of Falâsyân. The missionaries who converted them came from Egypt. Their translation of the Bible was made from the Greek version. The Falâsyân are not Israelites by blood.
21. John xii. 20; Acts x. 2.
22. See *Deut.* xxiii. 1. It is true that εὐνοῦχος might be taken by catachresis to designate a chamberlain as functionary of the Oriental Court. But δυνάστης was sufficient to render this idea; εὐνοῦχος ought then to be taken here in its proper sense.
23. *Acts* viii. 26, 29.
24. To conclude thence that all this history was invented by the author of the *Acts* seems to us rash. The author of the *Acts* insists with satisfaction upon the facts which support his opinions; but we do not believe that he introduces into his narrative facts purely symbolical or deliberately invented. See *Introd.*
25. For the analogous state of the first Mormons, see Jules Remy *Voyage au pays des Mormons* (Paris, 1860), i. p. 195, and following.
26. *Acts* viii. 39–40. Compare *Luke* iv. 14.
27. *Acts* ix. 32, 38.
28. Ib. viii. 40; xi. 11.
29. Ib. xxi. 8.

30. Jos. *B. J* III. ix. 1.
31. *Acts* xxiii. 23, and following; xxv. 1, 5; Tacitus *Hist.* ii. 79.
32. Jos. *B. J.* III. ix. 1.
33. Jos. *Ant.* XX. viii. 7; *B. J.* II. xiii. 5; xiv. 5; xviii. 1.
34. Palm. of Jerusalem, *Sota*, 21 b.
35. Jos. *Ant.* XIX. vii. 3-4; viii. 2.
36. *Acts* xi. 19.
37. Ib. ix. 2, 10, 19.

CHAPTER X.

1. This date resulted from the comparison of chapters ix., xi., xii. of the *Acts* with Gal. i. 18; ii. 1, and from the synchronism presented by Chapter xii. of the *Acts* with profane history, a synchronism which fixes the date of the incidents detailed in this chapter at the year 44.
2. *Acts* ix. 11: xxi. 39; xxii. 3.
3. In the Epistle to Philemon, written about the year 61, he calls himself an "old man" (v. 9); *Acts* vii. 57, he calls himself a young man.
4. In the same way that those named "Jesus" often called themselves "Jason;" the "Josephs," "Hegesippe;" the "Eliacim," "Alcime," etc. St. Jerome (*De Viris Ill.* 5) supposes Paul took his name from the proconsul Sergius Paulus (*Acts* xiii. 9). Such an explanation seems hardly admissible. If the *Acts* only give to Saul the name of "Paul," after his relations with that personage, that would argue that the supposed conversion of Sergius was the first important act of Paul as apostle of the Gentiles.
5. *Acts* xiii. 9, and following. The closing phrases of all the Epistles; II. Peter iii. 15.
6. The Ebionite calumnies (Epiphan. *Adv. hær.* xxx. 16, 25) should not be seriously taken.
7. St. Jerome, *loc. cit.* Inadmissible as the present St. Jerome, though this tradition appears to have some foundation.
8 Rom. xi. 1; Phil. iii. 5.
9. *Acts* xxii. 28.
10. *Acts* xxiii. 6.
11. Phil. iii. 5; *Acts* xxvi. 5.
12. *Acts* vi. 9; Philo, *Leg. ad Caium*, § 36.
13. Strabo XIV. x. 13.
14. *Ibid.* XIV. x. 14, 15; Philostratus *Vie d'Apollonius*, 1, 7.
15. Jos. *Ant.*, last paragraph, Cf. *Vie de Jésus.*
16. Philostratus, *loc. cit.*

17. *Acts* xvii. 22, e c.; xxi. 37.
18. Gal. vi. 11; Rom. xvi. 22.
19. II. Cor. xi. 6.
20. *Acts* xxi. 40. I have elsewhere explained the sense of the word 'Ἑβραϊστί. *Hist. des Langes Sémit.* ii. 1, 5; iii. 1, 2.
21. *Acts* xxvi. 14.
22. I. Cor. xv. 33, Cf. Meinecke. *Menandri fragm.* p. 75.
23. Tit. i. 12; *Acts* xvii. 28. The authenticity of the Epistle to Titus is very doubtful. As to the discourse in chapter xvii. of the *Acts*, it is the work of the author of the *Acts* rather than of St. Paul.
24. The verse quoted from Aratus (Phænom. 5) is really found in Cleanthes (*Hymn to Jupiter*, 5). Both are doubtless taken from some anonymous religious hymn.
25. Gal. i. 14.
26. *Acts* xvii. 22, etc. Observe note 23.
27. See *Vie de Jésus*, p. 72.
28. *Acts* xviii. 3.
29. *Ibid.* xviii. 3; I. Cor. iv. 12; I. Thess. ii. 9; II. Thess. iii. 8.
30. *Acts* xxiii. 16.
31. II. Cor. viii. 18, 22; xii. 18.
32. Rom. xvi. 7, 11, 21.
33. See above all the Epistle to Philemon.
34. Gal. v. 12; Phil. iii. 2.
35. II. Cor. x. 10.
36. *Acta Pauli et Theclæ* 3, in Tischendorf, *Acta Apost.*, apocr. (Leipzig, 1851), p. 41, and the notes (an ancient text perhaps, the original spoken of by Tertullian); the *Philopatris*, 12 (composed about 363); Malala Chronogr. p. 257, edit. Bonn; Nicephore, *Hist. Eccl.* ii. 37. All these passages, above all that of *Philopatris*, admit that these were ancient portraits.
37. I. Cor. ii. 1, etc.; II. Cor. x. 1, 2, 10; xi. 6.
38. I. Cor. ii. 3; II. Cor. x. 10.
39. II. Cor. xi. 30; xii. 5, 9, 10.
40. I. Cor. ii. 3; II. Cor. i. 8, 9; x. 10; xi. 30; xii. 5, 9, 10; Gal. iv. 13, 14.
41. II. Cor. xii. 7–10.
42. I Cor. vii. 7, 8, and the context.
43. I. Cor. vii. 7, 8; ix. 5. This second passage is far from being demonstrative. Phil. iv. 3, would imply the contrary. Comp. Clement of Alexandria, *Strom.* iii. 6, and Euseb. *Hist. Eccl.* iii. 30. The passage I. Cor. vii. 7, 8 alone has any weight on this point.
44. I. Cor. vii. 7–9.
45. *Acts* xxii. 3; xxvi. 4.

46. Ibid. xxii. 3. Paul does not speak of this matter in certain parts of his Epistles where he would naturally mention him (Phil. iii. 5). There is an absolute contradiction between the principles of Gamaliel (*Acts* v. 34, etc.) and the conduct of Paul before his conversion

47. Gal. i. 13, 14; *Acts* xxii. 3; xxvi. 5.

48 II. Cor. v. 16, does not implicate him. The passages *Acts* xxii. 3, xxvi. 4, give reason to believe that Paul was at Jerusalem at the same time as Jesus. But it does not follow that he saw him.

49. *Acts* xxii. 4, 19; xxvi. 10, 11.

50. Ibid. xxvi. 11.

51. High-Priest from 37 to 42; Jos. *Ant.* XVIII. v. 3; XIX. vi. 2.

52. *Acts* ix. 1, 2, 14; xxii. 5; xxvi. 12.

53. See *Revue Numismatique*, new series, vol. iii. (1858), p. 296, etc.; 362, etc.; *Revue Archéol.*, April, 1864, p. 284, etc.

54. Jos. B. J. II. xx. 2.

55. II. Cor. xi. 32. The Roman money at Damascus is wanting during the reigns of Caligula and Claud. Eckhel, *Doctrina num. vet.*, part 1, vol. iii. p. 330. Damascus money, stamped "Arétas Philhellenius" (ibid.), seems to be of our Hâreth (communication of M. Waddington).

56. Jos. *Ant.* XVIII. v. 1, 3.

57. Comp. *Acts* xii. 3; xxiv. 27; xxv. 9.

58. *Acts* v. 34, etc.

59. See an analogous trait in the conversion of Omar. Ibn-Hiseham. *Sirat errasoul*, p. 226 (Wüstenfeld edition).

60. *Acts* ix. 3; xxii. 6; xxvi. 13.

61. *Acts* ix. 4, 8; xxii. 7, 11; xxvi. 14, 16.

62. It is here that the tradition of the middle ages locates the miracle.

63. This results from *Acts* ix. 3, 8; xxii. 6, 11.

64. Nahr el-Aroadj.

65. The plain is really more than seventeen hundred feet above the level of the sea.

66. *Acts* xxvi. 14.

67. From Jerusalem to Damascus is over eight days' journey.

68. *Acts* ix. 8, 9, 18; xxii. 11, 13.

69. II. Cor. xii. 1, etc.

70. I experienced a crisis of this kind at Byblos; and with other principles I would certainly have taken the hallucinations that I had then for visions.

71. We possess thirteen accounts of this important episode: *Acts* ix. 1, etc.; xxii. 5, etc.; xxvi. 12, etc. The differences remarked between these passages prove that the apostle himself varied in the accounts he gave of his conversion. That in *Acts* ix. itself is not homogeneous, as we shall soon see. Comp. Gal. i. 15–17; I. Cor. ix. 1; xv 8; *Acts* ix. 27.

72. With the Mormons, and in the American trances, almost all the conversions are also induced by nervous excitement, producing hallucinations.

73. The circumstance that the companions of Paul saw and heard as he did may be legendary, especially as the accounts are on this point, being in direct contradiction. Comp. *Acts* ix. 7; xxii. 9; xxvi. 13 The hypothesis of a fall from a horse is refuted by these accounts. The opinion which rejects entirely the narration in the *Acts*, founded on ἐν ἐμοί of Gal. i. 16, is exaggerated, ἐν 'Ἐμοί in this passage, has the sense of "for me." Comp. Gal. i. 24. Paul surely had at a fixed moment, a vision which resulted in his conversion.

74. *Acts* ix. 3, 7; xxii. 6, 9, 11; xxvi. 13.

75. This was my experience during my illness at Byblos. My recollections of the evening preceding the day of the trance are totally effaced.

76. II. Cor. xii. 1, etc.

77. *Acts* ix. 27; Gal. i. 16; I. Cor. ix. 1; xv. 8; Hom. Pseudo-Clem. xvii. 13—19. Comp. the experience of Omar, *Sirat errasoul*, p. 226, etc.

78. *Acts* ix. 8; xxii. 11.

79. Its ancient Arabic name was *Tarik el Adhwa.* It is now called *Tarik el Mustekim*, answering to Ῥύμη εὐθεῖα. The eastern gate (*Bâb Sharki*) and a few vestiges of the colonnades yet remain. See the Arabic texts given by Wustenfield in the *Zeitschrift für vergleschende Erakunde* of Lüdde for the year 1842, p. 168; Porter, *Syria and Palestine*, p. 477; Wilson, *The Lands of the Bible*, II., 345, 355–52.

80. *Acts* xxii. 11.

81. The account given in *Acts* ix. appears to have been formed from two mingled narratives. One, the more original, comprises vv. 9, &c. The other more developed, containing more dialogue and legend, includes verses 9, 10, 11, 13, 14, 15, 16, 17, 18. The 12th verse belongs neither to that which precedes nor to that which follows it. The account in chapter xxii. 12–16, is more conformed to the above-mentioned texts.

82. *Acts* ix. 12. It should read ἄνδρα ἐν ὁράματι according to manuscript B. of the Vatican. Comp. verse 10.

83. *Acts* ix. 18; comp. *Tobit*, ii. 9; vi. 10; xi. 13.

84. *Acts* ix. 18; xxii. 16.

85. Gal. i. 2, 8–9, 11, &c.; I. Cor. ix. 1; xi. 23; xv. 8, 9; Col. i. 25; Ephes. i. 19; iii. 3, 7, 8; *Acts* xx. 24; xxii. 14–15, 21; xxvi. 16; Homiliæ Pseudo-Clem., xvii. 13–19.

86. Gal. i. 17.

87. 'Αραβία is "the province of Arabia," principally composed of the Hauran.

88. Gal. i. 17, &c.; *Acts* ix. 19, &c.; xxvi. 20. The author of the *Acts* believes that this first sojourn at Damascus was short, and that

Paul, shortly after his conversion, came to Jerusalem and preached there. (Comp. xxii. 17.) But the passage of the epistle to the Galatians is peremptory.

89. Insc. discovered by Waddington and De Vogüé (Revue Archéol., April, 1864, p. 284, &c., *Comptes Rendus* de l'Acad. des Inscr. et B. L., 1865, p. 106-108).

90. Dion Cass. lix. 12.

91. I have discussed this in the *Bulletin Archéologique* of Langperier and De Wette, September, 1856.

92. Gal. i. 16, with following verses, prove that Paul preached immediately after his conversion.

93. Jos. B. J., I., ii. 25; II., xx. 2.

94. *Acts* ix. 20–22.

95. Gal. i. 16. It is the sense of οὐ προσανεθέμην σαρκὶ καὶ αἵματι.

CHAPTER XI.

1. Acts ix. 31.
2. See the atrociously naïve avowal of 3 Macc. vii. 12, 13.
3. Read the 3d Book (apocryphal) of Maccabees, entire, and compare it with that of Esther.
4. Suetonius, *Caius*, 22, 52; Dion Cassius, lix. 26, 28; Philo, *Leg. ad Caium*, § 25, &c.; Josephus, *Ant.* XVIII., viii.; XIX., i. 1-2; *B. J.*, II. x.
5. Philo, *Leg. ad Caium*, § 30.
6. Philo, *In Flaccum*, § 7; *Leg. ad Caium*, § 18, 20, 26, 43.
7. Philo, *Leg. ad Caium*, § 29; Josephus, *Ant.* XVIII. viii.; *B. J.* II. x. Tacitus, *Ann.* XII. 54; *Hist.* V. 9, completing the first passage by the second.
8. Philo, *Leg. ad Caium*, § 27, 30, 44, and following.
9. Acts ix. 31.
10. Gal. i. 18, 19; ii. 9.
11. Acts xi. 29, 30.
12. Acts ix. 32.
13. At this day, *Ludd.*
14. Acts ix. 32–35.
15. Jaffa.
16. Jos. *Ant.* XIV., x. 6.
17. Acts ix. 43; x. 6, 17, 32.
18. Mischna, *Ketuboth*, vii. 10.
19. Compare Gruter, p. 891, 4; Reinesius, *Inscript.*, XIV. 61; Mommsen, *Inscr. regni Neap.*, 622, 2094, 3052, 4985; Pape, *Wört der Griech Eigenn.*, on this word Cf. Jos. *B. J.* IV., iii. 6.
20. Acts ix. 36, and following.

21. Ibid. ix. 39. The Greek runs: ὅσα ἐποίει μετ' αὐτῶν οὖσα.

23. Acts x. 9–16; xi. 5-10.

24. Ibid. x. 1; xi. 18.

25. There were at least thirty-two. (Orelli & Heuzen, *Inscr. Lat.*, Nos 90, 512, 6756.)

26. Compare Acts xxvii. 1. and Heuzen, No. 6709.

27. Compare Luke vii. 2, and following. Luke is priding himself, it is true, upon this idea of virtuous centurions, Jews in heart without circumcision (see Introduction). But the example of Izates (Jos. *Ant.*, xx., ii. 5), proves that such situations were possible. Compare Jos. *B. J.*, II., xxviii. 2; Orelli, *Inscr.*, No. 2523.

28. Acts x. 2, 7.

29. This seems, it is true, in contradiction to Gal. ii. 7-9. But the conduct of Peter in that which relates to the admission of the Gentiles was never very consistent. Gal. ii. 12.

30. Acts xi. 18.

31. Ibid. xv. 1, and following.

32. II. Cor. ii. 32, 33; Acts ix. 23–25.

33. Gal. i. 18.

34. Ibid. i. 18.

35. Ibid. i. 23.

36. *Acts* ix. 26.

37. Gal. i. 18.

38. *Acts* ix. 26.

39. Acts ix. 27. All this portion of the Acts has too little historical value to enable us to affirm that this fine action of Barnabas took place during the fifteen days that Paul passed at Jerusalem. But there is no doubt, in the manner in which the *Acts* present the case, a true sentiment of the relations of Paul and Barnabas.

40. Gal. i. 19, 20.

41. Ibid. i. 18. Impossible, consequently, to admit as exact the 28th and 29th verses of Acts ix. The author of the *Acts* makes an abusive employment of these ambushes and murderous projects. The Acts vary from the Epistle to the Galatians in supposing the sojourn of St. Paul at Jerusalem too long, and too near to his conversion. Naturally the Epistle merits our preference, at least, as to its chronology and the material circumstances.

42. See especially the Epistle to the Galatians.

43. Epistle to the Galatians, i. 11, 12, and nearly throughout; I. Cor. ix. 1, and following; xv. 1, and following; II. Cor. xi. 21, and following.

44. We find this sentiment more or less directly; Rom. xii. 14; I. Cor xiii. 2; II. Cor. iii. 6; I. Thess. iv. 8; v. 2, 6.

45. Gal. i. 22, 23.

46. *Acts* xx. 17, 21.

47 *Acts* ix. 29, 30.

48 Gal. i. 21.

49. Acts ix. 30; xi. 25. The capital chronological datum for this epoch of the life of St. Paul is Gal. i. 18; ii. 1.

50. Cilicia had a church in the year 51. *Acts* xv. 23, 41.

51 It is in the Epistle to the Galatians (towards 56), that Paul places himself for the first time openly in the rank of the apostles (i. 1, and the following). According to Gal. ii. 7–10, he had received this title in 51. Still he did not assume it, even in the subscription of the two Epistles to the Thessalonians, which are of the year 53. I. Thess. ii. 6, does not imply an official title. The author of the *Acts* never gives Paul the name of "apostle." "The apostles," for the author of the *Acts*, are "the Twelve." Acts xiv. 4, 14, is an exception.

CHAPTER XII.

1. Acts xi. 19.
2. Josephus, *Wars of the Jews*, ii. 4. Rome and Alexandria were the two chief ones; compare Strabo xvi. ii. 5.
3. Compare Otfried Müller, *Antiochian Antiquities*, Göttingen, 1839, p. 68. John Chrysostom, on *Saint Ignatius*, 4 (opp. t. ii. p. 597, edit. Montfaucon): *On Matthew*, Homilies lxxxv. 4. (vol. viii. p.810). He estimates the population of Antioch at two hundred thousand souls, without counting slaves, infants, and the immense suburbs. The present city has a population of not more than seven thousand.
4. The corresponding streets of Palmyra, Gerasium, Gadara, and Sebaste, were probably imitations of the grand *Corso* of Antioch.
5. Some traces of it are found in the direction of *Bâb Bolos.*
6. Dion Chrysostome, Orat. xlvii. (vol. ii. p. 229, edit. Reiske), Libanius, *Antiochicus*, p. 337, 340, 342, 356 (edit. Reiske), Malala, p. 232, et seq., 276, 280, et seq. (Bonn, edition.) The constructor of these great works was Antiochus Epiphanes.
7. Libanius, *Antioch.* 342, 344.
8. Pausanias, vi. ii. 7; Malala, p. 201; Visconti Mus. Pio-clemen., vol. iii. 46. See especially the medals of Antioch.
9. Pierian, Bottian, Penean, Tempean, Castalian, Olympic games, Jopolis (which was referred to Io). The city pretended to be indebted for its celebrity to Inachus, to Orestes, to Daphne and to Triptolemus.
10. See Malala, p. 199; Spartian, *Life of Adrian.* p. 14; Julian, *Misopogon*, p. 361, 362; Ammian Marcellin., xxii. 14; Eckhel, *Doct. num vet.* part i. 3, p. 326; Guigniaut, *Religions de l'Ant.* planches No. 268.
11. John Chrysostom, *Ad pop. Antioch.* homil. xix. 1; (vol. ii. p. 189.) De sanctis martyr. i. (vol. ii. p. 651.)
12. Libanius, Antioch., p. 348.

13. Act. SS. Maii, v. p. 383, 409, 414, 415, 416; Assemani, Bib. or., ii. 323.

14. Juvenal Sat., iii. 62, et seq.; Stacc. *Silves*, i. vi. 72.

15 Tacitus *Ann.* ii. 69.

16. Malala, p. 284, 287, et seq.; Libanius, *De Angariis*, p. 555, et seq.; *De carcere vinctis*, p. 445, et seq.; *ad Timocratem*, p. 385; *Antioch*, 323; Philost., *Vit Apoll.* i. 16; Lucian, *De Saltatione*, 76; Diod. Sic. fragm. lib. xxxiv. No. 34 (p. 358, ed. Dindorf); John Chrysos. Homil. vii. in Matt. 5 (vol. vii. p. 113); lxxiii. *in Matt.* 3 (ibid. p. 712); *De consubst. contra Anon.*, 1 (vol. i., p. 501); *De Anna*, 1 (vol. iv. p. 730), *De David et Saüle* iii. 1 (vol. iv. 768, 770); Julian Misopogon, p. 343, 350, edit. Spanheim; *Actes de Sainte Thècle*, attributed to Basil of Seleucia, published by P. Pantius (Auvers, 1608) p. 70.

17. Philostr. *Apoll.* iii. 58; Ausonius, *Clar. Urb.*, 2; J. Capitolin *Verus*, 7; *Marcus Aurelius*, 25; Herodian ii. 10; John of Antioch in the Excerpta Valesiana, p. 844; Suidas, at the word [illegible].

18. Julian *Misopogon*, p. 344, 365, etc.; Eunap. *Vie des Soph.*, p. 496, edit. Boissònade (Didot); *Ammien Marcellin* xxii. 14.

19. John Chrysos. *De Lazaro*, ii. 11 (vol. 1. p. 722, 723).

20. Cic. pro. Archiâ, 3, making allowance for the usual exaggeration of an advocate.

21. Philostrat us *Vie d'Apollonius*, iii. 58.

22. Malala, p. 287, 289.

23. John Chrysos., Homil. vii. *On Matt.* 5, 6. (vol. vii. p. 113); See O. Müller, *Antiq. Antioch.*, p. 33 note.

24. Libanius, *Antiochichus*, p. 355–366.

25. Juvenal, iii. 62 et seq. and Forcellini, in the word *ambubaja*, where he observes that the word *ambuba* is Syriac.

26. Libanius, *Antioch* p. 315; *De carcere vinctis*, p. 455; Julian Misopogon, p. 367, edit. Spanheim.

27. Libanius, *Pro rhetoribus*, p. 211.

28. Libanius, *Antiochichus*, p 363.

29. Libanius, *Antiochichus*, p 354 et seq.

30. The actual enclosure, which is of the time of Justinian, presents the same particulars.

31. Libanius, *Antioch.*, p. 337, 338, 339.

32. The lake *Ak Denir*, which forms on this side the actual limit of the territory of Antakieh, had, as it appears, no existence in olden times. See Ritter, *Erdkunde*, xvii. p 1149, 1613 et seq.

33. Josephus *Ant.*, xii iii. 1; xiv. xii. 6; *Wars of the Jews*, ii. xviii. 5 vii iii. 2–4.

34. Josephus, *against Apion*, ii. 4; *Wars of the Jews*, vii. iii. 2–4.

35. Malala, p. 244, 245; Jos., *Wars of the Jews*, vii. v. 2.

36. *Acts* vi 5.

37. Ibid. xi. 19, et seq.

38 Compare Josephus, *Wars of the Jews*, ii. xviii. 2.

39. *Acts* xv 20, 21. The proper reading is Ἕλληνας Ἑλληνιστας comes from a false agreement with ix. 29.

40. Malala, p. 245. The narrative of Malala cannot, indeed, be exact, Josephus says not a word respecting the invasion of which the chronographer makes mention.

41. Malala, p 243, 265–266. Compare "*Memoirs of Academy of Inscriptions and Belles-Lettres*," session of 17 August, 1865.

42. S Athanasius, *Tomus ad Antioch.* (Opp. vol. i. p. 771, edit. Montfaucon); S. John Chrysostom, *Ad pop. Antioch*, Homil i. and ii. beginning (vol. ii. p. i. and xx.); *In Inscr.* Act. ii. beginning (vol. iii. 60); *Chron. Pasch.*, p. 296 (Paris); Theodoret, Hist. Eccl., ii. 27; iii. 2. 8. 9. The agreement of these passages does not permit of ἐν τῇ καλουμένῃ Παλαιᾷ being rendered by "in that which was called the old town," as the editors have sometimes done.

43. Malala, p. 242.

44. Pococke, *Descript. of the East*, vol. ii. part i. p. 192 (London 1745), Chesney, *Expedition for the Survey of the Rivers Euphrates and Tigris*, i. 425, et seq.

45. That is to say, opposite to that part of the old town which is still inhabited.

46. See below.

47. The type of the Maronites is reproduced in a striking manner in the country of Antakieh, Soneideieb, and Beylan.

48 F. Naironi, *Anoplia fidei Cathol.* (Rome, 1694), p 58, et seq., and the work of S. Em. Paul Peter Masad, present patriarch of the Maronites, entitled Kitab ed. durr ed. manzoum (in Arabic, printed at the convent of Zamisch in the Kesronan, 1863).

49. *Acts* xi. 19, 20; xiii. 1.

50. Gal. ii. 11, et seq., presumes it to be so.

CHAPTER XIII.

1. *Acts* xi. 22, &c.

2. *Acts* xi. 25.

3. *Acts* xi. 26.

4. Libanius. *Pro templis*, p. 164, &c.; *De carcere vinctis*, p. 458.; Theodoret, *Hist. Eccl.* iv. 28; Jean Chrysost.; Homil. lxxii. *in Matt.* 3 (vol. vii. p. 705). *In Epist. ad Ephes.* Hom. vi. 4 (vol. xi. p. 44); In i. Tim. Hom. xiv. 3 &c. (ibid. p. 628, &c.); Nicephore xii. 44; Glycas p. 257 (Paris edition).

5. *Acts* xi. 26.

6. The passages I. Petri iv. 16, and James ii. 7, compared with Suet *Nero* 16, and with Tac. *Ann.* xv. 44, confirm this idea. See also *Acts* xxvi. 28.

7. It is true that we find Ἀσιανός (*Acts* xx. 4; Philo. Legatio, 36; Strabo, etc.). But it seems to be a Latinism like Δαλδιανοί, and the names of the sects Σιμωνιανοί, Κηρινθιανοί, Σηθιανοί, etc. The Greek derivative χριστός had been χρίστειος. It serves nothing to say that the termination *anus* is a Doric form of the Greek ανος; this was not known at all during the first century.

8. Tac. (loc. cit.) so interprets it.

9. Suet. *Claud.* 25. We shall discuss this passage in our next book.

10. Corpus *Inscr. Gr.* Nos. 2883 d., 3857 g., 3857 p., 3865 l. Tertul. *Apol.* 3; Lactance Divin. Inst. iv. 7. Comp. the French form *chrestien.*

11. James ii. 7, only implies an occasional usage.

12. *Acts* xxiv. 5; Tertull. *Adv. Marcionem* iv. 8.

13. *Nesârâ.* The names of *meschihoio* in Syriac, *mesihi* in Arabic, are relatively modern, and outlined from χριστιανός. The name of "Galileans" is much more recent. Julian gave it an official signification. Jul. *Epist.* vii.; Gregory, Orat. iv. (Invect. i.), 76; S. Cyrille d'Alex. *Contre Julien* ii. p. 39, Spanheim ed.); *Philopatris*, dialogue falsely attributed to Lucian, though really of the time of Julien, § 12; Theodoret *Hist. Eccl.* iii. 4. I believe that in Epictetus (Arrien, *Dissert.* iv., vii., 6) and in Marcus Aurelius (*Pensées* xi. 3), this name does not designate Christians, but rather "assassins" (*Sicaires*), fanatical disciples of Judas the Galilean or the Gaulonite, and of John of Gischala.

14. I. Petri iv. 16; James ii. 7.

15. *Acts* xiii. 2.

16. Ibid xiii. 1.

17. See chapter vi.

18. *Acts* xiii. 1.

19. Euseb. *Chron.* at the year 43; *Hist. Eccl.* iii. 22. Ignatii *Epist. ad Antioch.* (apocr.) 7.

20. I. Cor. xiv. entire.

21. II. Cor. xii. 15.

22. It places this vision fourteen years before he wrote the second Epistle to the Corinthians, which dates about the year 57. It is not impossible, however, that he was still at Tarsus.

23. For Jewish ideas about the heavens, see *Testam. des* 12 *patr.* Levi. 3; *Ascension d'Isaie*, vi. 13; viii. 8, and all the rest of the book; Talm. of Babyl., *Chagiga* 12 b.; Midraschim *Bereschith rabba*, sect xix. fol. 19 c.; *Schemoth rabba*, sect. xv. fol. 115 d.; *Bammiabar rabba*, sect. xiii. fol. 218 a.; *Debarim rabba*, sect. ii. fol. 253 a.; *Schir hasschirim rabba*, fol. 24 d.

24. Comp. Talmud of Babylon, *Chagiga*, 14 b.

25. Comp. *Ascension d'Isaie*, vi. 15; vii. 3, &c.

26. II. Cor. xii. 12; Rom. xv. 19.

27. I. Cor. xii. entire.

28. *Acts* xi. 29; xxiv. 17; Gal ii. 10; Rom. xv. 26; I. Cor. xvi. 1; II. Cor. viii. 4, 14; ix. 1, 12.
29. Jos. *Ant.* XVIII., vi., 3, 4; XX., v. 2.
30. James ii. 5, &c.
31. *Acts* xi. 28; Jos. *Ant.* XX., ii. 6; v 2; Euseb. *Hist. Eccl.* ii. 8, 12. Comp. *Acts* xii. 20; Tac. Ann. xii. 43; Suet. *Claud.* 18; Dion Cass. lx. 11. Aurelius Victor, Cas., 4; Euseb. *Chron.* year 43, &c. The reign of Claudius was afflicted almost every year by partial famines.
32. *Acts* xi. 27, &c.
33. The book of *Acts* (xi. 30; xii. 25) includes Paul in this journey. But Paul declares that between his first sojourn of two weeks and his journey for the affair of the circumcision, he did not visit Jerusalem. (Gal. ii. 1.) See Introduction.
34. Gal. i., 17–19.
35 *Acts* xiii. 3; xv. 36; xviii. 23.
36. Ibid. xiv. 25; xviii. 22.

CHAPTER XIV.

1. The inscriptions of these countries fully confirm the indications of Josephus. (Comptes Rendus de l'Acad. des Inscr. *I. B. L.*, 1865. pp. 106, 109.)
2. Josephus, *Ant.* xix. iv. *B. J.*, ii. xi.
3. *Ib.* xix. v. i.; vi. i.; *B. J.*, II. xi. 5; Dion Cassius, LX. 8.
4. Dion Cassius, LIX. 24.
5. Jos. *Ant.* xix. ix. 1.
6. Ibid. XIX. vi. 1, 3; ii. 3, 4; viii. 2; ix. 1.
7. Ibid. XIX. vii. 4.
8. Ibid. XIX. vi. 3.
9. Juvenal, Sat. vi. 158, 159; Persius, Sat. v. 180.
10. Philo. *In Flaccum*, § 5, and following.
11. Jos. *Ant.* XIX. v. 2, and sequel; xx. vi. 3.; *B. J.*, II. xii. 7. The restrictive measures which he took against the Jews of Rome (*Acts* xviii. 2; Suetonius *Claude*, 25; Dion Cassius, LX. 6) were connected with local circumstances.
12. Jos. *Ant.* xix. vi. 3.
13. Ibid. xix. vii. 2; *B. J.* ii. xi. 6; V. iv. 2. Tacitus, Hist. v. 12.
14. Tacitus, *Ann.* vi. 47.
15. Jos. *Ant.* XIX. vii. 2; vii. 21, viii. 1; XX. i. 1.
16. Ibid. XIX. viii. 1.
17. Suetonius, *Caius*, 22, 26, 35; Dion Cassius, lix. 24; lx. 8. Tacitus

Ann. xi. 8. As a type of the part these little Eastern Kings played, study the career of Herod Agrippa I. in Josephus (*Ant.* xviii. and xix.) Compare Horace, *Sat.* I. vii.

18. Supra.
19. Acts xii. 3.
20. Ibid. xii. 1, and following.
21. James was in fact beheaded, and not stoned to death.
22. Acts xii. 3, and following.
23. *Ibid.* xii. 9, 11. The account in the Acts is so lively and just, that it is difficult to find any place in it for any prolonged legendary elaboration.
24. Jos. *Ant.* xix. viii. 2; Acts xii. 18, 23.
25. Ibid. xix. vii. 4.
26. *Acts.* xii. 23. Compare 2 Macc. ix. 9; Jos. *B. J.* I. xxxiii. 5; Talmud of Bab. *Sota*, 35 *a.*
27. Jos. *Ant.* XIX. vi. 1; XX. i. 1, 2.
28. Ibid. xx. v. 2; *B. J.* ii. xv. 1; xviii. 7, and following; IV. x. 6; V. i. 6; Tacitus. *Ann.*, xv 28. *Hist.* i. 11; ii. 79; Suetonius, *Vesp.* 6; *Corpus Inscr. Græc.* No. 4957. (cf. ibid. iii. p. 311.)
29. Jos. *Ant.* XX. i. 3.
30. Ibid. XX. v. 4, *B. J.* II. xii.
31. Josephus, who relates with so much care, the history of these agitations in all its details, never mixes up the Christians with them.
32. Jos. *Against Apion*, ii. 39; Dion Cassius, lxvi. 4.
33. Jos., *B. J.*, IV., iv. 3; V., xiii. 6; Suetonius, *Aug.*, 93; Strabo, XVI., ii. 34, 37; Tacitus, *Hist.*, v. 5.
34. Jos., *Ant.*, XIII., ix. 1; xi. 3; xv. 4; XV., vii. 9.
35. Jos., *B. J.*, II., xvii. 10; *Vita*, 23.
36. Matt. xxiii. 13.
37. Jos., *Ant.*, XX., vii. 1, 3; Compare XVI., vii. 6.
38. Ibid. XX., ii. 4.
39. Ibid. XX., ii. 5, 6; iv. 1.
40. Jos., *B. J.*, II., xx. 2.
41. Seneca, fragment in St. Augustin. *De civ. Dei*, vi. 11.
42. Jos., *Ant.*, XX., ii.–iv.
43. Tacitus, *Ann.*, xii. 13, 14. The greater part of the names of this family are Persian.
44. The name of "Helen" proves this. Still, it is remarkable that the Greek does not figure upon the bi-lingual inscription (Syriac and Syro-Chaldaic) of the tomb of a princess of the family, discovered and brought to Paris by M. de Saulcy. See *Journal Asiatique*, Dec., 1865.
45. Cf. Bereschith rabba. xlvi. 51 d.

46. It is according to all appearances the monument known at this day under the name of "Tomb of the Kings." See *Journal Asiatique*, passage cited.

47. Jos., *B. J.*, ii., xix. 2; vi., vi. 4.

48. Talmud of Jerusalem, *Peah*, 15 b., where there are put into the mouth of one of the Monobazo maxims that exactly recall the Gospel (Matt. vi. 19 and following). Talmud of Bab., *Baba Bathra*, 11 a; *Joma*, 37 a; *Nazir*, 19 b; *Schabbath*, 68 b; *Sifra*, 70 a; *Bereschith rabba*, xlvi., fol. 51 d.

49. Moses of Khorene, ii. 35; Orose, vii. 6.

50. Luke, xxi. 21.

51. Τὰ πάτρια ἔθη, an expression so familiar with Josephus, when he defends the position of the Jews in the pagan world.

CHAPTER XV.

1. It is well known that no MS. of the Talmud is extant to control the printed editions.

2. Jos., *Ant.*, XX., v. 2.

3. Jos., *B. J.*, II., xvii. 8–10; *Vita*, 5.

4. The comparison of Christianity with the two movements of Judus and Theudas is made by the author of the *Acts* himself. (V. 36.)

5. Jos. *Ant.*, XX., v. 1; *Acts*, u. s. Remark the anachronism in *Acts*.

6. Jos. *Ant.*, XVIII., iv. 1, 2.

7. Jos. *Ant.*, XX., v. 3, 4; *B. J.*, ii., xii. 1, 2; Tacit, *Ann.*, xii. 54.

8. Jos. *Ant.*, XX., viii. 5.

9. Jos. *Ant.*, XX., viii. 5; *B. J.*, II., xiii. 3.

10. Jos. *B.*, *J.*, .VII. viii. 1; Mischna, *Sanhédrin*, ix. 6.

11. Jos. *Ant.*, XX., viii. 6, 10; *B. J.*, II., xiii. 4.

12. Jos. *Ant.*, XX., viii. 6; *B. J.*, II., xiii. 5: *Acts* xxi. 38.

13. Jos. *Ant.*, XX., viii. 6; *B. J.*, II., xiii. 6.

14. See ante, p. 153, note.

15. Justin, Apol., 1, 26, 56. It is singular that Josephus, so well informed on Samaritan affairs, does not mention him.

16. *Acts* viii. 9, etc.

17. It cannot be considered entirely apocryphal in view of the agreement between the system set forth in it, and what little we learn from the *Acts* concerning the doctrine of Simon upon miraculous powers.

18. Homil. Pseudo-Clem., ii. 22, 24.

19. Justin, *Apol.* 1, 26, 56; ii. 15. Dial. cum Tryphone, 120; Iren. *Adv* hær. I. xxiii. 2–5; xxvii. 4; II. præf; III. præf; Homiliæ pseudo-clem. i. 15; ii. 22, 25, etc.; Recogn. i. 72; ii. 7, etc.; iii. 47; Philosophumena IV. vii.; VI. i.; X. iv.; Epiph. *Adv. hær.* Lær. xxi.; Orig. *Cont*

Cels. v. 62; vi. 11; Tertull. *De Anima*, 34; *Constit. apost.* vi. 16; S. Jerome, *In Matt.* xxiv. 5; Theod. *Hæret. fab.* i. 1. It is from the quotations given in the *Philosophumena*, and not in the travesties of the Fathers, that an idea may be obtained of "The Great Exposition."

20 Philosophum., IV. vii.; VI. i. 9, 12, 13, 17, 18. Compare Revel. i. 4, 8; iv. 8; xi. 17.

21. *Philosophum.*, VI. i. 17.

22. Ibid. VI. i. 16.

23. *Act.* viii. 10; *Philosophum.*, VI. i. 18; Homil. Pseudo-Clem., ii. 22.

24. Allusion to the adventure of the poet Stesichorus.

25. Iren. *Adv.* hær. I. xxiii. 2–4; Homil. Pseudo-Clem., ii. 23.

26. Philosophum. VI. i. 16.

27. See *Vie de Jesus*, p. 247–249.

28. Ibid. p. 247, note 4.

29. *Chron. Samarit.* c. 10 (edit. Juynboll Leyden, 1848). Cf. Reland, *De Sam.* § 7; *Dissertat. miscell.* Part II. Gesenius, *Comment de Sam. Theol.* (Halle, 1824), p. 24, etc.

30. In a quotation given in the Philosophumena, VI. i. 16, is a citation from the synoptical gospels which seems to be given as from the text of the "Great Exposition." But this may be an error.

31. Homil. Pseudo-Clem. II. 23–24.

32. Iren. *Adv. hær.* I. xxiii. 3. *Philosophum.* VI. i. 19.

33. Homil. Pseudo-Clem. ii. 22. Recogn. II. 14.

34. Iren. *Adv.* hær. II. præf. III. præf.

35. See the Epistle (probably authentic) of Paul to the Colossians, i. 15, &c.

36. Epiph. *Adv.* hær. L. xxx. 1.

37. An argument for the latter hypothesis is, that Simon's sect soon changed into a school of fortune-tellers, and for the manufacture of philters and charms. *Philosoph.* VI. i. 20. Tertull. De Anima, 57.

38. Philosophum. VI. i. 20. Cf. Orig. *Contra Cels.* i. 57; vi. 11.

39. Hegesip. in Euseb. *Hist. Eccl.* iv. 22; Clem. Alex. *Strom.* vii. 17; *Constit. apost.* vi. 8, 16; xviii. 1, &c. Justin, Apol. i. 26, 56; Iren. *Adv. hær.* I. xxiii. init. Theod. Hær. fol. I. i. 2. Tertull. *De Præscr.* 47; De Anima, 50.

40. The most celebrated is that of Dositheus.

41. *Act.* viii. 9; Iren. *Adv. hær.* xxiii. 1.

42. *Philosophum.* VI. i. 19–20. The author attributes these perverse doctrines only to Simon's disciples; but if the disciples entertained them, the master must have shared them in some degree.

43. We shall hereafter see what these narrations signify.

44. The inscription SIMONI DEO SANCTO, stated by Justin to exist in the island (*Apol.* I. 26) of the Tiber, and mentioned also by other Fa-

thers, was a Latin inscription to the Sabine deity Semo Sancus, SEMONI-DEO-SANCO. There was in fact discovered under Gregory XIII. in the island of St. Bartholomew, an inscription now in the Vatican bearing that dedication. V. Baronius, *Ann. Eccl.* 44; Orelli, Inscr. Lat. No. 1860. There was at this spot on the island of the Tiber a college of *bidentales* in honor of Semo-Sancus, with many inscriptions of the same kind. Orelli, No. 1861. (Mommsen, Inscr. Lat. regni Neapol. No. 6770). Comp. Orelli, No. 1859. Henzen, No. 6999; Mabillon, *Museum Ital.* I. 1st part, p. 84. Orelli, No. 1862, is not to be relied on. (See *Corp.* Inscr. Lat. I. No. 542.)

45. This gross blunder could not have been detected without the discovery of the *Philosophumena*, which alone contains extracts from the *Apophasis magna* (VI. i. 19). Tyre was celebrated for its courtezans.

46. 'Εχθρὸς ἄνθρωπος, ἀντικείμενος. See Homil. Pseudo-Clem. hom. xvii. passim.

47. Thus in the Pseudo-Clementine literature, the name of Simon the Magician indicates sometimes the apostle Paul, against whom the writer had a spite.

48. It may be observed that in *Acts*, he is not treated as an enemy, but only reproached as of low sentiments, and room is left for repentance. (viii, 24).) Perhaps Simon was living when those lines were written, and his relations to Christianity had not yet become absolutely hostile.

CHAPTER XVI.

1. *Acts* xii. 1, 25. Remark the context.
2. 1 Peter v. 13; Papias in Euseb. *Hist. Acc.* iii. 39.
3. Acts xiii. 2.
4. Gal. i. 15, 16; Acts xvii. 15, 21; xxvi. 17-18; 1 Cor. i. 1; Rom. i, 1, 5; xv. 15, etc.
5. Acts xiii. 5.
6. The author of Acts, being a partisan of the hierarchy and of church-domination, has perhaps inserted this circumstance. Paul knew nothing of any such ordination or consecration. He received his commission from Christ, and did not consider himself any more especially the envoy of the church of Antioch than of that of Jerusalem.
7. *Acts* xiii. 3; xiv. 25.
8. In I. Peter v. 13, Babylon means Rome.
9. Cic. Pro Archia, 10.
10. Jos., B. J., II. xx. 2; VII. iii. 3.
11. *Acts* xviii. 24, &c.
12. See Philo. *De Vita Contempl.* passim.

13. Pseudo-Hermes. *Asclepius*, fol. 158, v. 159 r. (Florence Juntes, 15, 12.)

14. Cic. *Pro Flacco*, 28; Philo. *In Flaccum*, § 7; Leg. ad Caium, § 36: *Acts* ii. 5–11; vi. 9; Corp. Inscr. Gr. No. 5361.

15. Lex. Wisigoth; lib. xii., tit. ii. and iii. in Walter. Corp. jur. German Antiq. L. I. p. 630, &c.

16. See Vie de Jésus, p. 137.

17. Philo. *In Flacc.*, § 5 and 6; Jos. *Ant.* XVIII. viii. 1; XIX. v. 2, B. J. II. xviii. 7, etc.; VII. x. 1. Papyrus printed in *Notices et Extraits* XVIII., 2d part, p. 383, etc.

18. Dion Cass., XXXVII. 17; LX. 6. Philo. *Leg. ad Caium*, § 23. Jos. *Ant.* XIV. x. 8; XVII. xi. 1; XVIII. iii. 5; Hor. Sat. I. iv. 142–143; v. 100; ix. 69, &c.; Pers. 5, 179–184; Suet. *Lib.* 36; *Claud* 25; *Domit.* 12; Juv. iii. 14; vi. 542, &c.

19. *Pro. Flac.* 28.

20. Jos. *Ant.* XIV. x.; Suet. Jul. 84.

21. Suet. *Lib.* 36; Tac. *Ann.* ii. 85; Jos. *Ant.* XVIII. iii. 4, 5.

22. Dion Cass. LX. 6.

24. Jos. B. J., VII. iii. 3.

25. Seneca, fragment in Aug. *De Civ.* Dei, vi. 11; Rutilius Numatianus i. 395, &c.; Jos. Contr. Apion, ii. 39; Juv. Sat. vi. 544; xiv. 96, &c.

26. Philo. *In* Flacc. § 5; Tac. *Hist.* v. 4, 5, 8; Dion. Cass. xlix. 22; Juv. xiv. 103; Diod. Sic. fragm. 1 of lib. xxxiv. and iii. of lib. xl.; Philostr. *Vit. Apol.* v. 33; I. Thess. ii. 15.

27. Jos. Ant. XIV. x.; XVI. vi.; XX. viii. 7; Philo. *In Flacc.* and *Legatio ad Caium.*

28. Jos. *Ant.* XVIII. iii. 4, 3 Juv. vi. 543, &c.

29. Jos. *Contr. Apion*, passim; passages above cited from Tacitus and Diodorus Siculus; Trog. Pomp. (Justin) xxxvi. 411; Ptolem. Hephestion or Chennus, in Script. Poet. Hist. Græci of Westermann, p. 194. Cf. Quintilian, III. vii. 2.

30. Cic. *Pro Flacco*, 28; Tac. Hist. v. 5; Juv. xiv. 103–104; Diodorus Siculus and Philostratus, u. s.; Rutilius Numatianus i. 383, &c.

31. Martial, iv. 4; Amm. Marc. xxii. 5.

32. Suet. *Aug.* 76; Horace Sat. I. ix. 69, &c.; Juv. iii. 13–16, 296; vi. 156–160, 542–547; xiv. 96–107; Martial. Epigr. iv. 4; vii. 29, 34, 54; xi. 95; xii. 57; Rutilius Numat. l. c. Jos. *Contra Apion*, ii. 13; Philo. *Leg. ad* Caium. § 26–28.

33. Martial, Epigr. xii. 57.

34. Juvenal, Sat. iii. 14; vi. 542.

35. Juvenal, Sat. iii. 296; vi. 543, &c.; Martial, Epigr. i. 42; xii. 57.

36. Martial, Epigr. i. 42; xii. 57; Statius Silves, I. vi. 73–74, and Forcellini on word *sulphuratum.*

37. Horace, Sat. I. v. 100; Juvenal, Sat. vi. 544, &c., xiv. 96, &c; Apul. *Florida*, i. 6.

38. Dion Cass. lxviii. 32.

39. Tac. Hist. v. 5, 9; Dion Cass. lxvii. 14.

40. Hor. Sat. I. ix. 70; *Judæus* Apella, appears to be a joke of the same kind (see the scholiasts Acron and Porphyrion upon Hor. Sat. I. v. 100); compare the passage from S. Anitus, *Poemata*, v. 364, cited by Forcellini on the word Apella, but which I do not find either in the editions of this Father or in the ancient Latin manuscript, Bibl. Imp. No. 11320, as given by the learned lexicographer; Juv. Sat. xiv. 99, &c.; Martial Epigr. vii. 29, 34, 54; xi. 95.

41. Jos. Contr. Apion ii. 39; Tac. *Ann.* ii. 85, Hist. v. 5; Hor. Sat. I. iv 142, 143; Juv. xiv. 96, &c; Dion Cass. xxxvii. 17; lxvii. 14.

42. Martial, Epigr. i. 42; xii. 57.

43. Juv. Sat. vi. 546, &c.

44. Jos. *Ant.* xviii. iii. 5; xx. 11, 4; B. J. II. xx. 2; Act xiii. 50; xvi. 14

45. *Loc. cit.*

46. Jos. *Ant.*, xx. 11, 5; iv. 1.

47. Passages already cited. Strabo shows much greater justice and penetration (xvi. 11, 34, &c.) Comp. Dion. Cass. xxxvii. 17, &c.

48. Tac. Hist. v. 5.

49. Jos. Contr. Apion ii. 39.

50. Martial, xii. 57.

51. Jos. *Ant.* xiv. x. 6, 11, 14.

52. Eccl. x. 25, 27.

53. Rom. i. 24, &c.

54. Zach. viii. 23.

55. Hor. Sat. I. ix. 69; Pers. v. 179, &c. Juv. Sat. vi. 159; xiv. 96, &c.

56. Contr. Apion ii. 39.

57. Pers. v. 179–184; Juv. vi. 157–160. The remarkable preoccupation about Judaism which may be observed in the Roman writers of the first century, especially the satirists, arises from this circumstance.

58. Juv. Sat. iii. 62, &c.

59. Cic. *De Prov.* consul, 5.

60. The children whose appearance had most pleased me on my first visit, I found four years later, ugly, vulgar, and stupid.

61. Πατρῷος θεός is a very frequent formula in the inscriptions of the Syrians (Corp. Inscr. Græc. Nos. 4449, 4450, 4451, 4463, 4479, 4480, 6015.

62. Corp. Inscr. Græc. Nos. 4474, 4475, 5936; *Mission de Phenicie*, I. ii. c. ii. (in press), inscription of Abeda. Comp. Corpus, Nos. 2271, 5853.

63. Ζεὺς οὐράνιος, ἐπουράνιος, ὕψιστος, μέγιστος, θεὸς σατράπης, Corpus Inscr. Gr. Nos. 4500, 4501, 4502, 4503, 6012; Lepsius, Denkmæler, t. xii. fol. 100. No. 590. Mission de Phenicie, p. 103, 104

64. I have developed this in the *Journal Asiatique* for February 1859, p 259, &c., and in *Mission de Phenicie*, 1. II. c. ii.

65. Syrian code in Land, *Anecdota Syriaca*, i. p. 152, and different facts which I have witnessed.

66. Born in Haran.

67 See Forcellini, word *Syrus.* This word designates Orientals generally. Leblant, *Inscript.* Chret. de la Gaule, i. p. 207, 328, 329.

68. Juvenal, iii. 62–63.

69. Such is at this day the temperament of the Syrian Christian.

70 Inscriptions in *Mem.* de la Soc. des Antiquaires de Fr. t. xxviii. 4, &c. Leblant, Inscript. Chrét. de la Gaule, i. p. cxliv. 207, 324, &c. 353, &c. ii. 259, 459, &c.

71. The Maronites colonize still in nearly all the Levant like the Jews, Armenians, and Greeks, though on a smaller scale.

72. Cic. *De Offic.* i. 42; Dion. Hal. ii. 28; ix. 28.

73. See the characters of slaves in Plautus and Terence.

74. II. Cor. xii. 9.

75. Tacit. *Ann.* ii. 85.

CHAPTER XVII.

1. Tacit. *Ann.* i. 2; Florus, iv. 3; Pomponius in the Digest, 1; I. Tit. ii., fr. 2.

2. Helicon. Apelles, Euceres, etc. The Oriental kings were considered by the Romans to surpass in tyranny the worst of the emperors. Dion. Cassius lix. 24.

3. See inscription of the Parasite of Antony in the *Comptes Rendus de l'Acad. des Inscr. et B. L.*, 1864, p. 166, etc. Comp. Tacit. *Ann.* iv. 55, 56.

4. See for example the funeral oration on Turia by her husband Q. Lucretius Vespillo, of which the complete epigraphic text was first published by Mommsen in *Memoires de l'Academie de Berlin*, 1863, p. 455, &c. Compare funeral oration on Murdia (Orelli, Inscr. Lat. No. 4860), and on Matilda by the emperor Adrian (*Mem. de l'Acad. de Berlin*, u. s. 483, &c.). We are too much preoccupied by passages of the Latin satirists in which the vices of women are sharply exposed. It is as if we were to design a general tableau of the morals of the seventeenth century from Mathurin, Regnier, and Boileau.

5. Orelli, Nos. 2647, &c., especially 2677, 2742, 4530, 4860; Henzen, Nos. 7382, &c., especially No. 7406; Renier, Inscr. de l'Algerie, No. 1987. They may have been false epithets, but they prove at least the estimation of virtue.

6. Plin. *Epist.* vii. 19; ix. 13; Appian, Bell. Civ. iv. 36. Fannia twice followed to exile her husband, Helvidius Priscus, and was banished a third time after his death.

7. The heroism of Arria is well known.

8. Suet. *Aug.* 73; Fun. Orat. on Turia, i., line 30
9. Ib. 31.
10. The too severe opinion of Paul (Rom. i. 24, &c.) is explicable in the same way. Paul was not acquainted with the higher social life of Rome. Besides, these clerical invectives are not to be taken literally.
11. Sen. Ep. xii., xxiv., xxvi., lviii., lxx.; De Ira. iii. 15. De Tranq. anim. 10.
12. Apoc. xvii.; Cf. Sen. Ep. xcv. 16, &c.
13. Suet. *Aug.* 48.
14. The inscriptions contain countless examples.
15. Plut. Græc. Ger. Reipubl xv. 3–4; An seni sit ger. resp., passim.
16. Jos. Ant. xiv., x. 22, 23; Comp. Tacit. *Ann.* iv. 55, 56. Rutilius Numatianus, *Itin.* i. 63, &c.
17. "Immensa romanæ pacis majestas." Plin. *Hist. Nat.* xxvii. 1.
18. Ælius Arist. *Eloge de Rome*, passim; Plut. *Fortune* des *Romains;* Philo. *Leg. ad Caium*, § 21, 22, 39, 40.
19. Dion. Hal. Antiq. Rom. i., comm.
20. Plut. Solon. 20.
21. See Athen. xii. 68; Ælian, *Var.* Hist. ix. 12; Suidas, word Επίχουρος.
22. Tacit. *Ann.* i. 2.
23. Study the character of Euthyphron in Plato.
24. Diog. Laert. ii. 101, 116; v. 5, 6, 37, 38; ix. 52; Athen. xiii. 92; xv. 52; Ælian, *Var. Hist.* ii. 23; iii. 36; Plut. Pericles, 32; De Plac. Philos. I., vii. 2; Diod. Sic. XIII., vi 7; Aristoph. in Aves, 1073.
25. Particularly under Vespasian, as in the case of Helvidius Priscus.
26. We shall show later that these persecutions, at least until that of Decius, have been much exaggerated.
27. The early Christians were in fact very respectful towards Roman authority. Rom. xiii. i., &c.; I. Peter iv. 14, 16. As to St. Luke, see the Introduction to this work.
28. Diog. Laert. vii. 1, 32, 33; Euseb. Prepar. Evang. xv. 15, and in general the *De Legibus* and *De Officiis* of Cicero.
29. Terence, *Heautont.* I. i. 77, Cic. De Finibus Bon. et Mal., v. 23; *Partit. Orat.*, 16, 24: Ovid, Fasti, ii. 684; Lucian vi. 54, &c.; Sen., Epist. xlviii, xcv 51, &c.; De Ira, i. 5; iii. 43; Arrian. Dissert. Epict. I. ix. 6; ii. v. 26; Plut. Roman. 2; Alexander, i. 8, 9.
30. Virg. Eclog. iv.; Sen. Medea, 375, &c.
31. Tac. *Ann.* ii. 85; Suet. Tib 35; Ovid. Fast ii. 497–514.
32. The inscriptions for women contain the most touching expressions. "Mater omnium hominum, parens omnibus subveniens," in Renier, Inscr. de l'Algerie, No. 1987, Comp ibid. No. 2756; Mommsen, Inscr. R. N, No. 1431. "Duobus virtutis et castitatis exemplis." *Not. et*

Mem. de la Soc. de Constantine, 1865, p. 158 See inscription of Urbanilla in Guerin, Voy. Archéol. in Tunis, i. 289, and a beautiful one, Orelli. No. 4648. Some of these texts are subsequent to the first century: but the sentiments they express were not new when they were written.

33. Table-Talk I., v. 1; Demosth. 2; the Dialogue on Love, 2; and Consol. ad Uxorem.

34. "Caritas generis humani." Cic. *De Finibus*, v. 23. "Homo sacra res homini," Sen. Epist. xcv. 33.

35. Sen. Epist. xxxi., xlvii.; De Benef., iii. 18, &c.

36. Tac. *Ann.* xiv. 42. &c.; Suet. Claud. 25; Dion Cass. lx. 29; Plin Ep. viii. 16; Inscr. Lanuv. col. 2 lines, 1–4 (Mommsen *De Coll et Sodal.* Rom., ad calcem); Sen. Rhet. Controv. iii. 21; vii. 6; Sen. Phil. Epist. xlvii; De Benef. iii., 18, &c, Columella. *De re rustica*, i. 8; Plut. the Elder, 5; *De Ira*, 11.

37. Epist. xlvii., 13.

38. Cato. *De re rustica*, 58, 59, 104: Plut Cato, 4, 5. Compare the severe maxims of Ecclesiasticus xxxiii. 25, &c.

39. Tac. Ann. xiv. 60; Dion Cass. xlvii 10: lx. 16; lxii. 13; lxvi 14. Suet. Caius, 16; Appia, Bell. Civ. iv., from ch. xvii. (especially ch. xxxvi. &c.), to ch. li. Juv. vi. 476 &c., describes the manners of the worst class.

40. Hor. Sat. i. vi. 1, &c.; Cic. Epist. iii. 7; Sen. Rhet. *Controv.* i. 6.

41. Suet. Caius, 15, 16; Claud 19, 23, 25; Nero, 16; Dion Cass. lx. 25–29.

42. Tac. *Ann.* vi 17; comp. iv. 6.

43. Tac. *Ann.* xiii. 50, 51; Suet Nero, 10.

44. Epitaph of the jeweller. Evhodus (hominis boni, misericordis, amatis pauperis). *Corp. Inscr. Lat.* No. 1027, and inscription of the age of Augustus (Cf. Egger, *Mem. d'Histoire et de Phil*, p 351, &c.); Perrot, *Exploration de la Galatie*, &c., p 118, 119, πτωχοὺς φιλέοντα; Funeral Oration of Matilda by Adrian (*Mem. de l'Acad de Berlin* for 1863, p. 489); Mommsen, Inscr Regni Neap. Nos. 1431, 2868, 4880; Seneca Rhet., *Controv* I i.; iii 19; iv. 27, viii. 6; Sen Phil. *De Elem* ii. 5, 6. De Benef. i 1; ii. 11; iv. 14; vii. 31. Compare Leblant Inscr. Chret. de la Gaule, ii. p. 23, &c; Orelli, No. 4657, Fea *Framm de Frasti Consol.*, p. 90; R. Garrucci, *Cimitera degli ant. Ebrei*, p. 44.

45. Corp. Inscr. Græc, No. 2758

46. Ibid. Nos. 2194 b. 2511, 2759 b

47. It must be borne in mind that Corinth in the Roman epoch was a colony of foreigners, formed upon the site of the ancient city by Cæsar and Augustus.

48. Lucian, Demonax, 37.

49. Dion Cassius, lxvi. 15.

50. See Ælius Aristides. Treatise against Comedy, 751, &c., ed. Dindorf.

51. It is worthy of note that in several cities of Asia Minor the remains

of the ancient theatres are at this day haunts of debauchery. Comp Ov. Amor. i. 89, &c.

52. Orelli-Henzen Nos. 1172, 3362, &c., 6669; Guerin, Voy. en Tunisie, 11, p. 59; Borghesi, *Œuvres Completes*, iv. p. 269, &c; E. Desjardins. *De tabulis alimentariis* (Paris 1854); Aurelius Victor. Epitome, Nerva; Plin. Epist. i. 8; vii. 18.

53. Inscriptions in Desjardins, op. cit. pars ii. cap. 1.

54. Suet. *Aug* 41, 46; Dion Cass li. 21; lviii. 2.

55. Tac. *Ann.* ii. 87; vi. 13; xv. Suet. Aug. 41, 42; Claud. 18. Comp. Dion Cass. lxii. 18; Orelli, No. 3358 &c.; Henzen, 6662, &c.; Forcellini, article *Tessera frumentaria.*

56. Odyss. vi. 207.

57. Eurip. *Suppl.* v. 773, &c.; Aristotle Rhetor. II. v. iii. and Nicomachus viii. 1; IX. x. See Stobeus Florilegus xxxvii. cxiii. and in general the fragments of Menander, and the Greek comedians.

58. Aristotle Polit. VI. iii. 4. 5.

59. Cic. Tusc. iv. 7–8; Sen. De Clem. ii. 5. 6.

60. Papyrus at the Louvre, No. 37, col. 1. line 21. Notices et Extraits xviii 2d part, p. 298.

61. V. ante.

62. Apoc. xvii. &c.

63. Virg. Ec. iv. Georg. i. 463, &c.; Horace Od. I. ii; Tac. *Ann.* vi. 12; Suet. Aug. 31.

64. See for example De Republ. iii. 22, cited and preserved by Lactantius Instit. div. vi. 8.

65. See the admirable letter, xxxi. to Lucilius.

66. Suet. Vesp. 18; Dion Cass. t. vi. p. 558 (edit. Sturz); Euseb. Chron. A D. 89. Plin. Epist. i. 8; Henzen, Suppl to Orelli, p 124, No. 1172.

67. Funeral Oration of Turia, i. lines 30–31.

68. See first book of Valerius Maximus; Julius Obsequens on Prodigies; and *Discours Sacrés* of Ælius Aristides.

69. Augustus (Suet. Aug. 90–92) and even Cæsar, it is said, (but I doubt,) (Plin. Hist Nat. xxviii. iv. 7) did not escape it.

70. Manilius, Hygin. translations from Aratus.

71. Cic Pro Archia, 10.

72. Suet. Claud. 25.

73. Jos. *Ant.* XIX. v. 3

74. *Bereschith rabba* ch. lxv. fol. 65b; Du Cange, word *matricularius.*

75. Cic. *De Legibus*, ii. 8; Vopiscus. Aurelian, 19.

76 Religio sine superstitione, Orat. fun. Turia i. lines 30–31. See Plu. de Superstit.

77. See Melito, Περὶ ἀληθείας, in *Spicilegium Syriacum* of Cureto, p. 43, or *Spicil. Solesmense* of dom Pitra, t. ii. p. xli., to get a good idea of The impression made by it upon the Jews and Christians.

78 Suet. Aug. 52; Dion Cass li 20; Tac *Ann.* i. 10; Aurel. Victor Ceas, i. Appian. Bell. Civ. v. 132; Jos. B. J., I. xxi. 2, 3, 4, 7. Noris, *Cenotaphia Pisana*, dissert. i. cap. 4; *Kalendarium Cumanum*, in Corpus Inscr. Lat. i. p. 310; Eckhel. Doctrina Num. Vet. pars 2d. vol. vi. p. 100 124, &c.

79 Tac. *Ann.* iv. 55–56. Comp. Valer. Maxim. prol.

80 Ante, p. 193, &c.

81 Corinth. the only Grecian town which was considerably Christianized during the first century, was no longer at this period a Hellenic city.

82. Heracl. Corn. Comp. Cic. De Nat. Deorum, iii. 23, 25, 60, 62, 64.

83. Plut. Consol ad ux. 10; *De sera numinis vindicta*, 22; Heuzey. *Mission de Macedoine*, p. 128 *Revue Archéologique*. April, 1864, p. 282.

84. Lucret, i. 63, &c.; Sallust. Catil. 52; Cic. De Nat. Deorum. ii 24, 28. *De Divinat.* ii. 33 35. 57; *De Haruspicorum Responsis*, passim; Tuscul. i. 16; Juvenal, Sat. ii. 149, 152; Sen. Epist. xxiv. 17.

85. Sua cuique civitati religio est, nostra nobis. Cic. Pro Flacco, 28.

86. Cic. *De Nat. Deorum*, i. 30. 42; De Divinat. ii. 12, 33, 35, 72. *De* Harusp. Resp. 6. etc.; Liv. i. 19, Quint Curt. iv. 10. Plut *De plac. phil.* I. vii. 2; Diod. Sic. I. ii. 2. Varro. in Aug. *De civit. Dei*, iv. 31. 32; vi. 6. Dion Halic. ii. 20. viii. 5 Valer. Maxim. I. ii.

87 Cic. De Divinat. ii. 15; Juvenal, ii. 149, &c.

88. Tac. *Ann* xi. 15. Plin. Epist. x. 97. *sub fin.* Serapin in Plut. *De Pythiæ Oraculis.* Comp. *De EI apud Delphos*, init. See also Valer. Maxim I., *passim.*

89. Juv. Sat. vi. 489, 527, &c. Tac. *Ann.* xi. 15. Comp. Lucian *Conv. Deorum*; Tertull. *Apolog.* 6.

90. Jos. *Ant.* xviii iii. 4; Tac. *Ann.* ii. 85; Le Bas, *Inscr.* part v. No. 395.

91. Plut. De Pyth orac. 25.

92. See Lucian, *Alexander seu pseudomantis* and *De morte Peregrini.*

93. Sen. Epist. xii. xxiv. lxv. Inscr. Lanuv. 2d col. lines 5–6; Orelli, 4404.

94. Dion Cass. lxvi. 13; lxvii. 13; Suet Domit. 10. Tac. *Agricola.* 2.45; Plin *Epist.* III. ii; Philostr. Vit. Apollon. I. vii. passim. Euseb. *Chron.* A.D. 90.

95. Dion Cass lxii. 29.

96. Arrian, Dissert. de Epictet. I. ii. 21.

97. Ibid. I. xxv. 22.

CHAPTER XVIII.

1. Val. Max., I. iii; Liv. XXXIX. 8–18; Cic., *De Legibus*, II. 8; Dion Halic., II. 20; Dion Cass., XL. 47; XLII. 26; Tertull., *Apol.* 6; *Adv. nationes*, I. 10.

2. Propert., IV. i. 17; Lucian. VIII. 831; Dion Cass., XLVII. 15 Arnob ii. 73.
3. Val. Maxim. I. iii. 3.
4. Dion Cass. XLVII. 15
5. Jos., XLV. x. Comp. Cic., *Pro Flacco*, 28.
6. Suet., *Aug.*, 31, 93; Dion Cass., lii. 36.
7. Suet., *Aug.*, 93.
8. Dion Cass., LVI. 6.
9. Jos. *Ant.* XVI. vi.
10. Ibid. XVI. vi. 2.
11. Dion Cass., LII. 36.
12. Jos., B. J., V. xiii. 6. Comp. Suet, Aug, 93.
13. Suet. Tib., 36; Tac., Ann., ii, 85; Jos., Ant. XVII, iii, 4, 5; Philo., In Flaccum, § 4; Leg. ad Caium, § 24; Sen. Epist. cviii. 22. The assertion of Tertullian (Apol. 5), repeated by other ecclesiastical writers, that Tiberius had formed the intention of placing Jesus Christ on the list of gods, is not worth discussion.
14. Dion Cass., lx. 6.
15. Tacit. Ann., xi. 15.
16. Dion Cass., lx. 6; Suet., Claud. 25; Acts xviii. 2.
17. Dion Cass., lx. 6.
18. Jos. Ant., XIX. v. 2; XX. vi. 3; B. J. II. xii. 7.
19. Suet. Nero 56.
20. Tac. Ann. xv. 44; Suet. Nero. 16. This will be developed hereafter.
21. Tac. Ann. xiii. 32.
22 Comp Dion Cass. Domit. sub fin; Suet. Domit. 15 This distinction is formally made in the digest, I. xlvii., tit. xxii., de Coll. et Corp. i. 3.
23. Cic. Pro Flacco, 28.
24 This distinction is indicated in the *Acts* xvi 20, 21; Cf. xviii. 13.
25. Cic. Pro Flacco, 28; Juv. xiv. 100 &c; Tac. Hist. v, 4, 5; Plin. Epist. x, 97; Dion Cass. L. ii. 36.
26. Jos. B. J. VII. v. 2.
27. Ælius Arist. Pro Serapide, 53. Jul. Orat iv., p. 136, of Spanheim's Ed, and the sculptures copied by Leblant in the Bull. de la Soc. des Ant. de Fr, 1859, p. 19 -193.
28. Tac. Ann. ii 85; Suet. Tib. 37; Jos. Ant. XVIII. iii. 4-5; letter of Adrian in Vopisc. Vit. Saturn, 8.
29 Dion Cass. xxxvii. 17.
30. See the inscriptions collected in the Rev. Archéol. Nov. 1864, 391, &c; Dec, 1864, p. 460, &c; June, 1865, p. 451-452, and p. 497, &c.; Sept., 1865, p 214, &c.; Apr., 1866; Ross. Inscr. Græc. ined. fasc., ii., No. 282. 291. 292; Hamilton, Researches in Asia Minor, Vol. ii., No. 301. Corp. Inscr. Græc. Nos. 120, 126, 2525 b. 2562;

Rhangabe Antiq Hellen No 811. Henzen, No. 6082; Virg. Ecl v., 30. Comp. Harpocration Lex. art ἐρανιστής. Festus art. Thiastas: Digest XLVII, xxii., de Coll. et Corp. 4; Plin. Epist. x, 93, 94.

31. Aristot. Mor. Nicom. VIII., ix., 5. Plut. Quest. Græc. 44.

32 Wescher, Archives des missions scientif. 2d series, v., i, p. 432, and Rev. Arch., Sept., 1865, p. 221, 222. Cf. Aristot. Œconom. ii. 3. Strab. ix., i., 15. Corp. inscr. gr, No. 2271, lines 13–14.

33. Κληρωτοί.

34. Κλῆρος. The ecclesiastical etymology of κλῆρος is different, and implies an allusion to the position of the tribe of Levi in Israel. But it is not impossible that the word was primarily derived from the Greek confraternities (cf Act i. 25, 26; I. Petri, v. 3. Clem Alex. in Euseb H. E. iii. 23). M. Wescher finds among the dignitaries of these societies an ἐπίσκοπος (Revue Arch., April, 1866). See ante, p. 86. The assembly was also called σύναγωγή (Revue Arch., Sept., 1865, p. 216; Pollux IV. viii, 143).

35. Corp. inscr. Gr. No. 126. Comp. Rev. Arch. Sept. 1865, p. 216.

36. Wescher in Revue Archeol. Dec. 1864, p. 460, &c.

37. See ante, p. 338, note 2.

38. The Greek confraternities were not entirely exempt. Inscr. in Revue Archeol., Dec. 1864, p. 462, &c.

39. Digest XLVII. xxii. de Coll. et Corp. 4.

40. Liv. XXIX. 10, &c. Orell. and Henzen, Inscr. Lat. c. v. § 21.

41. Dion. Cass. lii. 36; lx. 6.

42. Liv. XXXIX. 8–18. Comp. decree in Corp. Inscr. Lat. I. p. 43–44. Cf. Cic. De Legibus ii. 8.

43. Cic. Pro Sext. 25; In Pis. 4; Asconius, in Cornelianam 75 (edit. Orelli); In Pison. p. 7–8; Dion. Cass. XXXVIII. 13, 14; Digest. III. iv. Quod cujusc. 1; XLVII. xxii. de Coll. et. Corp. passim.

44. Suet. Domit. 1; Dion. Cass. XLVII. 15; LX. 6, LXVI. 24; passages of Tertullian and Arnobius before cited.

45. Suet. Cass. 42; Aug. 32; Jos. Ant. XVI. x. 8; Dion. Cass. LII. 36.

46. "Kaput ex. S. C. P. K. Quibus coire, convenire, collegiumque habere liceat. Qui stipem menstruam conferre volent in funera, ii. in collegium coeant, neque sub specie ejus colleginisi semel in mense vocant conferendi causa unde defuncti sepeliantur." Inscr. Lanuv. 1st col. lines 10–13 in Mommsen, De collegiis et sodalitiis Romanorum (Kiliæ, 1843), p. 81–82 and ad calcem. Cf. Digest. XLVII. xxii. de Coll. et. Corp. 1; Tertull. Apol. 39.

47. Inscr. Lanuv. 2d col. lines 3, 7; Digest. XLVII. xxii. de Coll. et Corp. 3.

48. Digest. XLVII. xi. de Extr. crim. 2.

49. Ibid. XLVII. xxii. de Coll. et. Corp. 1 and 3.

50. Heuzey, Mission de Macedoine, p. 71, &c.; Orelli, Inscr. No. 4093

51. Orelli, 2409; Melchior et P. Visconti, Silloge d'iscrizioni antiche, p. 6.

52. See article relative to colleges of Esculapius and Hygiens, of Jupiter

Corninus, and of Dian and Antinous, in Mommsen, op. cit. p. 93 &c. Comp. Orelli, Inscr. Lat. Nos. 1710, &c., 2394, 2395, 2413, 4075, 4079, 4107, 4207, 4938, 5044; Mommsen, op. cit. p. 96, 113, 114; de Rossi, Bulletin di Archeol. Cristiana, 2d year, No. 8.

53. Inscr. Lanuv., 1st col., lines 6–7; Orelli. 2270; de Rossi, Bullett. di archeol. crist. 2d year, No. 8.

54. Inscr. Lanuv., 2d col., lines 11–13; Orelli, 4420.

55. Inscr. Lanuv., 1st col. lines 3, 9, 21; 2d col. lines 7–17; Mommsen, Inscr. regni Neap. 2559; Marini. Atti. p. 598; Muratori, 491, 7; Mommsen. De coll. et sod. p. 109, &c. 113, Comy. I. Cor. xi, 20, &c. The president of the Christian Churches was called by the pagans θιασάρχης. Lucien, Peregrinus, II.

56. Inscr. Lanuv. 2d col. line 7.

57. Inscr. Lanuv. 2d col. lines 24–25.

58. Ibid. 2d col. lines 26–29. Cf. Corpus Inscr. Gr. No. 126.

59. Orelli, Inscr. Lat Nos. 2399, 2400, 2405, 4093, 4103. Mommsen, De Coll. et Sod; Rom. p. 97; Heuzey u. s. Compare at this day the little cemeteries of the societies at Rome.

60. Hor. Sat. I. viii. 8.

61. *Funeraticium.*

62. Inscr. Lanuv. 1st col., lines 24, 25, 32.

63. Ib. 2d col. lines 3, 5.

64. Cic. De Offic. 1, 17. Schol. Bibb. ad Cic. Pro Archia, x. 1. Comp. Plut. De frat. amore, 7; Digest XLVII. xxii. de Coll. et Corp. 4. In a Roman inscription the founder of a sepulchre provides that only those of his own faith shall be buried there, *ad religionem pertinentes meam* (de Rossi, Bull. di Archeol. Crist. 53d year No. 7, p. 64.

65. Tertull. Ad Scap. 3; de Rossi, op. cit. 3d year, No. 12.

66. St. Justin, Apol. 1, 67; Tertull. Apollog. 39.

67. Ulpi. Fragm. xxii. 6. Digest III. iv. Quod cujusc. 1; XLVI. 1, de Fid; et Mand 22. XLVII. ii. de Furtis, 31; XLVII. xxii. de Coll. et Corp. 1, 3; Gruter. 322, 3. 4; 424, 12; Orelli. 4080; Marini, Atti. p. 95. Muratori, 516, 1; Mem. de la Soc. des Antiq. de Fr. XX. p. 78.

68. Dig. XLVII. xxii. de Coll. et Corp. passim; Inscr. Lanuv. 1st col. lines 10–13; Marini. Atti. p. 552; Muratori, 520, 3; Orelli 4075, 4115, 1567. 2797, 3140, 3913; Heuzen 6633, 6745; Mommsen op. cit p. 80, etc.

69. Digest XLVII. xi de Extr. crim. 2.

79. Ibid. XLVII. xxii. de Coll. et Corp. 2; XLVIII. iv. ad Leg. Jul. majest. 1.

71. Dion Cass. LX. 6. Comp. Suet. Nero 16.

72. See administrative correspondence of Pliny and Trajan. Plin. Epist. X. 43, 93, 94, 97, 98.

73. "Permittitur tenuioribus stipem menstruam conferre, dum tamen semel in mense coeant, ne sub prætextu hujusmodi illicitum collegium

cocant (Dig. XLVII. xxii. *de Coll. et Corp.* 1)." "Servos quoque licet in collegio tenuiorum recipi volentibus dominis (*ibid.* 3)." Cf. Plin. Epist. X. 94; Tertull. Apol. 39.

74. Digest I. xii. de Off præf. urbi, 1. § 14 (Cf. Mommsen op. cit p. 127); III.i v. Quod cujusc. 1; XLVII. xx. de Coll. et Corp 3. The excellent Marcus Aurelius extended as far as possible the right of association. Dig. XXXIV. v. de Rebus dubiis, 20; XL. iii. de Manumissionibus, 1; XLVII. xxii. de Coll. et Corp. 1.

CHAPTER XIX.

1. See de Rossi. Bull. di Arch. Crist 3d year, Nos 3, 5, 6, 12, Eg. Pomponia Græcina (Tac. Ann. xiii. 32) under Nero as already characteristic; but it is not certain that she was a Christian.
2. See de Rossi, *Roma Sotteranea* I. p. 309; and pl. xxi. No. 12 and the epigraphic collations of Leon Renier, Comptes Rend. de l'Acad. des Inscr. et B. L 1865, p. 289, etc., and of Creuly, Rev. Arch. Jan. 1866, p. 63–64. Comp. de Rossi, Bull. 3d year, No. 10, p. 77–79.
3. I. Cor. i. 26, etc.; Jac. ii. 5, etc.
4. Aἶος τοῖς θ ς. See relation of martyrdom of Polycarp. § 3, 9, 12. Ruinart. Acta sincera, p. 31, etc.
5. Ebionim. See Vie de Jésus. Jac. ii. 5, etc. Comp. πτωχοὶ τῷ πνεύματι, Matth. v. 3.
6. See *ante.*
7. Tac. Ann. XV. 44, Plin. Epist. X. 97; Suet. Nero 16; Domit. 15; Philopatris, passim. Rutil. Numat. 1, 389, etc.; 440, etc.
8. John xv. 17, etc.; xvi. 8, etc., 33; xvii. 15, etc.
9. James i. 27.
10. I allude to the essential and primitive tendencies of Christianity, not to the transformed Christianity now preached, especially that of the Jesuits.
11. See history of the origin of Babism by M. de Gobineau. *Les Relig. et les Philos. dans l'Asie Centrale* (Paris, 1865), p. 141, etc.; and by Mirza Kazem-beg in the *Journal Asiatique* (in press) I myself have received information from two individuals at Constantinople, who were personally mixed in the affairs of Babism, which confirms the narration of these two *savants.*
12. M. de Gobineau. p. 301, etc.
13. Another detail which I have from original sources is as follows: Several of the sectaries, to compel them to retract, were tied to the mouths of cannon, with a lighted slow-match attached. The offer was made to them to cut off the match if they would renounce Bab. In reply, they only stretched out their hands towards the creeping spark, and besought it to hasten and consummate their happiness.

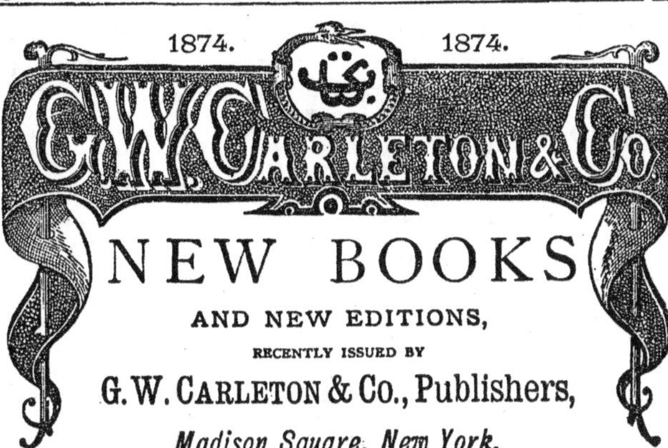

The Publishers, upon receipt of the price in advance, will send any book on this Catalogue by mail, *postage free*, to any part of the United States.

All books in this list [unless otherwise specified] are handsomely bound in cloth board binding, with gilt backs, suitable for libraries.

Mary J. Holmes' Works.

TEMPEST AND SUNSHINE	$1 50	DARKNESS AND DAYLIGHT	$1 50
ENGLISH ORPHANS	1 50	HUGH WORTHINGTON	1 50
HOMESTEAD ON THE HILLSIDE	1 50	CAMERON PRIDE	1 50
LENA RIVERS	1 50	ROSE MATHER	1 50
MEADOW BROOK	1 50	ETHELYN'S MISTAKE	1 50
DORA DEANE	1 50	MILLBANK	1 50
COUSIN MAUDE	1 50	EDNA BROWNING	1 50
MARIAN GRAY	1 50	WEST LAWN (new)	1 50

Marion Harland's Works.

ALONE	$1 50	SUNNYBANK	$1 50
HIDDEN PATH	1 50	HUSBANDS AND HOMES	1 50
MOSS SIDE	1 50	RUBY'S HUSBAND	1 50
NEMESIS	1 50	PHEMIE'S TEMPTATION	1 50
MIRIAM	1 50	THE EMPTY HEART	1 50
AT LAST	1 50	TRUE AS STEEL (new)	1 50
HELEN GARDNER	1 50	JESSAMAINE (just published)	1 50

Charles Dickens' Works.

"Carleton's New Illustrated Edition."

THE PICKWICK PAPERS	$1 50	MARTIN CHUZZLEWIT	$1 50
OLIVER TWIST	1 50	OUR MUTUAL FRIEND	1 50
DAVID COPPERFIELD	1 50	TALE OF TWO CITIES	1 50
GREAT EXPECTATIONS	1 50	CHRISTMAS BOOKS	1 50
DOMBEY AND SON	1 50	SKETCHES BY "BOZ"	1 50
BARNABY RUDGE	1 50	HARD TIMES, etc.	1 50
NICHOLAS NICKLEBY	1 50	PICTURES OF ITALY, etc	1 50
OLD CURIOSITY SHOP	1 50	UNCOMMERCIAL TRAVELLER	1 50
BLEAK HOUSE	1 50	EDWIN DROOD, etc.	1 50
LITTLE DORRIT	1 50	CHILD'S ENGLAND, and CATALOGUE	1 50

Augusta J. Evans' Novels.

BEULAH	$1 75	ST. ELMO	$2 00
MACARIA	1 75	VASHTI (new)	2 00
INEZ	1 75		

Captain Mayne Reid—Illustrated.

SCALP HUNTERS	$1 50	WHITE CHIEF	$1 50
WAR TRAIL	1 50	HEADLESS HORSEMAN	1 50
HUNTER'S FEAST	1 50	LOST LENORE	1 50
TIGER HUNTER	1 50	WOOD RANGERS	1 50
OSCEOLA THE SEMINOLE	1 50	WILD HUNTRESS	1 50
THE QUADROON	1 50	THE MAROON	1 50
RANGERS AND REGULATORS	1 50	RIFLE RANGERS	1 50
WHITE GAUNTLET	1 50	WILD LIFE	1 50

A. S. Roe's Works.

A LONG LOOK AHEAD	$1 50	TRUE TO THE LAST	$1 50
TO LOVE AND TO BE LOVED	1 50	LIKE AND UNLIKE	1 50
TIME AND TIDE	1 50	LOOKING AROUND	1 50
I'VE BEEN THINKING	1 50	WOMAN OUR ANGEL	1 50
THE STAR AND THE CLOUD	1 50	THE CLOUD ON THE HEART	1 50
HOW COULD HE HELP IT	1 50	RESOLUTION (new)	1 50

Hand-Books of Society.

THE HABITS OF GOOD SOCIETY. The nice points of taste and good manners, and the art of making oneself agreeable $1 75

THE ART OF CONVERSATION.—A sensible work, for every one who wishes to be either an agreeable talker or listener 1 50

THE ARTS OF WRITING, READING, AND SPEAKING.—An excellent book for self-instruction and improvement 1 50

A NEW DIAMOND EDITION of the above three popular books.—Small size, elegantly bound, and put in a box 3 00

Mrs. Hill's Cook Book.

MRS. A. P. HILL'S NEW COOKERY BOOK, and family domestic receipts $2 00

Charlotte Bronte and Miss Muloch.

SHIRLEY.—Author of Jane Eyre .... $1 75 | JOHN HALIFAX, GENTLEMAN $1 75

Mrs. N. S. Emerson.

BETSEY AND I ARE OUT—And other Poems. A Thanksgiving Story $1 50

Louisa M. Alcott.

MORNING GLORIES—A beautiful juvenile, by the author of "Little Women" 1 50

The Crusoe Books—Famous "Star Edition."

ROBINSON CRUSOE.—New illustrated edition $1 50

SWISS FAMILY ROBINSON. Do. Do 1 50

THE ARABIAN NIGHTS. Do. Do 1 50

Julie P. Smith's Novels.

WIDOW GOLDSMITH'S DAUGHTER	$1 75	THE WIDOWER	$1 75
CHRIS AND OTHO	1 75	THE MARRIED BELLE	1 75
TEN OLD MAIDS [in press]	1 75		

Artemus Ward's Comic Works.

ARTEMUS WARD—HIS BOOK	$1 50	ARTEMUS WARD—IN LONDON	$1 50
ARTEMUS WARD—HIS TRAVELS	1 50	ARTEMUS WARD—HIS PANORAMA	1 50

Fanny Fern's Works.

FOLLY AS IT FLIES	$1 50	CAPER-SAUCE (new)	$1 50
GINGERSNAPS	1 50	A MEMORIAL.—By JAMES PARTON	2 00

Josh Billings' Comic Works.

JOSH BILLINGS' PROVERBS	$1 50	JOSH BILLINGS FARMER'S ALMINAX, 15 cts.
JOSH BILLINGS ON ICE	1 50	(In paper covers.)

Verdant Green.

A racy English college story—with numerous comic illustrations $1 50

Popular Italian Novels.

DOCTOR ANTONIO.—A love story of Italy. By Ruffini $1 75

BEATRICE CENCI.—By Guerrazzi. With a steel Portrait 1 75

M. Michelet's Remarkable Works.

LOVE (L'AMOUR).—English translation from the original French $1 50

WOMAN (LA FEMME). Do. Do. Do. 1 50

May Agnes Fleming's Novels.

GUY EARLSCOURT'S WIFE. . . . . . $1 75 | A WONDERFUL WOMAN $1 75
A TERRIBLE SECRET 1 75

Ernest Renan's French Works.

THE LIFE OF JESUS . . . . $1 75 | LIFE OF SAINT PAUL $1 75
LIVES OF THE APOSTLES . . . . 1 75 | BIBLE IN INDIA. By Jacolliot 2 00

Geo. W. Carleton.

OUR ARTIST IN CUBA . . . . $1 50 | OUR ARTIST IN AFRICA. (In press.) $1 50
OUR ARTIST IN PERU . . . . 1 50 | OUR ARTIST IN MEXICO. Do. 1 50

Popular Novels, from the French.

SHE LOVED HIM MADLY. Borys . . . $1 75 | SO FAIR YET FALSE. By Chavette. $1 75
A FATAL PASSION. By Bernard. 1 75

Maria J. Westmoreland's Novels.

HEART HUNGRY . . . . $1 75 | CLIFFORD TROUPE. (New) $1 75

Sallie A. Brock's Novels.

KENNETH, MY KING . . . . $1 75 | A NEW BOOK. (In press.) . . . .

Don Quixote.

A BEAUTIFUL NEW 12MO EDITION. With illustrations by Gustave Dore $1 50

Victor Hugo.

LES MISERABLES.—English translation from the French. Octavo $2 50
LES MISERABLES.—In the Spanish language 5 00

Algernon Charles Swinburne.

LAUS VENERIS, AND OTHER POEMS.—An elegant new edition $1 50
FRENCH LOVE-SONGS.—Selected from the best French authors 1 50

Robert Dale Owen.

THE DEBATEABLE LAND BETWEEN THIS WORLD AND THE NEXT $2 00
THREADING MY WAY.—Twenty-five years of Autobiography 1 50

The Game of Whist.

POLE ON WHIST.—The late English standard work $1 00

Mansfield T. Walworth's Novels.

WARWICK . . . . $1 75 | STORMCLIFF $1 75
LULU . . . . 1 75 | DELAPLAINE 1 75
HOTSPUR . . . . 1 75 | BEVERLY. (New.) 1 75

Mother Goose Set to Music.

MOTHER GOOSE MELODIES.—With music for singing, and illustrations $1 50

M. M. Pomeroy "Brick."

SENSE—(a serious book) . . . . $1 50 | NONSENSE—(a comic book) $1 50
GOLD-DUST do. . . . . 1 50 | BRICK-DUST do. 1 50
OUR SATURDAY NIGHTS . . . . 1 50 | LIFE OF M. M. POMEROY 1 50

John Esten Cooke.

FAIRFAX . . . . $1 50 | HAMMER AND RAPIER $1 50
HILT TO HILT . . . . 1 50 | OUT OF THE FOAM 1 50

Feydeau and Cazenave.

FEMALE BEAUTY AND THE ARTS OF PLEASING.—From the French $1 50

Joseph Rodman Drake.

THE CULPRIT FAY.—The well-known fairy poem, with 100 illustrations $2 00
THE CULPRIT FAY. Do. superbly bound in turkey morocco . . 5 00

Richard B. Kimball.

WAS HE SUCCESSFUL? . . . . $1 75 | LIFE IN SAN DOMINGO $1 50
UNDERCURRENTS OF WALL STREET. 1 75 | HENRY POWERS, BANKER 1 75
SAINT LEGER . . . . 1 75 | TO-DAY 1 75
ROMANCE OF STUDENT LIFE . . . . . . 1 75 | EMILIE. (In press.) . . . .

Author "New Gospel of Peace."

CHRONICLES OF GOTHAM.—A rich modern satire. (Paper covers) . . . . 25 cts
THE FALL OF MAN.—A satire on the Darwin theory. Do. . . . . 50 cts

Celia E. Gardner's Novels.

STOLEN WATERS (in verse) . . . . $1 50 | TESTED. . . . . . . (in prose) $1 75
BROKEN DREAMS do. . . . . 1 50 | RICH MEDWAY . . . . do. 1 75

Ann S. Stephens.

PHEMIE FROST'S EXPERIENCES.—Author of "Fashion and Famine"........$1 75

Anna Cora Mowatt.

ITALIAN LIFE AND LEGENDS......$1 50 | THE CLERGYMAN'S WIFE —A novel.$1 75

Mrs. C. L. McIlvain.

EBON AND GOLD.—A new American novel.................................$1 50

Dr. Cummings's Works.

THE GREAT TRIBULATION........$2 00 | THE GREAT CONSUMMATION......$2 00
THE GREAT PREPARATION........ 2 00 | THE SEVENTH VIAL. 2 00

Cecelia Cleveland.

THE STORY OF A SUMMER; OR, JOURNAL LEAVES FROM CHAPPAQUA.........$1 50

Olive Logan.

WOMEN AND THEATRES.—And other miscellaneous sketches and topics.......$1 50

Miscellaneous Works.

TALES FROM THE OPERAS........$1 50
FELDAZZLE'S BACHELOR STUDIES.. 1 00
LITTLE WANDERERS.—Illustrated.. 1 50
GENESIS DISCLOSED.—T. A. Davies 1 50
COMMODORE ROLLINGPIN'S LOG.... 1 50
BRAZEN GATES.—A juvenile 1 50
ANTIDOTE TO GATES AJAR ......25 cts
THE RUSSIAN BALL (paper)........25 cts
THE SNOBLACE BALL do ....25 cts
DEAFNESS.—Dr. E. B. Lighthill... 1 00
A BOOK ABOUT LAWYERS.......... 2 00
A BOOK ABOUT DOCTORS.......... 2 00
SQUIBOB PAPERS.—John Phœnix .. 1 50
NORTHERN BALLADS.—Anderson...$1 00
PLYMOUTH CHURCH.—1847 to 1873. 2 00
O. C. KERR PAPERS.—4 vols. in 1... 2 00
CHRISTMAS HOLLY—Marion Harland 1 50
DREAM MUSIC.—F. R. Marvin... 1 50
POEMS.—By L. G. Thomas...... 1 50
VICTOR HUGO.—His life... .... 2 00
BEAUTY IS POWER............. .. 1 50
WOMAN, LOVE, AND MARRIAGE . .. 1 50
WICKEDEST WOMAN in New York..25 cts
SANDWICHES.—By Artemus Ward.25 cts
REGINA.—Poems by Eliza Cruger.. 1 50
WIDOW SPRIGGINS.—Widow Bedott 1 75

Miscellaneous Novels.

A CHARMING WIDOW.—Macquoid..$1 75
TRUE TO HIM EVER.—By F. W. R. 1 50
THE FORGIVING KISS.—By M. Loth. 1 75
LOYAL UNTO DEATH.............. 1 75
BESSIE WILMERTON.—Westcott.... 1 75
PURPLE AND FINE LINEN.—Fawcett. 1 75
EDMUND DAWN.—By Ravenswood. 1 50
CACHET.—Mrs. M. J. R. Hamilton, 1 75
MARK GILDERSLEEVE.–J. S. Sauzade 1 75
FERNANDO DE LEMOS.—C. Gayaree 2 00
CROWN JEWELS.—Mrs. Moffat..... 1 75
A LOST LIFE.—By Emily Moore... 1 50
AVERY GLIBUN.—Orpheus C. Kerr. 2 00
THE CLOVEN FOOT.— Do. . 1 50
ROMANCE OF RAILROAD.—Smith... 1 50
ROBERT GREATHOUSE.—J. F. Swift $2 00
FAUSTINA.—From the German.... 1 50
MAURICE.—From the French...... 1 50
GUSTAV ADOLF.—From the Swedish 1 50
ADRIFT WITH A VENGEANCE....... 1 50
UP BROADWAY.—By Eleanor Kirk. 1 50
MONTALBAN..................... 1 75
LIFE AND DEATH................ 1 50
CLAUDE GUEUX.—By Victor Hugo. 1 50
FOUR OAKS.—By Kamba Thorpe.. 1 75
ADRIFT IN DIXIE.—Edmund Kirke. 1 50
AMONG THE GUERILLAS. Do. . 1 50
AMONG THE PINES Do. . 1 50
MY SOUTHERN FRIENDS. Do. . 1 50
DOWN IN TENNESSEE. Do. . 1 50

Miscellaneous Works.

WOOD'S GUIDE TO THE CITY OF NEW YORK.—Beautifully and fully illustrated..$1 00
BILL ARP'S PEACE PAPERS.—Full of comic illustrations...................... 1 50
A BOOK OF EPITAPHS.—Amusing, quaint, and curious. (New)......... .... 1 50
SOUVENIRS OF TRAVEL.—By Madame Octavia Walton LeVert............... 2 00
THE ART OF AMUSING.—A book of home amusements, with illustrations...... 1 50
HOW TO MAKE MONEY; and how to keep it.—By Thomas A. Davies......... 1 50
BALLAD OF LORD BATEMAN.—With illustrations by Cruikshank (paper).......25 cts
BEHIND THE SCENES; at the "White House."—By Elizabeth Keckley....... 2 00
THE YACHTSMAN'S PRIMER.—For amateur sailors. T. R. Warren (paper)....50 cts
RURAL ARCHITECTURE.—By M Field. With plans and illustrations......... 2 00
LIFE OF HORACE GREELEY.—By L. U. Reavis. With a new steel Portrait .. 2 00
WHAT I KNOW OF FARMING —By Horace Greeley.......................... 1 50
PRACTICAL TREATISE ON LABOR.—By Hendrick B. Wright............... .. 2 00
TWELVE VIEWS OF HEAVEN.—By Twelve Distinguished English Divines...... 1 50
HOUSES NOT MADE WITH HANDS.—An illustrated juvenile, illust'd by Hoppin. 1 00
CRUISE OF THE SHENANDOAH—The Last Confederate Steamer............... 1 50
MILITARY RECORD OF CIVILIAN APPOINTMENTS in the U. S. Army 5 00
IMPENDING CRISIS OF THE SOUTH.—By Hinton Rowan Helper... .... 2 00
NEGROES IN NEGROLAND Do. Do. Do. (paper covers).. 1 00

www.ingramcontent.com/pod-product-compliance
Lightning Source LLC
LaVergne TN
LVHW010149110826
845151LV00002B/471

* 9 7 8 1 4 2 5 5 3 7 4 4 9 *